Gertrude Stein AND THE REINVENTION OF RHETORIC

Gertrude Stein AND THE REINVENTION OF RHETORIC

SHARON J. KIRSCH

THE UNIVERSITY OF ALABAMA PRESS
Tuscaloosa

The University of Alabama Press
Tuscaloosa, Alabama 35487-0380
uapress.ua.edu

Typeface: Garamond and Corbel

Manufactured in the United States of America
Cover photograph: *Gertrude Stein* by Jo Davidson, 1922–1923, terra cotta.
Photo courtesy of National Portrait Gallery, Smithsonian Institution.
Cover design: Michele Myatt Quinn

∞

The paper on which this book is printed meets the minimum requirements
of American National Standard for Information Sciences—Permanence of
Paper for Printed Library Materials, ANSI Z39.48-1984.

Library of Congress Cataloging-in-Publication Data

Kirsch, Sharon, 1966–
Gertrude Stein and the reinvention of rhetoric / Sharon J. Kirsch.
pages cm
Includes bibliographical references and index.
ISBN 978-0-8173-1852-9 (hardback) — ISBN 978-0-8173-8794-5
(e book) 1. Stein, Gertrude, 1874–1946—Criticism and interpretation.
I. Title.
PS3537.T323Z7163 2014
818'.5209—dc23
2014015788

Contents

Acknowledgments vii
1. Introduction: Gertrude Stein Reinvents Rhetoric 1
2. "Suppose a Grammar Uses Invention" 21
3. Compositional Form after Arrangement 41
4. An Exacting Style 59
5. Troubling Memory 75
6. Gertrude Stein Delivers 97
7. Supposing Stein: Toward a Conclusion 115
Notes 123
Works Cited 143
Index 159

Acknowledgments

It is an honor, even in its most challenging moments, to have the opportunity to write about writing, to trace Gertrude Stein's lessons through a different history, and to explore the inventive potential of language. I am grateful for the opportunity, an opportunity that would not have been possible without the help and support of many people over many years.

Very early in the process, before I could see a connection between Stein and rhetoric, Neil Schmitz recommended *How to Write* as a place to begin; since then this book has been responsible for the reinvention of my thinking. My colleagues in the School of Humanities, Arts and Cultural Studies at Arizona State University served as excellent intellectual interlocutors, offering helpful advice and generous feedback: Marlene Tromp, Duku Anokye, Patrick Bixby, Annika Mann, Julia Sarreal, and Eric Wertheimer. Risa Applegarth, Diane Gruber, Karla Murphy, and Lisa Lucenti provided exquisite close readings and invaluable feedback that sharpened my arguments significantly. My gratitude also goes to the members of the Cyber Stein Writing Group who deepened my understanding of Stein, offered insightful commentary, and continue to make conferences enjoyable: Amy Moorman Robbins, Emily Setina, and Janet Boyd. A special thanks to Janet for supporting this project and opening doors to new ones.

The New College of Interdisciplinary Arts and Sciences at Arizona State University generously provided grant funding and research leave to support the completion of the manuscript. I also appreciate the support of the New College's Center for Critical Inquiry and Cultural Studies. The anonymous reviewers for the University of Alabama Press provided detailed and insightful responses and recommendations, which helped to strengthen the manuscript as well. I would also like to extend a special thanks to Dan Waterman for so graciously ushering the project through the editorial process.

My students, who have fearlessly joined conversations of potentially daunting complexity and managed to ask intelligent, creative, and critical questions, continue to challenge and influence my approach to Stein and rhetorical studies. My research assistants, Nanette Schuster and Haran Phaneuf, provided research and editorial support and deserve special recognition as well. A heartfelt thanks also to my friends who have helped in countless ways over many years through their intellectual generosity and friendship: Caroline M. J. Fisher, Suzy Beemer, Terri Hartman, Alisa Messer, and Aaron Vick.

As an undergraduate at the University of Nebraska, Lincoln, George Wolf, Kate Ronald, Les Whipp, and Sue Rosowski were teachers who opened the door to a world of inquiry and possibility filled with thoughtful questions about writing, reading, teaching, and living. I remain ever grateful for their gifts.

My deepest gratitude goes to my partner in all things, Michael Stancliff, for his tireless generosity, enthusiasm, and humor and for reminding me, at just the right moments, that even Gertrude Stein struggled with sentences and paragraphs and that she enjoyed it. I dedicate this project to my children, Willa Jane and Samuel Bodhi, who, in the midst of it all, kept me focused on the joys of the smallest things: playing with single letters of the alphabet, learning to read words on the page, and already perfecting the art of parental persuasion.

Earlier versions of two chapters appeared elsewhere. Chapter 2, "Suppose a grammar uses invention," was originally published in *Rhetoric Society Quarterly* 38.3 (2008): 283–310. Chapter 6 is an expanded version of "Gertrude Stein Delivers," which was originally published in *Rhetoric Review* 31.3 (2012): 254–270. I am grateful for permission to reprint these.

1
Introduction
Gertrude Stein Reinvents Rhetoric

> Invention: "Suppose a grammar uses invention"
> Arrangement: "With which arrangement are they in agreement"
> Style: "Think of how do you do as very necessary"
> Memory: "She is the articulation of forgetting"
> Delivery: "Do you understand. Do you any or all of you understand. . . . It makes an awful lot of difference to me"[1]

Although Gertrude Stein has been labeled many things—a poet; a lecturer; a novelist; a publicity hound; a mind-numbing, exhilarating, difficult, philosophical writer; a lesbian icon; a great teacher; a genius; a Vichy sympathizer; a survivor—few have recognized her as a rhetorician or sought a place for her in the history of twentieth-century rhetoric. Stein is often seen as a premier modernist or proto-postmodernist innovator. However, Stein's interest in language in all its possible forms exceeds contemporary critical categories and modern disciplinary boundaries in spite of, or perhaps because of, its grounding in rhetorical culture. This book reassesses an iconic literary figure as a major twentieth-century rhetorician, not a spin doctor, as the word might suggest to some; it identifies Stein as a writer who reinterpreted classical traditions of rhetoric to which she was heir even as she anticipated what was to come in the theoretical and literary study of discourse. Stein's career unfolds at t)he crossroads of literary composition and rhetorical theory, a site where she alternately challenges, satirizes, and reinvents the five classical canons of rhetoric—invention, arrangement, style, memory, and delivery—as surely as she invented new trajectories of literary experimentation.

Although rhetoric is often defined and taught as persuasive speaking and writing, its definition has repeatedly expanded and contracted since its inception in ancient Greece nearly 2500 years ago. Wayne Booth acknowledges this definitional challenge, noting "My first problem lies of course in the very word 'rhetoric'" (*Vocation* 309). Beyond and within academic circles the word *rhetoric* tends to evoke negative and narrow connotations: spin, deceit, empty words. John Locke's warning that rhetoric is sophistry, "a powerful instrument of error and deceit," still seems to hold sway (*Essay* Book II, 34). Locke's castigation of rhetoric is epistemologically neo-Platonic; in its obsession with clarity and certainty it echoes Plato's fear of Sophist theory and practice. Ancient Greek and Roman rhetoricians, however, offer more extensive and nuanced definitions. For example, Plato identifies rhetoric as the "art of winning the soul by discourse," Aristotle famously sees it as the "faculty of discovering in any particular case all of the available means of persuasion," Quintilian describes it as a "good man speaking well," and Cicero designates it as "one great art comprised of five lesser arts [canons]." These definitions all view rhetoric as an expansive, teachable art. As such, it can teach, delight, and persuade audiences; it can perform, mediate, and construct ideas and knowledge; it can induce, generate, clarify, or shape belief and action; it can articulate complexity in situations that resist easy answers or answers at all.

For nearly half a century, Stein's writing explored the limits and possibilities of language. Her reinvention of the classical canons embraces the rhetoricity of time itself as a cognitive and textual sensibility while continually calling into question how or if understanding is conveyed. As the titles of her works suggest, Stein is particularly interested in "How Writing is Written," in *Composition as Explanation*, in location (*Geography and Plays* and *The Geographical History of America*), in *How to Write*, in *Narration*, in *The Making of Americans*, in *Stanzas, portraits*, and autobiographies. Although she did not explicitly locate herself in what we have come to call the rhetorical tradition, her writing investigates many of the major and defining concerns of the classical rhetoric. In particular, Stein's writing shares the Sophists' focus on how uses of language arise in particular circumstances and through particular practices and how uses of language can be *kairotic*—that is, responsive to what is happening right here, right now and to those with whom we communicate. For Stein, particular moments include both the historical context for the writing as well as what she calls the "continuous present" of the writing itself. I read Stein's continuous present, a core Steinian concept, as the productive and ongoing kairotic art of rhetoric, the dynamically open process of situated language practices including their potentialities and outcomes.

Like all discursive practices, rhetorics, however defined, are always grounded in and reflective of particular moments in history, and as such, they are intricately bound up with prevailing and shifting cultural and linguistic norms.[2] The remarkable range of Gertrude Stein's writing—from poems, plays, and novels to valentines, portraits, operas, and texts that confound ready classification—explores what James Berlin calls "dispositions of discourse at a particular moment" ("Revisionary Histories" 116). For Stein, dispositions of discourse include history, time, knowledge, geography, grammar, and genre. They also include explorations of dispositions of words: their arrangement, positioning, tendencies, and inclinations across time and space, lexically and syntactically, epistemologically and ontologically.

In this book I cast Stein as a contemporary Sophist, an itinerant teacher wandering from town to town, text to text, offering lessons in the arts of discourse and a theory of rhetoric that stretches across the canons. Rather than enter into a philosophical debate about transcendent truth or the existence of Platonic universal forms, the Sophists turn their attention to the contingencies of human affairs; Sophists work within the realm of the probable, displaying the creative, playful, powerful, and kairotic elements of language. John Poulakos defines sophistic rhetoric as "an art which seeks to capture in opportune moments that which is appropriate and attempts to suggest that which is possible" (36).[3] The Sophists were popular in ancient Greece not only because they offered important skills to the populace in a burgeoning democracy but also because they put on a good show. Audiences enjoyed the entertainment of a bombastic, grandiloquent spectacle of language. Greece's best-known Sophist, Gorgias, tells his audience outright that "To tell the knowing what they know shows it is right but brings no delight" (*Encomium of Helen* section 5). Speech is indeed a powerful lord, as Gorgias's audience well knew, and his *Encomium of Helen* provides persuasive evidence and offers an entertaining exhibition of his skill.

Stein, like the Sophists, puts on a good show. Whether filling lecture halls across the United States as she did during her 1934–35 lecture tour or tantalizing readers with the domestic, tactile atmospheres of *Tender Buttons*, Stein mesmerizes and confounds audiences and readers. She does, indeed, want her work to be enjoyed. She points out, "If you enjoy it you understand it," and in this she follows a tradition dating back to the Sophists and recurring throughout literary and rhetorical history, a tradition that includes Sir Philip Sidney's sense of poetry as an "arte of imitation" used "to teach and delight" as well as George Campbell's view that an end or purpose of speaking is "to please the imagination" (Lundell 88, 86, and Sidney 1). Stein's writing revels in the pleasures of the text even when or, perhaps, especially when the meanings of the text are not immediately apparent or clearly bound by normative rationality.

It is not my intention in this work to reify canonical rhetorical concepts; in fact, my aim is nearly the opposite. The canons of rhetoric are an artificial taxonomy, a classical system that divides the study of rhetoric into five parts, a sequential compositional process.[4] This ordering is and has always been (in spite of Ciceronian efforts to explain otherwise) an invented structure. My organization of this book around the ancient canons is intended to be productive and provocative and to reveal Stein as a Sophistic provocateur whose writing career makes an inventive mess of canonical rhetoric and modernist categories of thought. Whether examining the institutionalization of belletristic literature through the canons of arrangement and style as she does in her *Lectures in America*, establishing the connections between rhetorical invention and grammar as she does in her primer *How to Write,* or reinventing rhetoric's lost canon of memory as more than mnemonics as she does in *The Geographical History of America,* Stein's kairotic and theoretical provocations make textual, critical, and historicizing turns as she works through and reinvents theories of invention, arrangement, style, delivery, and memory.

Although interest in the canons of rhetoric, individually and together, has waxed and waned throughout the history of rhetoric, the canons regained popularity in the late nineteenth and early twentieth century as the organizational structure for the dissemination of modern rhetorical theory. Attributed to Cicero and the unknown author of *Rhetorica ad Herennium* (80 BCE), the canons facilitate a rhetorical process that enables the rhetor to communicate effectively. Beginning with invention (*inventio* in Latin, *heuresis* in Greek) and following the classical definitions, the rhetor discovers appropriate arguments for a particular rhetorical situation. The canon of arrangement (*dispositio* in Latin, *taxis* in Greek) offers organizing principles to structure the argument effectively. After determining what to say and how to arrange it, the rhetor turns to the rhetorical canon of style (*elocution* in Latin, *lexis* in Greek), which in its narrow sense refers to ornamentation, or dressing up language with figures of speech. The rhetorical canon of memory (*memoria* in Latin, *mneme* in Greek) offers methods and devices for retaining and recalling information. Finally, the canon of delivery (*pronuntiato* in Latin, *hypocrisis* in Greek) focuses on the physical performance of the speech.

Stein's oeuvre constitutes a cultural poetics of communication and compositional theory that reinvigorates all five canons of classical rhetoric but in a radically changed intellectual environment. Her approach to composition demonstrates a particular interest in the first canon, invention, defined in its classical sense as a starting point for discovering available resources for rhetorical action. I use these divisions primarily because Stein's writing so fully addresses each and also to offer a new investigative lens for how we might understand Stein's unyielding sense that in every moment, the continuous present, our language practices confound and create possibilities of what she repeatedly calls "being existing."[5] Although I devote one chapter to each of the classical canons of rhetoric, I do not mean to suggest that they are definitive, finite, or distinct in any way. Of interest here is their overlap or, more specifically, their convergence in the canon of invention, which is present in each of Stein's canonical inquiries. For Stein, invention becomes a catalyst for the other canons. Drawing on many of her well-known and lesser-known texts, I place Stein in a pedagogical and historicizing key to demonstrate how she crafts a rhetorical theory across the classical canons that helps to explain and expand our understanding of the liminal space between rhetoric and poetics.

Coming to Writing

Gertrude Stein came of age and learned to write during a time when academic culture was still firmly rooted in nineteenth-century rhetorical thought. Her formal education in composition at Radcliffe College, the women's college of Harvard University, occurred before the turn of the century. Many nineteenth-century habits linger in her twentieth-century writing: her focus, albeit critical, is on the mechanics of writing, on the inventiveness of grammar, the imperative of arrangement and style, the centrality of imaginative articulations of memory, and the necessity of effective and generative delivery. The rhetorical milieu prevalent in the last decades of the nineteenth century provides a productive lens through which to consider how Stein's compositional practices variously reflect, appropriate, revise, and sometimes reject nineteenth-century rhetorical theory and practice across rhetoric's five canons. Locating Stein, the grande dame of modernist poetics, within the rhetorical traditions in which she was educated highlights the residual habits of composition and discourse theory she rejected or revised as well as habits she never expunged from her writing practices.

Although most scholars have focused on Stein as a twentieth-century experimental, modernist literary figure, some have acknowledged the prolific writer's connection with and debt to the nineteenth century. In "Gertrude Stein and the Twentieth Century," Donald Sutherland notes that Stein "was determined, in her time, to stay with the twentieth century, come what might" (15). In *Language & Time & Gertrude Stein*, Carolyn Faunce Copeland locates Stein's break from nineteenth-century literary conventions in her "mature narrative prose" produced between 1913 and 1932 (74–75). Stein's discovery of the modernist literary technique of repetition is, according to Lisa Ruddick, what "leads her away from nineteenth-century family structures and cultural values" (x). Stein herself describes "Melanctha," the second story in *Three Lives*, as "a definite step away from the nineteenth century and into the twentieth century in literature" (*Autobiography* 66). For Charles Bernstein, however, Stein "moved into the twentieth century grounded in the nineteenth," and her "use of the family as a microcosm for the state or church or world" made *The Making of Americans* "very much a work of, or rooted in, the nineteenth century" ("Inventing" 59, 58). Stein's connections to the nineteenth century are not limited to her early work written just after the turn of the twentieth century. The imprint of the nineteenth century remains apparent even in her most hermetic writing from the 1930s, including *Stanzas in Meditation* and *How to Write*, where she theorizes the function of grammar—a late nineteenth-century obsession cannily reimagined and resituated at the center of her rhetorical theory.

Stein, of course, was aware of herself as a *fin de siècle* writer. She was particularly interested in locating her ideas within this liminal space, this movement from one century to the next: "Of course after all there was the nineteenth century and there is the twentieth century, that is undeniable and I began then when evolution was still exciting very exciting" (*Everybody's Autobiography* 249). She was excited about what was happening in her time, especially as the century ended and a new one began, when the theory of evolution provided a new narrative of beginnings, a new way of telling human history in which nature proved to be inventive and dynamically adaptable within the passage of time. Stein also often thought of herself and her writing as historical. Late in her life in the preface to the *Modern Library* edition of her selected writings, Stein quips: "I always wanted to be historical, from almost a baby on" ("A Message" vii).

Scholars disagree about the ways in which Stein's nineteenth-century roots factor into her twentieth-century writing. Lisa Ruddick argues that after the turn of the century William James, Stein's professor at Radcliffe, "had come to represent to her everything she now questioned about the nineteenth century, and as she went about 'killing the nineteenth century' through a modernist literary practice, she pulverized the ideals that had once drawn her to James but now repelled her—specifically, the nineteenth-century faith in progress, in science, and in 'character'" (1). But Stein realized that the past cannot simply be killed off, nor will it disappear; it continues to lurk, even in a continuous present. Her explorations of memory, in particular, suggest a continuous present that has not forgotten the past but rather positions it as necessary and generative. The "articulation of forgetting," as Stein says in the early portrait "Two: Gertrude Stein and Her Brother," is central to her investigation of memory and time, which I address in chapter 5. And while she certainly did not reiterate Jamesian social theory, she acknowledged, later in her life, the importance of his thinking to hers when she called him "the really lasting impression of her Radcliffe life" (*Autobiography* 96).[6]

The conundrum of how to write is a problem that both includes and exceeds literary form in the same way that writing may exceed history while at the same time remaining located within it. Neil Schmitz traces the change in Stein's conception of herself as a writer to the period when she wrote *Tender Buttons* (1914). In this work "she ceased to ask the technical questions about story and character so desperately current in modern writing. Yet in this withdrawal from the instrumentality of narrative, her refusal to employ any language other than her own, she did not, curiously enough, abandon the socio-political realm, rise, as Barthes puts it, 'above History'" ("The Rhetoric" 1218). Even when working within or against literary genre, her principal project is the problem of language, which, for Stein, entails crafting a relationship between writing and culture, between the writer and her culture, between the writer and her audience. By the time Stein gave her *Lectures in America* in the mid-1930s, she began to contemplate more overtly the circulation of language in culture as the titles of her essays suggest: "How Writing is Written," "American Education and Colleges," and "American Newspapers."[7] Thus, Stein doesn't "kill the nineteenth century dead, dead dead," as she says in *Wars I Have Seen* (79); rather, she consistently and deliberately works within rhetorical and literary terms while reinventing them.

Claiming Stein as a Rhetorician

Even attempting to place Gertrude Stein within the history of modernity and literary modernism proves difficult, complicated by the fact her spheres of influence extend well beyond literary innovation into painting, photography, fashion, printing, and managing her public image. Just as surely as her literary innovations helped to define a new phase in literary history, her roles as a cultural networker and a literary ambassador also deeply influenced the canon of modernism.[8] In addition, shifting definitions of modernism also make it difficult to locate Stein definitively. Susan Stanford Friedman teases out the definitional challenges of modernity in "Definitional Excursions: The Meanings of Modern/Modernity/Modernism." Whether defined as rebellion, resistance to tradition ("make it new"), rupture from the past as it was in the 1950s, or as elitist, high culture—"the supreme fiction, master narrative, the great white hope" as it tended to be in the 1990s (494)—the shifting definitions of modernism have both helped and hindered Stein's canonical position. Although she gained mainstream celebrity status following the success of *The Autobiography of Alice B. Toklas,* her other writing, particularly the more hermetic texts from the 1930s, remained marginalized partially due to their difficulty, even though difficulty did not diminish Joyce or Eliot's place in the pantheon of modernists. Stein's mainstream success and celebrity during her lifetime along with her interest in the ordinary also put her at odds with "high" modernism.[9]

Stein played an active role in shaping her place in the canon of modernism that she helped to create but from which she was often excluded or overshadowed by some of the very artists she helped to promote. At the same time, Stein and her writing were long excluded from the patrilineal high modernist canon grounded in the work of Eliot, Yeats, Pound, Lawrence, Joyce, authors who were considered exemplars in the academy through the 1970s. Even in the mid-1980s, Stein's canonical position remained tenuous as Susan Howe notes in a comparison with Emily Dickinson: "Emily Dickinson and Gertrude Stein are clearly among the most innovative precursors of modernist poetry and prose, yet to this day canonical criticism from Harold Bloom to Hugh Kenner persists in dropping their names and ignoring their work" (*My Emily* 11).[10] Marianne DeKoven concurs, arguing that Stein's writing "went further than any other twentieth-century writer in English (perhaps in any language) in reinventing literary language and form, undoing conventional, hierarchical, sense-making modes of signification" ("Modernism and Gender" 223). Although I agree with DeKoven's assessment, I would add that Stein's investigations and reinventions of language extend well beyond the literary.

Stein's rhetorical approaches to composition collapse distinctions and open up possibilities between poetry and prose, philosophy and literature, knowing and enjoying, the modern and postmodern, the literal and figurative, the public and the private, and the intelligible and the unintelligible. Her innovative writing serves as a prescient precursor to contemporary poetics, particularly the rise of Language poetry in the late twentieth century. In turn, many Language poets took Stein's work as a conceptual resource in reassessments of and generative investigations into language. Stein's influence is evident, for example, in Ron Silliman's influential collection of critical essays, *The New Sentence*, Charles Bernstein's cross disciplinary, cross genre, groundbreaking oeuvre, Lyn Hejinian's "Two Stein Talks," Juliana Spahr's *Everybody's Autonomy: Connective Reading and Collective Identity*, and Joan Retallack's *Gertrude Stein: Selections* with its illuminating introduction.

It is not surprising that Gertrude Stein, modernist icon, has been so completely overlooked by the field of rhetorical studies. Claimed by literature departments, Stein continues to be interpreted primarily as a twentieth-century belletristic literary figure and a premier modernist who prefigures and often exceeds antifoundational postmodern sensibilities. Likewise, rhetoricians have not attempted to claim Stein, especially not as one of the twentieth century's premier and most challenging rhetoricians.[11] In the early twenty-first century, Wayne Booth identified numerous "major rescuers" of rhetoric in the twentieth century who "labored to rescue the study of rhetorical issues and methods." The names include William James, John Dewey, J. L. Austin, I. A. Richards, Jacques Derrida, among others, but Booth did not mention Stein. Stein, however, deserves inclusion because Booth based his criteria for identifying these rescuing rhetoricians on their "serious criticism of various positivisms" and "separation of knowledge/rationality/proof from the resources of argument that rhetoric (and life) provide" (*The Rhetoric* 56). Stein, like other twentieth-century rescuers of rhetoric, challenges a study of rhetoric that reduces it to logical proof and privileges reason above all other rhetorical concerns and modes of persuasion. Although Booth's rescuers often "do not employ rhetorical terms," Stein does.

It may be that Stein continues to be overlooked by the field of rhetorical studies because of the sheer difficulty of much of her work. While it is certainly true that readers find the demanding nature of Stein's writing off putting, it ought not deter those who study Greek and Roman texts in translation, authors with no extant writings, grammar textbooks, and postmodern theory as rhetoric. As Ulla Dydo, the premier scholar of Stein's manuscripts, asserts, "Stein *is* hard work, for she challenges our capacity to read and our expectations of what written words and sentences are, what they do and how they do it" (12). Perhaps Stein has also been overlooked by "the rhetorical tradition" because she is a woman, and the history of rhetoric has only recently begun to know what to do with women in its traditions, particularly women who actively theorize uses of language.

Recent attention to the place of women in rhetorical studies is a veritable drop in the bucket of a more than two-thousand-year-old history. Beginning with Karlyn Kohrs Campbell's important anthology of women speakers, *Man Cannot Speak for Her: Key Texts of Early Feminists*, the focus on women in the tradition of rhetoric has a rich and varied history that includes the 1992–1993 Campbell/Bieseceker debate, the special issues of *Rhetoric Society Quarterly* in 1992 and 2002, book-length studies in the mid- to late 1990s, and anthologies in the early twenty-first century.[12] Although women are increasingly included in "the rhetorical tradition" even as the concept of tradition is deconstructed, feminist historians of rhetoric tend to recover women *rhetors,* women who composed or even spoke publicly, but not those who studied, theorized, or taught the arts of rhetoric.[13] Jane Donawerth maintains that women can and do produce rhetorical *theory,* but she finds that these theories constitute a "counter-discourse, an alternative to the dominant rhetorical theory of the time" (12). Stein, however, works within the dominant rhetorical discourse of the turn of the twentieth century so often excluded from discussions of modernism and literary history. From her earliest portraits in the first decade of the twentieth century in which she playfully loosens the connection between words and objects to the theoretical suppositions about grammar in *How to Write,* Stein explores, more thoroughly, theoretically, and creatively than most, the limits and possibilities of language through the lens of rhetoric's classical canons.

To make my case for Stein as a rhetorical theorist who develops a poetics of invention that works across literary, rhetorical, and philosophical registers, I assess the manner in which the various fields of contemporary theory overlook their debt to rhetoric. At a time when English studies shifted away from rhetoric toward literature, from Greek and Latin toward English, from oratory toward composition, Stein brackets epistemological questions of stable, universal truth and writes within the realm of the probable, exploring the connections and contradictions between epistemic and ontologic functions of language. To illustrate the stakes of such a discussion of rhetoric, I offer in what follows a brief history of rhetoric in English studies, which demonstrates the degree to which contemporary theory writ large, whether literary, critical or philosophical, claims or fails to claim its historical associations with rhetoric.

The institutional and historical context I consider positions Gertrude Stein as a preeminent rhetorical *theorist* who engages debates about the place and scope of rhetoric in its contemporary cultural manifestations and across the five canons of invention, arrangement, style, memory, and delivery. Stein's theories of rhetoric and composition keep rhetoric, poetics, and philosophy in dialogue, never privileging one at the expense of the others, and always exploring the historical and psychological dynamics of thinking and writing. Both Stein and rhetorical studies have much to teach us about the importance of theoretical knowledge regarding language; perhaps the most powerful lesson is the way both decenter theory by avoiding any single or dominant orientation. Theoretical knowledge in Stein's work emerges as a source of both quotidian and essential lessons, not just about making or interpreting art, though that is certainly possible, but also about living more fully and effectively within the languages that define us and our worlds.

A Poetics of Invention: *Critical Inquiry*, Rhetorical History, Gertrude Stein

Recognizing Gertrude Stein as a preeminent twentieth-century rhetorician poses historical and theoretical challenges. Although the case has been made that Stein's writing contributes to twentieth-century *literary* theory and criticism—her inclusion in *The Cambridge History of Literary Criticism* makes this case—and that her writing anticipates contemporary theory's poststructuralist feminist critiques of patriarchy—Stein scholarship from the 1980s and 1990s makes this case—her contributions to rhetorical studies remain obscured by a disciplinary history that separates the study of literature, rhetoric, and theory.[14] The figure of Gertrude Stein allows an interdisciplinary reconfiguration by redefining rhetorical studies not as the handmaiden to composition or public speaking—largely its position in the academy throughout the twentieth century—and not as the forgotten sidekick to philosophy within the history of Western intellectual traditions, where philosophy's search for truth has historically trumped rhetoric's willingness to explore the realm of the probable and the contingent. Rather, we can think generatively of Gertrude Stein as the eccentric aunt of the rhetorical tradition who remains independent of established traditions even as she engages and revises them. Her literary and philosophic interests in composition are rooted in the rhetorical theory inherited from the nineteenth century during which a codified emphasis on style and arrangement eclipsed rhetorical invention. Rhetoric was, at best, reconceived in a way that separated it from its civic and communal roots and located it within a sovereign authorial mind.

In order to address Gertrude Stein, the quintessential literary modernist, as a rhetorical theorist, a clearer sense of what constitutes theory, particularly the kind of theory toward which rhetoric has always gravitated, is necessary to better understand who might count as a rhetorical theorist. Within the explosion of "theory" in the last quarter of the twentieth century, the hybridity of literary and rhetorical theory has attracted little attention.[15] Scholars have been bumping up against this quarrel between philosophy and rhetoric, either elaborating it like Stanley Fish; denying it like Ed Schiappa; approaching it like Nietzsche, Derrida, and De Man; re-contextualizing it within the Sophist revival like Steven Mailloux, Susan Jarratt, Sharon Crowley, and Bruce McComiskey; or ignoring it like the premier theory journal in the humanities, *Critical Inquiry.*

In the complicated historical lineages of what are called with varying degrees of precision philosophy, theory, and critical inquiry, I turn to *Critical Inquiry*, the journal that prides itself on a half century of publishing "the best critical thought in the arts and humanities," in the hopes of clarifying the place—or seeming absence—of rhetoric in the practice of critical inquiry and the world of contemporary theory. Given its broad definitions of theory and its founding board member's affiliation with rhetoric, I choose *Critical Inquiry* as an exemplar of theory's arbitration and rhetoric's elision. Other journals like *Philosophy and Rhetoric* or *PRE/TEXT* foreground theory and rhetoric but overlook literature and literary theory, which only extends the perception that these fields of inquiry are distinct. Rather than parse similarities and differences among theory journals in the humanities, I use *Critical Inquiry* synecdochically for a current state of "theory" in the late twentieth- and early twenty-first-century humanities.

Despite a pervasive consensus among theoretical schools across the humanities and social sciences that we ought to or already have done away with the governing binaries of Western thought—a consensus we might broadly classify as deconstructive—we have yet to disentangle rhetoric from the philosophical and literary structures that have gained intelligibility through, I argue, distinctions from and denials of rhetoric. With some of the twentieth century's most celebrated, often controversial, and sometimes vilified theorist-thinkers as it founders, editorial board members, and contributors, *Critical Inquiry* has thoughtfully and consistently interrogated, among other things, the shifting but tenacious role of theory in the humanities.[16] Because Wayne Booth, recognized in the field of rhetorical studies as one of the twentieth century's foremost rhetoricians, was a founding member of the journal, one might expect to find in the pages of *Critical Inquiry* interrogations and discussions of rhetorical history and theory or at least discussions about the lack of discussion. Instead, one finds very little mention of rhetoric. Interestingly, while Booth called himself a rhetorician and included the word "rhetoric" in the titles of many of his book-length and most famous studies, he is rarely referred to or remembered as a rhetorician; rather he is seen as an American *literary* critic, one of the twentieth century's most "prominent and influential" ones.[17] A similar story could be told about another of *Critical Inquiry's* original editorial board members and another of the twentieth century's premier rhetoricians, Kenneth Burke.

In 2006, the journal editors at the time, Anne H. Stevens and Jay Williams, analyzed the story of theory as told through three decades of footnotes in *Critical Inquiry*. In "The Footnote, in Theory," Stevens and Williams "sought to investigate how theory is transmitted through notes, what sorts of conversations are held below the main text" (208).[18] Not only would the subtext clarify the "identity of [their] journal," it would also help to answer the abiding question, "What is theory?" (209). I expected clarification and information regarding these unwritten "conversations" in the text; instead I found confusion about the pervasive definitional problem facing theory, next to nothing about rhetoric, and its editors "stunned" to find no women in their top twenty "Citations of Theorists," with only Judith Butler in the top twenty-five.[19] As a result, my inquiry here seeks to understand the absence of rhetoric from *Critical Inquiry* and theory more generally as well as the absence of women from both.

The absence of rhetorical studies in the pages of *Critical Inquiry* helps to explain how the rise of theory in the late twentieth century further marginalized the study of rhetoric. Stevens and Williams claim that "*CI* [*Critical Inquiry*], and theory more generally, has always been philosophically inclined" (223). They note that the data gathered and analyzed in the article was compiled "in the hopes of creating *a* history of literary theory over the last thirty years" (218). While their italics indicate "*a*" multiplicity of possible histories of which they are offering one, I would also italicize "literary" to indicate a further assumption on their part, namely, that the theory they address is *literary.* Thus, even though this subtextual definition is "philosophically inclined," it is, specifically, philosophically inclined *literary* theory. Because it is *literary* theory, it fails to recognize or account for its deep historical connection with rhetoric. This commonplace elision of rhetoric and rhetorical theory is not at all surprising, particularly in conjunction with philosophy, which has condemned rhetoric at least as far back as Plato's *Gorgias*.

Stevens and Williams's hope "of creating *a* history of literary theory" is consistent with the intellectual origins of the founders of the journal, a group of Neo-Aristotelian literary critics, who, in 1974, sat more comfortably within their disciplinary home of literature. These might be and have been characterized as the good old days when English departments taught what J. Hillis Miller calls literature "in the old-fashioned sense of novels, poems and plays" (415), that is, the prelapsarian days of British and American literature when a poem was just a poem, standing still in time, so to speak, and criticism was still largely "practical." It may also be the case that literature professors sit so comfortably in English departments, chatting from time to time with their colleagues in comparative literature and ignoring the compositionists that we forget English departments as such have only existed for little more than 50 years.[20] There is a hint of nostalgia in Miller's quip, but, "old-fashioned" or not, neither the days of practical criticism nor its vanquishing by deconstruction acknowledge certain older prehistories, particularly literature's longstanding connection to rhetoric.

From its inception in the mid-1970s, merely a generation after English departments became permanent fixtures in American universities, *Critical Inquiry* has maintained a tacit adherence to what has become "literary theory" in spite of its gestures toward interdisciplinarity and its claim to offer "new grounds for theoretical debate."[21] The editors' articulated "hopes" in "The Footnote, in Theory" of "creating *a* history of literary theory over the last thirty years" reveals this literary grounding even as the footnotes themselves attest to the "wide interdisciplinary focus" proclaimed in the journal's self description (218). This discrepancy unmasks not only the perpetual quarrel between philosophy and rhetoric but also literature's forgotten historical and theoretical grounding in and connection with rhetoric at least institutionally speaking since the Enlightenment, although one might argue, as Richard McKeon has in the pages of *Critical Inquiry* itself, that this debate goes back much further to the Sophists, Aristotle, and Plato.[22] Critical inquirers forget to recognize that they are working in a rhetorical tradition both institutionally *and* historically located within "English studies" but with its origin in ancient Greece.

Stein's particular intellectual coming of age occurred just as the study of rhetoric—historically the systematic interdisciplinary investigation of the theory and practice of what we now call *discourse*—gave way to literature. Although Stein is and can continue to be read and remembered as *literary*, this work positions her as a liminal figure who signals what is to come in later twentieth-century philosophically inclined literary theory and early twenty-first-century rhetorical studies. However, making a strong argument for Stein as a theorist—

not just a philosophically inclined literary theorist but also a *rhetorical* theorist—requires fuller sense of the rhetorical landscape she inherited from the nineteenth century.

Lost in the Academy: Rhetoric from Whence?

Perhaps it is not surprising that *Critical Inquiry* forgets rhetoric. Like many other high cultural arbiters of the humanities, perhaps the journal does not know where rhetoric is from or where it might be going. Like the character Phaedrus in Plato's eponymous dialogue, rhetoric is too often cast as lost in the "pleasures of discourse" and in need of a teacher, "a master of the art," like the philosopher Socrates, who "understand[s] the real nature of everything" (20, 23). Socrates asks, "My dear Phaedrus, whence come you, and whither are you going?" With no disciplinary home of its own during the last century, the study of rhetoric remains lost in the intra- and inter-disciplinary shuffle within and across departments of English and communication studies. Understanding the recent history of rhetorics will help to clarify why *Critical Inquiry* and contemporary theory more generally forget rhetoric and how we might read Stein as what Wayne Booth calls a "rescuer of rhetoric."

The connection of rhetorical studies to literary studies remains largely unclaimed among literary artists and scholars due, in part, to rhetoric's modern affiliation with composition, rendering its institutional position as separate from, if not subordinate to, the study of literature.[23] In the nineteenth century, definitions of rhetoric included literature or "belles lettres," largely due to the sweeping influence of Hugh Blair's *Lectures on Rhetoric and Belles Lettres*.[24] Blair, a central figure in the Scottish Enlightenment, who was initially a professor of rhetoric, essentially became the first professor of English in 1762 when his title was changed to Chair of Rhetoric and Belles Lettres at the University of Edinburgh. The addition of belles lettres or fine writing to Blair's title marks an inaugural moment of literary study in the academy, a moment made possible through its coupling with rhetoric, which remained the pinnacle of a liberal arts education well into the mid-eighteenth century. Winifred Horner calls Scottish rhetoric "the missing link that forges the chain between classical rhetoric and contemporary language studies" (9). However, belletristic rhetorics shaped by Blair's *Lectures on Rhetoric and Belles Lettres* have been also identified also as "a negative theoretical and curricular force" because they "accelerated the erosion of rhetoric's historic function in society and the academy, a process completed by the early twentieth century" (Johnson 11).[25] As an influential figure in the rhetorical culture inherited by Stein, Blair, at least in compositional precept, is a kind of shadow figure in Stein's writing. Whereas Blair's yoking of rhetoric and fine writing led away from the canon of invention primarily toward style and arrangement, Stein's rhetorical theory elaborates a poetics of invention across each canon.

Modern rhetorical theory inherited from the nineteenth century dismissed invention as a key element of rhetoric or, at best, reconceived it in a way distanced from its ancient civic and communal roots and located within a sovereign authorial mind. When scholars of the history of rhetoric discuss the modern rhetorical theory that took hold in the nineteenth century and shaped our understanding of rhetoric through the following century, they do so with a kind of lament for the days gone by when classical rhetoricians served the public interest and recognized the communal rather than the singular function of communication. Founded on the philosophical tradition of Scottish Common Sense Realism, nineteenth-century rhetorical theory redefined the function of discourse through its incorporation of modern philosophic theories of the human mind. This reduced rhetoric to arrangement, style, belles letters, or, as Locke has it, "artificial and figurative applications of words," thereby removing it from the public sphere and placing it within a human mind that was capable of recognizing its own operations and communicating clearly. For Locke, we "make words serviceable" by ensuring "that they excite in the hearer *exactly* the same idea they stand for in the mind of the speaker" (*Essay* Book III, 9, 6, emphasis added). This precision requires not invention but clarity—getting it right, taking an idea in one head and depositing into another, where words are in the service of accurately representing and clearly transmitting ideas. Rhetoric, particularly when reduced to ornament, seemingly gets in the way of perspicuity, but rhetoric reduced to ornament forgets to inquire critically, to examine contingency and context, the central intellectual operations of invention. Stein's rhetorical reinventions examine assumptions about clarity and communication, and remain deeply invested in ornament, style, and arrangement, though not at the expense of a poetics of invention.

By the turn of the twentieth century, modern rhetorical theory had moved away from its roots in civic deliberation and became largely reduced to ornament (the canon of style), divorced from oratory, subsumed under composition, and rendered inessential to literature except as figures of speech. After the turn of the twentieth century, the study of rhetoric became institutionally fragmented just as disciplines were beginning to form. Oratory and public speaking migrated to departments of speech communication. Logic, a key element of rhetoric from the time of Aristotle, shifted to departments of philosophy or mathematics. The scientific study of language and its structures moved to new departments of linguistics. Within these new institutional structures, composition remained in departments of English, isolated from broader elements of rhetoric within a discipline moving toward the "practical" interpretation of literature. Thus, the inclusion of belles lettres with rhetoric was short lived as the rise of composition within departments of English reduced rhetoric primarily to rules of correct usage. Stein's rhetorical theory refuses these reductions by, for example, connecting grammar to invention (Stein says in *How to Write* we can "suppose a grammar uses invention") and by re-inscribing the canon of style as more than embellishments of or a supplement to content.

Early twentieth-century histories of rhetoric, written primarily by speech communication critics and practitioners, focused solely on oratory or the teaching of public speaking.[26] These histories dominated rhetorical studies for the first three-quarters of the twentieth century and overlooked the impact of the inclusion of written discourse and belles lettres on rhetoric.[27] But, as Victor Vitanza points out, this tension between speech communication and English, "either as oral versus written discourses or as rhetorical (political) versus rhetorical (poetic) is an ancient one" (194). The fragmentation of rhetoric into different disciplines and the uncoupling of speaking from writing undermined the study of rhetoric and the interdisciplinary study of language. Yet even in our more broadly construed contemporary inter- and trans-disciplinary field of humanities, a cogent historical account of rhetorical theory remains unarticulated, unintelligible within the pages of *Critical Inquiry* and other arbiters of theoretical knowledge.

Because historians of composition are among the few who care and have a vested interest, they have located the split between literature and composition at Harvard where, early in the nineteenth century, the first Boylston professor of rhetoric and oratory, John Quincy Adams, taught rhetoric as a necessary democratic skill for the future leaders of the nation. However when Edward Channing, a literary scholar, assumed the Boylston chair in 1819, he began to move away from rhetoric's classical roots. This erosion continued in 1851, when Francis Child took over and moved to banish the Greek and Roman classics all together; he also changed the title of the chair's lectures from "Rhetoric and Criticism" to "English Language and Literature." This shift away from rhetoric toward literature laid the foundation for departments of English throughout the twentieth century where the study of rhetoric, if it has remained at all, focuses on style, figures, and tropes used in the service of analyzing literature, or has become co-opted by the teaching of writing that emphasizes clarity and correct usage.[28] During the early part of the twentieth century, the period during which Stein wrote some of her most exacting texts, including *How to Write* and *Stanzas in Meditation*, I. A. Richards's *Practical Criticism* formalized literary analysis. Influenced by this movement, literary scholars increasingly began to turn to the "more important" theoretical work of literary analysis and criticism, identifying and analyzing "the best that is known and thought in the world" (Arnold 283). More recently, in the 1970s, literary scholars began deconstructing Arnoldian canon making.

While literary scholars spent a century defining and legitimating their field of study, they increasingly distanced themselves from the "skills-based" teaching of composition, a job still left primarily to graduate students, who likely entered graduate school to study literature.[29] These graduate students inherited the habit of distancing themselves from rhetoric, learned in a folkloric fashion; as a result they carry on the high-low split of literature (now understood as theory) and rhetoric (now reduced to instruction in composition). According to Susan Miller, the "uneasy relationship between 'composition' and 'literature,'" often departmentally and institutionally characterized as dividing "low" from "high," has perpetuated the "almost absolute separation" of literature and composition and has "in varying degrees overlooked the connection between a cultural history of composition and a cultural history of literary studies" (2, 45).[30]

This separation between literature and composition only further elided the place of rhetoric in English studies. The divide deepened with the rise of contemporary theory as seen in the pages of *Critical Inquiry* where any sustained discussion of rhetoric is absent. Given that English studies has yet to acknowledge theoretical connections across the scholarship within its own field, it becomes difficult for interdisciplinary approaches beyond English departments that recognize the place of rhetoric or remember the central role it played in liberal arts education for two millennia. Thus, disciplinary inclinations toward "literary" studies continue to trump the more inclusive "English" studies, a designation which would, at least, allow the possibility of including rhetoric. Gertrude Stein, the literary icon, allows us to rethink historical and theoretical connections between rhetoric and literature and to move toward a kind of interdisciplinarity promised by such venues as *Critical Inquiry*.

Tracing the history of English departments, James Berlin specifically analyzes the relationship between rhetoric and poetics. Initially, works like George Campbell's *The Philosophy of Rhetoric* (1776) regarded literary texts "as a subcategory in a hierarchy of discourses that culminates in the rhetorical" (*Rhetoric* 29). By the turn of the twentieth century, however, this hierarchy became inverted and placed canonized literary texts in opposition to rhetorical texts. Berlin's history of rhetoric and poetics finds that while the definitions and domains of rhetoric and poetry are "historically variable, these domains are usually established as a function of the relation to each other" (29). Although most often cast as a poet or literary writer, the version of Stein I offer demonstrates the ways in which she keeps the rhetoric/poetics dyad dancing, in dialogue historically, rhetorically, and literarily in a way that shifts scholarly understandings of both rhetorical and literary studies.

Where Plato sought to cast out the poets and condemn the rhetoricians so that philosophy and its search for Truth could take precedence, Stein complicates any clear distinctions between rhetoric and poetry, between speaking and writing, between what we say and how we say it. Although Stein received her formal writing instruction during a shift in the late nineteenth-century that emphasized the mechanics of writing—an apparent move away from broader rhetorical and theoretical concerns about language—her explorations of rhetoric's five canons refuse to do away with rhetoric's first canon, invention. Stein's inventional disposition toward language shifts the nineteenth-century emphasis on the primacy of logic and clarity toward a willingness to push language beyond its role of simply providing information toward what she calls "intellectual recreation"—a concept to which I return in the next chapter. In fact, Stein, who is inclined to systematic thought on a massive scale, offers a comprehensive rhetorical *theory* for the twentieth century that is rooted historically, institutionally, and culturally in each of rhetoric's traditional canons while also signaling what is to come in twentieth-century theory. Stein has much to teach about how to write by engaging or ignoring normative constraints. Like the ancient Sophists maligned by Plato for being "lovers of discourse" and losing sight of Truth, Stein brackets, at least occasionally, philosophical questions not by avoiding them but by constantly engaging them, refusing to settle or stop, even when a word is placed on the page or in a sentence, grammar, history, or theory. We must, says Stein, "stay with the language" ("Poetry and Grammar" 319). Her precept requires not a passive staying, not a surrender, but a critical abiding, a kairotic poetics of invention, continually responsive to the situation at hand. Throughout the pages that follow, I "stay with" Stein's language in just this way.

Beginning with "Suppose a Grammar Uses Invention," I elucidate Stein's theory of rhetorical grammar by grounding it in her study of composition at Radcliffe in the mid-1890s. Working primarily with Stein's experimental primer *How to Write,* a book about the craft of composition, I establish one of the central arguments of the book regarding Stein's status as a twentieth-century rhetorician who reconfigures past traditions around the canon of invention to teach a new century about shifts in rhetorical culture across the divide of a century. For Stein, a grammar that takes invention as both a means of discovering and creating does something much more than offer pre-existing rules for writers to follow. Moving into the other canons, Stein never leaves invention behind but rather integrates it into her formulation of each canon.

Chapter 3, "Compositional Form after Arrangement," demonstrates the ways in which arrangement was a central concern and a fundamental conundrum for Stein. Her writing actively explores and engages a wide range of genres—plays, novels, essays, lectures, poems, valentines, and portraits—all forms of literary arrangement. Writing is in itself an arrangement even as it attempts to forgo order. Stein's arrangements continually refer to the structure of the language, the grammar, the history, the mind and myriad culturally bound assumptions about what writing does, or more typically, assumptions about what it does not do. Regardless of *how* one writes, arrangement is always at play. Although Stein surely engages arrangement as sequencing or ordering, she is as interested in exploring and understanding arrangements as agreed upon actions or processes. Stein's abiding concern with arrangement should not surprise us. When she says, "It is by no means strange to arrange," she means it literally (*Stanzas* 246). Arrangement happens all the time, cognitively and ideologically as well as discursively. She held on tenaciously to the idea of order, but she heeded only ironically the assumptions of sender-receiver models of communication, exploring arrangement instead as a model of thinking.

Chapter 4, "An Exacting Style," examines Stein's approach to style through a rhetorical rather than literary lens to illuminate how deeply rooted Stein's thinking was in nineteenth-century conceptions of clarity, particularly the shift away from rhetorical invention and toward bellestristic aestheticism. Although Stein does not leave behind Hugh Blair's influential lessons in *Lectures in Rhetoric and Belles Lettres,* she does not adopt them without critical qualifications. In Stein's transformed canon, style becomes a means of, not divorced from, invention. Stein's writing explores the tensions and dynamics between innovations in literary form and rhetorical invention where style is a vital force in a rhetorical situation that neither exceeds nor is reducible to the event itself.

The fifth chapter, "Troubling Memory," turns to the canon of memory. Exploring the shift from *what* we know to *how* and *why* we know and remember it, Stein rejects memory as mimesis, a mere reiteration of the past, because "remembering *in itself* is not really an important enough thing to really need recalling" (*Narration*, 59; emphasis added). My readings of several key texts in Stein's oeuvre demonstrate that memory is not simply a problem for Stein, something to get out of the way in order to occupy and write the "continuous present." By locating her theorization of memory within the historical and philosophical shifts in the study of language at the turn of the century, this chapter demonstrates how memory in Stein's hands becomes a function of composition, a kairotic engagement with the moment even as it invokes the past.

The sixth chapter, "Gertrude Stein Delivers," examines how Stein's lecture tour during 1934 and 1935 marks her theoretical performance of the art of delivery. Stein's approach to the delivery of her lectures positions her as more akin to the Sophists; not a "mere Sophist" as Aristotle framed it or as a purely deceitful trickster as Plato saw the Sophists but an itinerant intellectual, traveling and teaching, questioning, giving public exhibitions of her skill, willing to privilege probability over the quest for certain truth, interested in exploring all things, all of Aristotle's categories, all the while maintaining an investigation of language-in-culture.

This final chapter ends with a meditation on Stein's legacy in academic and popular circles. We—culturally and academically speaking—continue to be drawn to the larger-than-life figure, which Stein took so much care to create and which has been subsequently taken up with often sensationalizing enthusiasm. Gaining facility with language, discovering one's available means, cultivating the ability to work across the registers of philosophy, poetry, history, and grammar are, for Stein, a cultural necessity "as long as humanity is anything" ("Poetry and Grammar" 238).

2

"Suppose a Grammar Uses Invention"

> Successions of words are so agreeable.
>
> It is about this. . .
>
> Grammar is a conditional expanse. . .
>
> A grammar has been called a grammar of diagram. This is not to be selfish. A grammar has been called a list of what is to be done with it. . .
>
> The question is if you have a vocabulary have you any need of grammar except for explanation that is the question, communication and direction repetition and intuition that is the question. Returned for grammar. . .
>
> Suppose a grammar uses invention.
>
> Stein, *How to Write*

In her experimental primer *How to Write* (1931), a book about the craft of composition, Gertrude Stein offers many lessons through chapters devoted to vocabulary, sentences, paragraphs, grammar, and forensics. In the excerpts used as an epigraph to this chapter, she examines the possibilities of grammar as "a conditional expanse." Stein considers what grammar has been in modernity thus far: formulaic, lists of rules to follow, diagrams to chart. She questions the use and function of vocabulary in relation to grammar. If "you have a vocabulary"—a list of words and phrases, a lexicon, names for things—then what purpose does grammar serve "except for explanation": to elucidate, to make our ideas clear in a Lockean sense, to get the right words to represent the ideas existing in an individual mind? If "a noun is a name of anything," inquires Stein, then "why after a thing is named write about it." Nouns name things and attempt to fix some objective reality in words. But Stein's primer supposes that language, even in its basic elements, works differently: "Suppose a grammar uses invention." Suppose we begin our study of composing as classical rhetoricians did with invention, with a search for specific things to say at particular moments, in particular rhetorical situations. For Stein, a grammar that supposes invention does something much more than offer pre-existing rules for writers to follow.

Many know that Gertrude Stein's language often appears dense and repetitious, as epitomized most famously by her gnomic pronouncement "A rose is a rose is a rose is a rose."[1] Most do not know that her peculiar and seemingly unconventional use of language also frustrated her composition teachers at Harvard University in the 1890s. Additionally, many do not realize that much of her prolific career explores shifts in rhetorical theory inherited from the nineteenth century, shifts that redefined and limited the role of invention.

In this chapter I elucidate Stein's theory of rhetorical grammar by analyzing her studies in the mid-1890s at Radcliffe, Harvard University's women's college, and by demonstrating how for Stein the study of grammar correlates with rhetoric's first canon, invention. In a sense, Stein learned her Harvard lessons well. I read her early experiments with literary form and her focus on grammar as contending with the institutional attempts to reduce composition to rules of correct usage, a reduction Stein was not willing to accept without investigation. Although she was influenced by the trend in the late nineteenth century that emphasizes prescriptive grammar, at the same time she made grammar matter by creating a rhetorical theory that took as its starting point the supposition that "grammar uses invention." As will become clear, what Stein calls invention includes a kind of discovery and creation that occurs during the composing process, in the midst of writing and at the level of grammar. Late in her life, she said that she wanted to "think of the writing in terms of discovery, which is to say the creation must take place between the pen and the paper, not before in a thought or afterwards in a recasting" (Preston 188). Placing Gertrude Stein's writing practices within rhetorical traditions of the nineteenth century reveals a Gertrude Stein who is not necessarily or not only a literary figure, but rather, a rhetor and a twentieth-century rhetorician who refigures past traditions to teach a new century how to write.

Stein's entire canon can be conceived as an extensive response to the changes taking place in the study of language and the shift from rhetoric to composition at the turn of the century when the institutional separation of rhetoric from literature took place. In *How to Write*, in particular, she examines sentences, paragraphs, and forensics as well as the manner in which language holds, rejects, or conveys meanings and perceptions and the ways acts of writing invent identity. I begin with Stein's experience of composition in her undergraduate courses at Radcliffe College in the mid-1890s when the Harvardization of English was firmly in place.[2] Harvard's entrance exams—curriculum reform efforts that led to the modern two-semester composition sequence—and the increased use of more "practical" textbooks offered lessons in ostensibly clear writing and proper grammar. While some literary scholars have ignored Stein's theoretical canon, reducing her composition theory to satire or just a spoof, I examine the connection between Stein's *How to Write* and the book Robert J. Connors calls the "prototype for all 'handbooks of composition' that came after," Edwin A. Abbott's *How to Write Clearly* (68). Although Stein was unwilling to reduce writing to mechanical correctness, she was increasingly willing to "reduce" composition to grammar by making grammar "do" and by supposing it uses invention that includes both discovery and creation. From her moment in history, Stein aimed to invent a kind of writing that was not uninterested in its own practices. She recognized that language cannot be deployed in a cultural or historical vacuum and that rules of usage—just like any usage itself—carry with them an ideological framework that empowers some to invent and others to follow rules.

"Your vehemence runs away with your syntax": Stein's Writing at Radcliffe and the Harvardization of English

Stein came of age and was asked to produce "college-level" writing during a time when academic culture was still firmly rooted in nineteenth-century rhetorical thought that either wholly dismissed invention as a key element of the writing process or reconceived it in light of developments in psychology and philosophy.[3] Her formal education in composition at Radcliffe College occurred before the turn of the century, and Stein cultivated nineteenth-century habits in her twentieth-century writing: her focus, albeit critical, is on the mechanics of writing, grammar, the human mind, and history. Locating Stein within the rhetorical traditions in which she was educated highlights the residual habits of composition and discourse theory that she rejected or revised, habits that she never fully expunged from her writing practices. Due in large part to what we now call the "current-traditional" first-year composition model put forward at Harvard in the last quarter of the nineteenth century, the study of rhetoric became less a theoretical study of language and much more the study of composition where good writing was a result of adhering to fixed rules, an approach that continues to dominate writing instruction in American colleges.[4]

Rhetoric as a field of study that entails all aspects of speaking and writing, including logic, philosophy, grammar, literature, poetry, and dialectic, fragmented under the restructuring of university curricula and the rise of new disciplines at the end of the nineteenth century. Logic, for example, had already migrated to departments of philosophy or mathematics, and philology and linguistics became housed in new departments of linguistics. The study of rhetoric was increasingly reduced to oratory, which became the cornerstone of newly formed departments of speech communication, a discipline made official in 1914 when the speech members of English departments walked out of a meeting of the National Council of Teachers of English to form their own organization and eventually their own departments. The split between speaking and writing further fractured the study of rhetoric, leaving only composition within departments of English and within a discipline increasingly focused on critical analysis and the interpretation of literature, not invention-based rhetoric. By century's end and largely due to Harvard's lead, first-year courses in written composition were widely required in universities throughout the United States.[5] These composition courses, generally offered in the first year for incoming students, focused on grammar and perspicuity. However, as the study of language fractured into different and developing institutional disciplines, Stein resisted even as an undergraduate at Radcliffe thinking about language, specifically about writing, as so easily compartmentalized.

By the time Stein reached Harvard in 1893, the shift from rhetoric to composition was complete. Composition had become a kind of writing instruction that focused largely on mechanics, much to the continued dismay of Harvard's faculty. To gain entrance to the "Harvard Annex," students were required to take an undergraduate entrance examination that required writing a short composition on a literary topic, which examined "works of standard authors," such as Shakespeare's *Tempest*, *Julius Caesar*, or Scott's *Ivanhoe*.[6] When first instituted in the mid-1870s, the exam included only a short composition, but by the time Stein arrived, students were also required to correct "specimens of bad English" (Briggs 57). During Stein's time as an undergraduate, the Committee on Composition and Rhetoric at Harvard prepared four reports on the status of writing instruction for the Board of Overseers. In the first report, written in 1892, likely the year Stein would have taken the entrance exam, the Committee bemoaned the "quantity" of work composition instructors performed that required "not only unremitted industry, but mental drudgery of the most exhausting nature" (Adams, Godkin, Quincy 75). The report squarely placed the blame on the preparatory schools for failing to adequately prepare their students for a university education. "It is obviously absurd that the College—the institution of higher education—should be called upon to turn aside from its proper functions, and devote its means and the time of its instructors to the task of imparting elementary instruction which should be given even in ordinary grammar schools" (Adams, Godkin, Quincy 77). Even "ordinary" elementary schools ought to provide their students with the elements of basic writing, including grammatical rules and theme writing. The report indicated that such basic writing skills were not the responsibility of higher education; however, colleges and universities even the caliber of Harvard continued to find that students required further instruction in grammar.

The shift away from rhetoric toward literature, away from Greek and Latin toward English, away from oratory toward composition began at Harvard under the oversight of Charles W. Eliot, who served as president of Harvard from 1869 to 1909. Eliot is credited with creating one of the first modern universities in the United States based on the German model and including a graduate school, electives, and additional far-reaching curricular reforms (Morison 329–399). These reforms established the kinds of English composition courses that continue to be widely required for first-year students. At the same moment rhetoric was fragmenting under the pressure of newly forming disciplines, Eliot set out to remedy "the prevailing neglect of the systematic study of the English language" (qtd in Kitzhaber 33). Initially, "the emphasis tended to be on rhetoric for its own sake, rhetoric as a body of principles worthy in themselves of being learned without regard for actual writing" (166–167). The focus on "actual writing" as manifested at Harvard was in practice a move that pulled rhetoric even further from its theoretical, multidisciplinary, and civic roots.

Furthermore, Kitzhaber notes that additional changes were taking place at Harvard in the 1890s, the period of Stein's tenure: "The almost unanimous interest in the paragraph as well as the growing attention to the whole composition were evidence of a shift of emphasis in rhetorical instruction in the 1890s," a shift from theoretical to practical rhetoric (166).[7] The increased focus on exercises in textbooks was "symptomatic of a desire to make the study of rhetoric more practical" (206). Titles of textbooks widely used in composition courses underscore this shift. Adams Sherman Hill's *The Principles of Rhetoric and Their Application*, one of the most influential textbooks used in the required composition courses offered at Harvard for over thirty years, replaced and reworked George Campbell's *Philosophy of Rhetoric.*[8] The change in the titles from "philosophy" to "principles" speaks to the move away from the theoretical underpinnings of rhetoric to a more "practical" approach to discourse. Whereas Hill's text begins with a chapter on "grammatical purity," Campbell's opens with "The Nature and Foundations of Eloquence." Hill notes that "the foundations of rhetoric rest upon grammar"(1). He highlights the importance of grammatical purity—what he labeled "correctness" in the first edition—as "the first requisite of discourse, whether spoken or written" (2). Additionally, John Franklin Genung's *The Practical Elements of Rhetoric, with Illustrative Examples* (1885), also widely used at the end of the nineteenth century, excluded, as Genung says, "extended philosophizing on principles and usages" (Brereton 328). Although Hill and Genung's handbooks emphasize correct usage and clear composition, they do so within the context of a larger discussion of the definition of rhetoric included in both of their opening chapters.[9] The inclusion of definitions of rhetoric in Hill and Genung's texts, no matter how diminished, suggests that these composition textbooks and their authors still recognized that they were beholden to the rhetorical tradition most immediately defined by Blair and Campbell, whom both Hill and Genung reference. Soon, however, textbooks in the twentieth century became so practical that many ceased to mention rhetoric at all.

Stein found herself negotiating the ostensible divide between composition and rhetoric in English 22, a two-semester writing course she took in 1894–1895. Her "Radcliffe themes," composed of essays, criticism, aphorisms, autobiographical narratives, and fictional stories, represent the rhetorical workshop of a nascent writer. Her early writing was important enough to her that she kept all fifty writing assignments and in 1939 sent them to Thornton Wilder, who later added them to Stein's archive at the Beinecke Library at Yale University. When editing the Radcliffe manuscripts, Rosalind Miller included the themes Stein wrote along with the comments her professor wrote on her papers. The vast majority of comments consist of single words or single phrases. Here is a sampling of the feedback Stein received: "Has humor—Some misuses"; "Pathetic but not convincing"; "Point of view nobly remote"; "Last sentence queer"; "?"; "Shows gain in descriptive power"; "Your vehemence runs away with your syntax"; "Interesting"; "Shows discernment"; "Hegelian"; "Perspicacious"; "appreciative"; "Arrives"; "A happy consummation"; "Shows acumen—"; "Seems forced"; "Makes a point"; "Caustic"; "Paragraph your dialogue"; "You are severe"; "Specific"; "Sympathetic"; "A rhapsody"; "Language a bit conventional"; "Ends well" (109–155). These comments demonstrate a current-traditional approach to responding to student writing because they focus on the product rather than process. Additionally, they emphasize her style and usage along with her clarity or lack thereof.[10]

Many of Stein's Radcliffe themes explore issues that would become central to her later writing.[11] The topics of her themes include psychology, human nature, literature, philosophy, family, and history. Her choice of topics suggests that even at this early date, writing functioned as a venue of inquiry for Stein. She used first- and third-person narrative, dialogue, humor, understatement, and exaggeration. The shorter themes often addressed issues of belief. Toward the end of the first semester in an untitled writing assignment, Stein commented: "It is a painful fact of human experience that each of us must go over the same old ground of mental struggle and development. To be sure it is a reflection old as the hills but it is still new for I have just rediscovered it. The worst of it is, that the recognition of it as fact is of no value" (122).

Even as an undergraduate, Stein's concerns include human experience, repetition, the relation between old and new, and most particularly, how to embody these concerns in language. Although the ideas presented in her college themes were not as developed as they would later become, the idea that something as "old as the hills" can seem new to someone who has yet to experience it and, further, that it can seem new as if it had been forgotten and rediscovered are themes Stein explored in many later writings including *The Making of Ameri-*

cans, Three Lives, The Geographical History of America or The Relation of Human Nature to the Human Mind, and *The Mother of Us All.*

While in college, Stein questioned the basis of belief: "Sometimes I fiercely and defiantly declare that I won't believe neither now nor in the future." This battle of belief divides the protagonist of her essay who responds to the battle of growing up and developing mentally. The narrator's "other mocking self" is quoted as saying "'Be still you fool . . . why struggle, you must submit sooner or later to be ground in the same mill with your fellows'" (122). The topic seems apropos for a college student, particularly a woman at the country's most elite institution of higher learning that as late as 1897 found a survey of essays by women writers to "show a marked superiority" in mechanical execution including "neatness, penmanship punctuation and orthography." On the level of "thought and form," however, the samples of women's writing were "less robust and less self-assertive" (Brereton 108).[12] But these ideas of repetition in human experience, of going over "the same old ground or mental struggle," of understanding what is "new" and how it relates to what is "old" are concerns of Stein's throughout her years as a mature writer. Similarly, her "disdain for the more necessary marks of punctuation," in the words of her professor William Vaughn Moody, also continued to develop to become a defining feature of her writing.

A decade after Stein's tenure, a young student at Radcliffe commented on the required writing course: "In English A we sink our individuality in a sea of criticism. . . . Whatever idea, whatever individuality of style we may naturally possess, we must drop under the red pencil of the section man. . . . English A does not teach us to write, it teaches us not to write" (qtd. in J. Campbell 475).[13] Stein certainly experienced "the red pencil of the section man," particularly when she received comments from her instructor that focused solely on the mechanics of her writing: "You are careless too about punctuation . . . the quotation marks . . . should be single—not double." Her professor continued, "It will pay you to review those parts of the textbook which treat of sentences and paragraphs" (113). Stein's own subsequent theory of writing would be anything but careless. Even if the result of her college writing course was learning how *not* to write, this early experience served as a pivotal base from which Stein's thinking on writing developed.

In *How to Write*, she formulated her own theory of rhetorical grammar, a theory that required being useful, making grammar do: "It is useless to know how to say so. Grammar. I made it do. . . . The subject is grammar" (106). The subject *is* grammar, but a grammar that necessitates practice, requires usefulness, and refuses mere recitation. Although she devoted a section in *How to Write* to "Sentences and Paragraphs," a response, perhaps, to her professor's request, she did not simply duplicate the lessons of her Radcliffe writing course. She was unwilling to limit the study of writing to a system of rules for arranging words because that alone was useless. A grammar that supposes invention becomes in Stein's hands a rhetorical grammar that attends not just to arrangement, style, or the rules of correct usage, but also and always to a kind of discovery that occurs during the composing process, a discovery made possible within the act of composing.

By the time Stein took her composition courses at Radcliffe, this preoccupation with grammar resulted in a proliferation of grammar books used to teach students how to write properly. Stein's primer *How to Write* reads like a grammar book, but not just any grammar book. Her arrangement of *How to Write* is reminiscent of conventional grammar books with sections on sentences, paragraphs, grammar, narrative, vocabulary, and finally forensics. The organization of the book, beginning with the basic elements of writing and then moving into argumentation, is a sequence followed in university and community college textbooks and classrooms throughout the twentieth and into the twenty-first century—a sequence adopted from the nineteenth century. Stein does not do away with the past or the late nineteenth-century's preoccupation with grammar; rather she rewrites it.

Where Rosalind Miller calls *How to Write* "a big spoof about words, grammar, textbooks on grammar" in which Stein is humorously "satirizing pedantic texts," I surmise that *How to Write* in its entirety may very well be satirizing not just any grammar book, but Edwin A. Abbott's *How to Write Clearly*, the grammar text widely used at Harvard during the 1870s and 1880s (Wozniak 11). Abbott's book was introduced and used extensively at Harvard and the University of Michigan, particularly after the poor showing of students on the Harvard entrance exam, when "specimens of bad English" plagued the writing of incoming students (Brereton 57). Robert J. Connors identifies Abbott's text, which was printed twenty-five times between 1874 and 1914, as "the earliest recognizable prototype for all 'handbooks of composition' that came after it" (68). Given how widely Abbott's text was used in first-year writing courses at Harvard, Stein may very likely have been aware of it; certainly her professors were.[14] Even if she did not actually use Abbott's text, she would have studied similar rules and exercises.

What Stein's *How to Write* takes as its point of departure is Abbott's peculiar pronouncements about writing. Brereton calls Abbott's *How to Write Clearly* "one of the oddest and most complicated textbooks" with "totally arbitrary" rules on clarity and exercises that are "extraordinarily complicated" (316). Abbott seemingly fails to heed his own warning on the opening page: "Ambiguity may arise, not only from bad arrangement, but also from other causes—from the misuse of single words, and from confused thought" (5). Although *How to Write Clearly* purports to be concerned with clarity and the rules for attaining it, Abbott acknowledged that his book was not a complete guide to writing. Rather, the only writing problems addressed in *How to Write Clearly* are those that are "removable by definite rules" (5). Clear writing was dependent on "the arrangement of words" and a "matter of rules" (5, 6). The ability to write clearly, according to Abbott, was "a mere matter of adverbs, conjunctions, prepositions, and auxiliary verbs, placed and repeated according to definite rules" (6). On the one hand, it is ironic that a grammar book that purports to help students write clearly is itself overly complicated and lacking clarity; on the other hand, it is further evidence of the difficulty of reducing writing practices to fifty-six rules, as Abbott does.

Several of Abbott's rules sound almost Steinian. For example, rule sixteen reads: "The subject, if unusually emphatic, should often be removed from the beginning of the sentence. The beginning of the sentence is an emphatic position, though mostly not so emphatic as the end. Therefore the principal subject of a sentence, being emphatic, and being wanted early in the sentence to tell us what the sentence is about, comes as a rule, at or near the beginning" (22). Stein agrees in the second chapter of *How to Write* entitled "Sentences and Paragraphs" when she says, "Every sentence has a beginning" and "Every sentence which has a beginning makes it be more left to them" (26). Her statement is quite literal and clear: when we write, sentences begin on the left. That makes sense. But her sentence says more. She also derides how little is learned by knowing the proper placement or order of sentences and their subjects. She further explains the challenge of working with sentences. "It is not very easy to save a sentence," she says, particularly from the likes of Abbott. While Stein's *How to Write* offers satiric commentary on Abbott's attempt at clarity, the folly she exposes is confusing rule-based composition with knowing how to write. "The great question" for Stein "is can you think a sentence," not can you follow rules (35). Stein plays with the Latin root of *sentence,* which suggests a faculty of perceiving thought, meaning, judgment, and opinion. She has moved us back into a rhetorical realm. Her corrective does not do away with structure or the rules of grammar; rather, sentences in Stein's hands make it so "more [is] left to them" by demonstrating that the structures matter little when disconnected from invention (26).

"Grammar. I made it do": Stein's Rhetoric of Grammar

Stein's lessons at Harvard translate into what became an extended meditation on language including the place of invention and the function of grammar, particularly in *How to Write.* Over the course of a decade, she wrote *How to Write* (1931), *Lectures in America* (1935), which she delivered across the United States, *Narration* (1935), *The Geographical History of America or The Relation of Human Nature to the Human Mind* (1936), *Everybody's Autobiography* (1937), and many of the essays in *How Writing is Written.* During the time she worked on *How to Write*, Stein wrote to Sherwood Anderson about her focus on syntax: "I am working fairly steadily on the sentence, I am making a desperate effort to find out what is and isn't a sentence, having been brought up in a good old public school grammar and sentences are a fascinating subject to me. I struggled all last year with grammar, vocabulary is easier, and now I think before more grammar I must find out what is the essence of a sentence, sometimes I almost know but not yet quite, I think it will interest you" (White 68). Stein's concerns—sentences, vocabulary, paragraphs, and grammar—reflect the late nineteenth-century shift in composition theory and practice that emphasized the mechanics of writing, a seeming move away from broader rhetorical concerns about language. Stein refused as she moved into the twentieth century to relinquish rhetoric's first canon, to reduce writing to composition or rule-governed mechanics, or to practice without theory. Rather, invention was central to her thinking about how to write. Stein recognizes grammar as a study and use of language that is generative, that requires participation from its users: readers and writers, audience and speakers. Stein's approach to grammar also developed through other lessons she learned at Harvard, most importantly through the philosophical challenges offered in courses taught by George Santayana and William James. Stein examines what is lost when the study of composition becomes rote memorization or mere application of predetermined rules. Stein draws on all her lessons at Harvard by devising her own way to "make a fuss about grammar," as she says, where making a fuss is at the same time making grammar do something, making it useful, and disclosing its generative properties through compositional experiments.

"I am I because my little dog knows me": Stein, Invention, and Rhetorical Identity

Following a classical model where the study of rhetoric began with invention, followed by arrangement, style, memory, and delivery, Stein, like a classical rhetorician, privileges rhetoric's first canon as a starting point for the study of discourse. Stein did so during a period often written off as "most responsible for the theoretical impoverishment of the rhetoric of composition," a period that "cannot in any sense be called one of the great eras of rhetoric" (Johnson 11, Kitzhaber 226). The rise of belletristic rhetoric, particularly through the enormously influential *Lectures on Rhetoric and Belles Lettres* by Hugh Blair, underscored the move away from the civic function of public discourse, a move that elided or even dismissed invention from rhetoric.[15] While some such as Blair were willing to eliminate invention from the domain of rhetoric, those who maintained the concept, according to Sharon Crowley, "devised an inventional theory explicitly designed to conform to current developments in philosophy, psychology, and logic" (11). In *The Methodical Memory: Invention in Current-Traditional Rhetoric*, Crowley notes a shift in eighteenth-century discourse theory and finds that the new rhetoricians put forward an "introspective theory of invention" that relied on three unspoken assumptions about the human mind: "first, that it could reliably investigate its own workings; second, that when a mind was engaged with a specific problem, it worked in an organized linear sequence, moving from specific to general or from general to specific; and third, that the mind's sequential workings were accurately inscribed in memory and could be accurately reproduced upon demand" (12). Stein, too, was troubled by the implications these assumptions brought to a now-diminished concept of invention. In several of her works from the 1930s including *How to Write*, *Narration* (1935), *The Geographical History of America or The Relation of Human Nature to the Human Mind* (1936), and *Everybody's Autobiography* (1937), Stein explored the relation between the human mind, how it understands its workings, and how ideas are conveyed in language. Investigating the workings of one's mind entailed for Stein "saving the sentence"—the chapter that opens *How to Write*—by thinking like a grammarian and understanding the sentence's function in relation to the empirical world. She says, "There is no use in finding out what is in anybody's mind" (*How to Write* 16). What is in someone's mind is always created through language, words, and sentences.[16] Although Stein's much discussed preoccupation with identity is often cast in psychoanalytic or poststructural terms, it can be seen as a response to the crisis classical invention faced by the end of the nineteenth century.[17]

For Stein, the function of the individual authorial mind that apprehends and authorizes its subject through reason was, at the same time, a problem of identity *and* a problem of invention. What the new rhetoricians brought to invention and to the inventional theory that dominated nineteenth-century rhetoric in North America was, according to Crowley, a relocation of its source to the mind of a single author, not the commonplaces of the community. Privileging the sovereign authorial mind removes language from the rhetorical equation by rendering language a transparent medium for representing and transmitting knowledge and ideas. Thus the study of rhetoric becomes the study of getting it right, of conveying with clarity one's ideas by correctly following rules. Rhetors who lack the ability to think clearly or to convey their ideas properly can refer to grammar books. Stein interrogates the difference between writing for an audience and writing (for) the self. Although there may be distinctions, Stein is more concerned with what she calls "entity" writing as it is contained within "identity" writing. She plays with the connection on the level of the word. *Entity,* the fact of existence or being, is connected to and contained within the word *identity,* the collective characteristics that make something or someone known. Regardless of how the connection or relation is defined, it is defined discursively, through the act of writing. It is not predetermined by one's mental faculties. It cannot "be accurately reproduced upon demand" as Crowley notes. In a discussion of "Sentences and Paragraphs" in *How to Write*, Stein considers a similar point: "Now think of the difference of repeat and of duplicate" (*How to Write* 110). A repetition underscores the contingency of language—the way it changes over time and depends on place even if we use the same words, the same sentence. While duplication may copy the past, it cannot simply repeat it. Duplication is always contemporaneous with itself; it is always present in its own time while at the same time acting as a witness to history.

Stein's interest in repetition and recreating ideas in language demonstrates a rhetorician's interest in how ideas are conveyed from writers to audiences, from past to present, from memory to words. These ideas stem from other rhetorical lessons Stein learned at Harvard in her philosophy and psychology courses with George Santayana and William James.[18] Her theory of rhetorical grammar repositions the role of the writer somewhere between these lessons in her philosophy courses and the lessons in her grammar books. Stein encountered contradictory ways of thinking about composition and its relation to knowledge. Stein biographer Linda Wagner-Martin notes that Santayana's theories of writing were important to Stein, particularly "his belief that writing, like the acquisition of all knowledge, started with mysticism—and that writing was in some ways itself an acquisition of knowledge" (32). Although Stein may have entertained the idea of realities beyond perceptual or intellectual apprehension, what remained central to her rhetorical theory was the belief that writing was an activity, an intellectual recreation, not a mere imitation or accurate reproduction. In an essay on "Literary Form," derived from lectures on aesthetics given at Harvard in 1890s, Santayana found the English language "remarkable for the intensity and variety of the colour of its words" (n. 345). He also commented that "grammar, philosophically studied, is akin to the deepest metaphysics, because in revealing the constitution of speech, it reveals the constitution of thought" (345). Stein shares Santayana's conviction that the interrelation of grammar, language (spoken or written), and thought is a philosophical endeavor. However, Santayana's approach to writing greatly differed from the prevailing model at Harvard put forward by Adams Sherman Hill. In the preface to his influential

Principles of Rhetoric, Hill claimed that rhetoric "does not undertake to furnish a person with something to say" (iv). Hill cautioned that as writers, we "must not attempt to express ourselves in language before we thoroughly know our own meaning" (iv). A writer's thinking, according to Hill, must be done prior to writing. The purpose of writing, therefore, is to arrange one's ideas stylistically and clearly. Although writing may have to do with arrangement and style, it also functions for Stein as a heuristic, a site of knowing, a place where meaning can be made.

William James's theory of pragmatism also offered Stein a way to think about grammar as connected to invention.[19] Jamesian pragmatism, like rhetoric, is about probability not certainty, about what works and how, not what is true and why. In Lecture VII of *Pragmatism*, entitled "Pragmatism and Humanism," James maintains that "the notion of *the* Truth, conceived as one answer, determinate and complete" is often understood as such due to the ways in which we talk about it, ways that make it seem as if we uphold a notion of absolute truth (115). James explains: "Common-law judges sometimes talk about the law, and schoolmasters talk about the latin [*sic*] tongue, in a way to make their hearers think they mean entities pre-existent to the decisions or to the words and syntax, determining them unequivocally and requiring them to obey" (116). James locates discourse in material circumstance. He is concerned with who is talking—judges and teachers—and with where the talking takes place—courtrooms and classrooms. He continues, "we pretend that the eternal is unrolling" and "the one previous justice, grammar or truth is simply fulgurating, and not being made" (116). James includes "grammar" with other concepts, like truth and justice, often considered eternal and unchanging rather than "being made" as we talk about them. Extending the pragmatic concept of multiplicity or variety from truth and justice to grammar creates a grammar consisting not just of pre-existent rules, but a grammar also dependent upon and defined by its use. This pragmatic notion of grammar as something that is made as we talk about it, not a pre-existent entity, echoes Stein's assertion that we must "suppose a grammar uses invention." If grammar uses invention, then grammar becomes not just a "man-made thing," as James calls "laws and languages," but things that change over time and place and depend on the rhetor.

A single Stein sentence repeated with variation in several works from the 1930s shows how she plays with rhetorical identity and explores the function of the writer reproducing ideas. In *How to Write* (1931), *The Geographical History of America or The Relation of Human Nature to the Human Mind* (1936), and *Everybody's Autobiography* (1937), Stein repeats "I am I because my little dog knows me" (113, 66, 19). This repetition challenges the sovereignty of an individual author/mind by calling into question the function of a sentence and the generative quality of language. Stein likely came across "the little dog" example, originally from *Mother Goose*, in Josiah Royce's metaphysics course at Radcliffe. Royce used the verse to illustrate Kant's transcendental theory of apperception, which, according to Royce, "depends on and involves self recognition" where "the phenomena of my sense-world . . . recognize the authority of my thought-forms, or categories'" (128).[20] For Kant, the mind apprehends and has knowledge not just of its own mental states, as Hume would have, but also of external objects. In *Talks to Teachers* (1892), William James also addresses apperception, defining it as "the act of taking a thing into the mind" in such a way that it becomes "a sort of fusion of the new with the old" (157). What Stein adds to theories of apperception— the relation between mind/object, new/old—is the sentence and the status of rhetorical identity, of knowing one's self in language. Her repetition of "I am I because by little dog knows me" draws on and extends Royce's Kantian lesson by examining the role of the sentence in an epistemological endeavor.

Stein's inquiry continues. In *Everybody's Autobiography*, she follows the original sentence with another problematizing one's identity by connecting it to invention and to writing: "But was I I when I had no written word inside me" (66). This sentence calls into question the epistemological validity of the preceding sentence: is one's identity shaped or known because "my little dog knows me," because something outside of myself and outside of the sentence provides empirical evidence, or, as the second sentence suggests, am I I only when my ideas exist with written words? If there are no written words, no invention in the act of writing, then what happens to the identity of "I"?

Stein addresses the issue more directly in *How to Write* by moving from words to sentences: "What is a sentence for if I am I then my little dog knows me" (19). The logical sequence of the sentence has changed from "I am I *because"* to a conditional proposition, "*If* I am I *then*" (emphasis added). The connection between the first and second parts of the sentence changed. "I am I" not *because* "my little dog knows me"; rather, because "I am I," my little dog knows me. In other words, the relationship of how one knows oneself is not determined by an external entity, by what a little dog knows; it exists in relation to it. Stein's variation in *How to Write* self-reflexively reframes the issue calling into question not just what is known, but also the function of a sentence in relation to what is known. She begins the iteration by asking "What is a sentence for." The question is less epistemological, less about who knows what and how, and more rhetorical, more an issue of how this knowing or being ("I am I") connects to language, to writing. Stein questions the founding epistemological assumption of modern philosophy, that knowledge exists independent of language, that it can reside in individual minds until it is attached to words and transmitted via a transparent conduit of language to other minds. Sentences and paragraphs, just like the rules of grammar, do not exist for Stein outside the rhetorical situation; they are situated within and responsive to particular moments and specific audiences, even of little dogs.

"Why make a fuss about it": Stein and Generative Grammar

By theorizing a rhetorical grammar, Stein addresses the crisis of invention in modern rhetorical theory and pedagogy not by adding a modern or postmodern twist, but by harkening back to a classical model and updating it for her current situation. In "The Gradual Making of the Making of Americans," one of her *Lectures in America,* Stein speaks to the importance of grammar to the English language: "English grammar is interesting because it is so simple. Once you really know how to diagram a sentence really know it, you know practically all you have to know about English grammar. In short any child thirteen years old properly taught can by that time have learned everything about English grammar. So why make a fuss about it. However, one does" (146–147). Stein agrees with the members of the Committee on Composition and Rhetoric at Harvard that by the age of thirteen children can learn the rules of grammar, but she problematizes the seeming simplicity of knowing the rules of correct usage. Harvard's Board of Overseers made a fuss about grammar when they implemented the entrance exam because they felt that the students coming to Harvard had failed to learn "the basics" adequately. They suggested that if students learn the rules, for example the fifty-six put forward by Abbott in *How to Write Clearly*, then they should know how to write. But Stein shows that knowing the rules, knowing "everything about English grammar," is not equivalent to knowing how to write. Stein also problematizes grammar but very differently than the educators at Harvard. "It is this that makes the English language such a vital language that the grammar of it is so simple and that one does make a fuss about it" (*Lectures* 147). She recognizes that the vitality of the English language is connected to grammar. Where the Harvard men imply a linear progression from grammar to rhetoric, from simple to sophisticated, where the study of language begins with mastery of the simple rules of grammar and then moves on to the more important aspects of the language, Stein denies a linear, binary model. The inventiveness of the English language is present even in its simplest forms, even in the rules of grammar. One simply needs to know how to make a fuss about it.

When Stein revises classical rhetoric's first canon, she recalls earlier definitions of grammar and differentiates her own thinking: "A grammar *has been* called a grammar of diagram. . . . A grammar *has been* called a list of what is to be done with it" (*How to Write* 56, emphasis added). Reducing grammar to a diagram or a list makes it useless. "Grammar is useless because there is nothing to say" (62). Without invention, grammar is useless; the writer merely follows rules and language merely mimes external objects or internal ideas. However, for Stein, there is, literally, nothing to say, until one invents it.

Stein's concept of invention works in between "discovery" and "creation." Invention as discovery, particularly in its Aristotelian sense, emphasizes finding appropriate means of persuasion. According to this view "means" or commonplaces exist in the world, and it is the job of the rhetor to find them and express them in language. In this model language is a tool for persuading audiences by representing things already existing in the world. Invention as creation, according to Yameng Liu, posits "bringing into being something that has never before existed, some strange entity snatched *ex nihilo* which is, presumably, completely different from whatever has been accepted as part of the 'reality'" (54). But for Stein, as for her teacher William James, the "new" always carries with it the "old," even when or especially when we create in language.[21] Drawing from James's theory of apperception, new experiences are always understood in light of old ones. For James, both "new" and "old" are mutually modified by their encounter: "In this gradual process of interaction between the new and the old, not only is the new modified and determined by the particular sort of old which apperceives it, but the apperceiving mass, the old itself, is modified by the particular kind of new which it assimilates" (*Talks to Teachers* 165). Thus, creating does not happen out of nothing, but within language, within the words in which we write and speak, words that carry histories within them that shape our understanding of both the present, the past, and ourselves. Although the writer herself in the act of writing appears temporally suspended in the present, the history and the context remain. In "We Came. A History," written in 1930, Stein clarifies: "Sentences are historical" (275). The act of writing itself occurs in the present, the continuous present as Stein has it. The processes of writing (its methods, practices, and grammars) and the written product itself are rooted in sentences and history. Many years later, Derrida suggests a similar idea about the relationship between language and history: "We have no language—no syntax, no lexicon—which is alien to history" (280). Invention always negotiates history and place, time and situation, past with present, and the rhetor within.

Stein's theory of rhetorical grammar can be illuminated through Debra Hawhee's account of Gorgias's theory of invention, which critiques the view that the two senses of invention are discovering and creating. Hawhee argues that both senses of invention—as a process of looking out into the world to discover arguments and as a generative process that creates new things to say—rely on the same model of modern subjectivity. According to Hawhee, both "the 'grasping' and 'generating' models of invention posit an active, sovereign subject who sets out either to 'find' or 'create' discursive 'stuff'" (16). This is the model of subjectivity borne of Descartes's *cogito ergo sum*, condensed by Hume's skepticism, and solidified by Kant's transcendental method. The discovery and creation models of invention presuppose an individual writer whose relationship to the rhetorical situation is linear. Hawhee offers a third term in the discursive encounter, what she calls "invention-in-the-middle" in which discovering and creating arguments are, at the same time, discovering and creating the rhetor. The shift moves from "'I invent' [to] 'I invent and am invented by myself and others' (in each encounter)" (17). Stein and her little dog agree. Stein clarifies the relation between the act of writing and invention when she says, "but think of the writing in terms of discovery, which is to say the creation must take place between the pen and the paper, not before in a thought or afterwards in a recasting. . . . You won't know how it was, even what it is, but it will be creation if it came out of the pen and out of you and not out of an architectural drawing of the thing you are doing" (Preston 188). Stein's comments use the defining terms of rhetorical invention—creation and discovery—and her language is precise. Invention does not merely reflect the past, "how it was," or the present, "what it is." The creation, for Stein, occurs in the midst of writing; it comes "out of the pen and out of you" by drawing on the past to shape the present. It creates and is created by the rhetor.

Grammatical Invention: Reading *How to Write*

In the fourth chapter of *How to Write*, entitled "A Grammarian," Stein identifies and rehearses the function of a grammarian by reinscribing her time's reductive preoccupation with grammar. Stein's grammarian does not simply work with pre-existent rules to which words and sentences are made to obey; rather, grammar becomes a heuristic. Thinking and writing in terms of grammar, working on the level of grammar, Stein's grammarian puts it this way:

> Now I am playing.
> And yielding.
> To not attempting.
> Think closely of how grammar is a folder.
> To look back in the way they came. Now think.
> Who stands.
> To look back in the direction in which they came.
> In the direction in which they came

> To look back in the direction in which they came.
> A grammarian is so.
> Afraid.
> Is a word.
> To look back in the direction in which they came.
> To look back in the way they had come. Now
> you see that means that others had come and
> others look back in the direction that others had
> come. (110)

Stein asks her readers to read closely, to listen carefully, to do more than correct "specimens of bad English." Toward the end, the first-person narrator asks, repeatedly, for the audience, the reader, to think: "Now think. . . . Think well of this. . . . Think of the difference. . . . Think of that" (109–111). Specifically, Stein asks her audience to "think closely of how grammar is a folder," about grammar as a container of language and its history. If grammar is the study of language, a composed body of words, their structure, arrangement, pronunciation, meaning, and history, then what is Stein asking? She defines a grammarian as one who considers all of these elements of language, just as she considers all these elements of writing or written language.[22]

Stein's grammarian theorizes the role of history to the work of writing by looking back in at least two ways. First, "to look back *in the direction* in which they came" and, second, "to look back *in the way* in which they came"—a subtle but Steinian distinction (emphasis added). She repeats this phrase and its variation several times. She also shifts the tense from "came" to "had come," from simple past to past perfect, from an action that occurred in the past to an action completed at some definite point in past time. Indefinite and definite pasts. Stein seizes the moment by playing with grammatical time, with history in grammar. She forgoes or at least calls into question chronological time, suggesting instead a more flexible, less linear sense of time where linearity and duration matter less than the opportunity made possible in a particular moment. Stein's kairotic sense of time recognizes the contingency of situations, a contingency based on contemporaneous and historical events. We teach our students, like Stein her audience, that a "kairos-based discourse does not seek certainty prior to writing, but rather views writing and speaking themselves as opportunities for exploring issues and making knowledge" (Crowley and Hawhee 35). When Stein says, "Anybody can see nearly what I mean," a reader, the student, learns to feel thankful for single words like "nearly" (110).

But Stein's grammatical shift from "came" to "had come" is almost lost in a clause. The verb, the action, has to do with looking back, with *where* to look and in what direction and with *how* to look and in what way. For Stein and for the grammarian, this is all apprehended through language. Grammar, as the grammarian knows and as Stein shows, is not outside of time or history. Looking back becomes a pedagogical moment when one learns not only of one's past but also that others have learned about the past, and furthermore, that they bring that learning into the present. Rhetoricians like Stein, who include kairos as a central principle of invention, acknowledge the importance of an issue's history as well as its shifts over time and their current ramifications. Although Stein's word choice of "direction" and "way" are similar, almost a duplication, they are also different. "Way" can indicate a road, a path or direction, a certain path, or going from one place to another; it can also suggest a manner of doing something culturally as in the "American way" or individually as in "my way." What happens when one looks back in the direction or in the way "*they* had come" (emphasis added)? Stein tells us what "that means": "Now you see that means that others had come and others look back in the direction that others had come." The act of looking back is a connective act, a communal move that connects one to the past by recognizing and remembering it. In Stein's rhetorical theory, invention does not occur ex nihilo.

Stein ends "A Grammarian" with a warning about not thinking, about stopping:

> It stops because you stop. Think of that. You stop because you have made other arrangements.
>
> Changes.
>
> Grammar in relation to a tree and two horses. (111)

The stopping is a result of something "you have made" in the past, perhaps a list of grammatical rules. The past tense is significant. Something is made, done, completed, and the invention has stopped because "other arrangements" have been made; thus the invention is finite, its job is done, the means discovered, the rules decreed. Therefore, when "it" stops, "you" also stop. But Stein doesn't stop. In Stein's rhetorical theory, invention is an intellectual re-creation, both discovering and creating, as Hawhee has it, a "discursive encounter [that] itself forges a different subject . . . and the emergent subject becomes a force in the emerging discourse" (17). There is no stopping for rhetoricians. For Stein, invention is ongoing, responsive to and informed by its discursive community. She ends the essay as a grammarian, thinking, continuing, and making "Changes," a word that stands, centered, by itself just before the final line that continues to connect grammar with specific objects: "Grammar in relation to a tree and two horses" (111). Grammar is not a set of a priori rules that govern language but can be used continually to discover and create relations between objects in the worlds in which we live and, in the process, help us discover and create ourselves. Stein's grammarian supposes that grammar uses invention. For anyone who is looking or trying to see, it cannot stop. Nor can she. Stein's rhetorical theory privileges a conversation that always continues and calls for rhetors to continue inventing and being invented by their rhetorical situations.

Gertrude Stein is a rhetorician, a teacher of rhetoric whose pedagogy relies on epistemic rhetoric, that, according to James Berlin, "posits a transaction that involves all elements of the rhetorical situation: interlocutor, audience, material reality, and language" (16). Throughout *How to Write,* Stein shows what epistemic rhetoric looks like by asking her audience to become aware of and to struggle with the syntax of language, its position in history, the lessons of the grammarian, and also the call to thought and action inherent in language. For Stein, our language use is always situated in particular times and places and has many functions: to instruct, to confound, to shape or unravel knowledge, to build community, to delight, to move us to thought and/or action. She marvels at the ways language communicates itself, and she enjoys how funny it is (as with little dogs and Kant).

Several years after the publication of *How to Write*, Stein gave her *Lectures in America*. These lectures include "Poetry and Grammar" in which she clarifies the cultural function of language: "Language as a real thing is not imitation either of sounds or colors or emotions it is an intellectual recreation and there is no possible doubt about it and it is going to go on being that as long as humanity is anything. So every one must stay with the language their language that has come to be spoken and written and which has in it all the history of its intellectual recreation" (238). The opening statement about language makes clear what language is not: imitation. Rather, it is "an intellectual recreation"—a phrase that, at first glance, might be dismissed as playful amusement. But recreation, as a noun, suggests refreshment as well as amusement, refreshment of the mind or body by engaging in enjoyable activities; it is part of what makes humanity something. And "there is no possible doubt about it and it is going to go on . . .". Language is creating anew, refreshing, rejuvenating, and it is collective. When Stein claims that "Grammar is in our power," she means it, for if it is not in our power, it will surely be in someone else's (73). Ulla Dydo confirms that Stein's work "is a demonstration of possibilities of grammar for democracy" (*The Language* 17). Stein insists on the importance of staying "with the language," on our ability to develop our facility with language, an intellectual recreation that, by its very nature, creates the possibility of a world not predicated on automatic, unquestioned deferral to authority or to the accepted wisdom of elders. Rather, to suppose a grammar uses invention, to *suppose* anything, asks that we enter into a rhetorical realm to explore the complexity and humanity of thinking and writing.

3
Compositional Form after Arrangement

> It is by no means strange to arrange.
>
> Stein, *Stanzas in Meditation*

> With which part of the arrangement are they in agreement.
>
> Stein, *How to Write*

Gertrude Stein, the premier experimental modernist, crafted *The Making of Americans* (1906–1908) a decade before T. S. Eliot began *The Waste Land.* She published *Tender Buttons* years before George Willard reported on *Winesburg, Ohio* (1919) and just as Ezra Pound made his first attempt in 1915 at what would become a touchstone in literary modernism, *The Cantos.* Pound's title refers to the poetic form he used, dividing the poem into 120 sections that resist coherent arrangement. Similarly, the sequenced stories in Sherwood Anderson's *Winesburg, Ohio* and Jean Toomer's genre-bending *Cane,* while interrelated, are arranged around a place—stable or shifting—rather than a central protagonist or a unified theme.[1] These examples indicate the ambitious, self-conscious formal experimentation of modernist writers, who reconceived the logical and aesthetic relations of the parts within the whole much like Stein's painter friends, Pablo Picasso and Georges Braque.

Just after the turn of the twentieth century, when artists were beginning to investigate and assess the functions of arrangement, the most influential philosophers and rhetoricians found arrangement to be so self-evident that it required no discussion. Philosophic discourse continued to follow the prescribed analytic order of logical argumentation, a form of writing assumed to be transparent and detached from the ideas presented, merely the most reasonable ordering of premises.[2] If language were simply a means of presentation, then proper order would clearly follow from clear thinking. Rhetoricians, if they addressed arrangement at all, taught it as the management of arguments, ordering them logically to make a persuasive case to a rational audience whose minds purportedly processed information in the same way regardless of the topic, social context, or differences in race, class, or gender. Thus, the arrangement of arguments would ostensibly mirror the universal processes of reason at work in the minds of both writer and reader.

Although modernism ushered in widespread literary innovation in the early twentieth century, writers including Stein often continued to work within traditional literary genres. Classifying literary texts into genres began as early as Aristotle's classifications of poetry in the *Poetics*. Calling classifications into question or challenging their definitional boundaries soon followed. Wai Chee Dimock has recently pointed out, "The membership—of any genre—is an open rather than closed set, because there is always another instance, another empirical bit of evidence to be added" (1378).[3] Thinking beyond the simplifying binary of open/closed form, Derrida addresses the ways in which "a limit is drawn" when the word, *genre,* is invoked (56). Derrida points out that genres always function as principles of arrangement: "The genre has always in all genres been able to play the role of order's principle: resemblance, analogy, identity and difference, taxonomic classification, organization and genealogical tree, order of reason, order of reasons, sense of sense, truth of truth, natural light and sense of history" (81). Derrida's principles of order bring us back tellingly to Stein's famous quip, "a rose is a rose is a rose is a rose." Although Stein's repetitive floral arrangement elucidates Derrida's principles of order, it also underscores that arrangements of words, like genres, draw limits, organize experience, and perform or define identity. Stein knew well that modern arrangement was often predetermined by genre conventions, cultural expectations, or historical convention; it is no wonder that she places the question of consensus or "agreement" at the center of her canonical plundering.

Shortly after Stein explored issues of form, cultural and individual identity, history, and geography in the genre-bending *The Geographical History of America or The Relation of Human Nature to the Human Mind* (1936), Kenneth Burke's *Philosophy of Literary Form* (1941) noted a connection between literary form and identity: "Implicit in poetic organization per se there is the assertion of an identity" (39).[4] Stein's explorations and constructions of "identity writing" for an audience as well as the more meditative, private "entity writing" work across genre; these works include the poetry in "Identity a Poem," the novel *The Making of Americans,* and perhaps even *Tender Buttons*, which is preoccupied with arrangement and a largely absent "I." Although Stein's writing often gives the appearance of adhering to literary genre, her engagement with form often deconstructs the very principles of generic order. She steps out from under the long shadow of the Enlightenment, outside of dialectic or systematic modes of argumentation, though the arrangements of her writing continue as inventive acts questioning and engaging the formative power of representational, philosophic, linguistic, and rhetorical frames.

For Stein, arrangement remained a central concern and a fundamental site of invention for the entirety of her writing life. Rather than simply assuming or rejecting conventions, she actively and self-reflexively investigated a wide range of genres—plays, novels, essays, lectures, poems, valentines, and portraits—all forms of literary arrangement. Adhering tenaciously to the idea of order, she heeded only ironically assumptions of sender-receiver models of communication, instead exploring arrangement heuristically. Her interest in form includes but also extends beyond arrangement's primary denotation of adapting to or rejecting a particular order or sequence. To arrange or to make arrangements can also entail preparing for a future event. We make plans, often with others, for a particular time in the future. These arrangements require coming to an agreement with someone. Stein's writing requires a certain arrangement among reader, writer, and text.

Although Stein surely engages arrangement as sequencing or ordering, she is just as interested in exploring and understanding arrangements as agreed upon actions or processes, as in the case of the tacit or troubled agreement to genre conventions or historical narratives in some writing. In *How to Write*, she queries, "With which arrangement are they in agreement" (136). Not only are multiple arrangements possible, as her omnipresent, sometimes communal, often patriarchal pronoun suggests, "they" agree with some and not with others. These textual arrangements extend to history as Stein elaborates in "We Came. A History" (1930), which opens with a self-assured interlocutor who notes, "We came and were pleased with what we saw" (274). The text goes on to discuss, perform, and rearrange history. Although concerned with "An attitude of being made agreeable" in part because "we found it agreeable to show them things" (275), the speaker, speaking for "we," goes on to question and define what constitutes history: "History is this anything that *they* say and that *they* do and anything that is made for them by them. . . . This is historical. . . . What is historical. Sentences are historical. . . . This is not historical. . . . This might be historical. . . . This is historical. . . ." (275 emphasis added). Initially claiming that "they" have a say over history, the speaker quickly takes over, identifying what is and what is not historical. Just before the text largely drops end-stopped sentences and opts instead to connect words, phrases, and occasionally sentences with equal signs, the speaker asks, "How do you like what you have heard.= . . . History is made by a very=Few who are important=And history is what that=One says" (275, 276). Stein frames the word and phrases with equal signs, calling attention to assumptions at work in historical sentences, in segments of narrative history. We have heard what "they say" and what "One says": "All this has=Been a history of pleasantness=In arrangement which=They made when they=Were pleased.=" (277). But now, "We came and were pleased," and the textual equations of history become contested, rearranged, and equalized. "We came" and established another history. Arrangements can be rearranged. We can agree with some and not others.

Stein's abiding concern with arrangement should not surprise us. To arrange, as Stein suggests in the otherwise confounding *Stanzas in Meditation,* is "by no means strange" (246). Arrangement happens all the time, visually, verbally, cognitively, and ideologically as well as discursively. She understood visual arrangement from an early age due in part from her interest in painting and sculpture and her friendship with Picasso. Painted by Picasso, photographed by Man Ray and Cecil Beaton, sculpted by Jacques Lipchitz and Jo Davidson, Stein's image became one of the early twentieth century's most famous. Wanda Corn and Tirza True Latimer credit Alice B. Toklas with rearranging Stein's image by creating her iconic, masculine, short-cropped haircut, a signature look not adopted until she was fifty-two. Developing a distinctive style as a lesbian couple in the late 1920s, Stein and Toklas "performed their partnership in front of a camera, saying pictorially what they could never discuss in public" (6).[5] More than a style, the visual arrangement of their lives, a kind of composition in the continuous present, also contributed to a new cultural order.

Writing is in itself an arrangement even as it attempts to forgo order; it continually refers to the structure of the language, the grammar, the history, the mind, and myriad of culturally bound assumptions about what writing does, or more typically, assumptions about what it does not do. Paragraphs and sentences are products of arrangement; history and time are abstract but normalized matters of arrangement just as surely. Thus, writing is by necessity the practice of arrangement whether or not prescribed rules are followed, broken, revised, or ignored.

Formal innovation obsessed modernist writers and artists and their critics. The dominant story of modernism depicts a heroic overthrow of received tradition in which syntactic unfamiliarity, paratactic structure, or the reworking of sacred or mythical texts seems to will a new age into existence. The early seeds of New Criticism moved away from biography, history, and culture toward conceptualizing an independent text. However, the burgeoning field of literary criticism maintained a sharp focus not just on the text itself but also increasingly on logical analysis of figurative textual components even when rendering ambiguity. In the end, perhaps in the intensity of critical attention to the innovations of modernist aesthetics, the idea of a "break" with past formal traditions has been reified. Stein's concerns exceed literary and modern rhetorical theory and practice that shaped early twentieth-century approaches to composition and literary experimentation. In order to understand how Gertrude Stein wove all these traditions, new and old, and their formal mandates into a theoretical treatment of textual arrangement, we must first attend to a chapter inevitably left out of accounts of high modernism's formal transgressions.

The Rhetorical Canon of Arrangement: Ancient and Modern

Arrangement is a kind of framework, an ordering that structures reading, writing, and rhetorical situations by framing the ways in which ideas, knowledge, constituted subjects, and time emerge. The canons of rhetoric are themselves an arrangement of steps for crafting effective communication. Of all the canons, arrangement has received the least scholarly attention until quite recently with the rise of computer-mediated hypertext and increased attention to taxis.[6] However, even with the prevalence of hypertext and the theoretical inquiries it has inspired in the last two decades, arrangement still continues to be subsumed by other canons. Collin Gifford Brooke argues that "the (hypertextual) collapse of arrangement into invention and delivery . . . is rapidly becoming commonplace among hypertext critics" (256). Earlier, W. Ross Winterowd argued, "Invention and arrangement are so nearly the same that they are almost indistinguishable; they are basically the same process" (*Rhetoric* 121). In the mid-1990s, Jeanne Fahnestock agreed, noting that the canon of "arrangement has received little *independent* treatment" (32 emphasis added).

Although Aristotle began to systematize the study of rhetoric in his *Rhetoric*, it was Roman rhetoricians who arranged rhetoric into five distinct parts, the canons of rhetoric. James Murphy notes, "In the two centuries between the death of Aristotle (332 BCE) and the appearance of the first major Roman treatises about 90 BCE the most important developments in classical rhetoric took place in codification and schematization" (128). The Roman *Rhetorica ad Herennium* is the first text to offer a detailed discussion of each of rhetoric's five canons. This work remains tremendously influential not only for the study of rhetoric but also as a still-recognized sequencing of the writing process. As the second canon, following invention, arrangement has to do with finding an effective order of arguments in a speech or writing. A writer or orator begins by exploring possible lines of argument (invention), which would then be arranged into the most persuasive order and styled to meet the needs of the audience. The canons of memory and delivery come last in the Roman schema as a matter of utility in assuring an effective presentation of the argument.

Classical rhetoricians established a general pattern of arrangement still recognized today. In *Phaedrus*, Plato calls proper arrangement necessary for finding truth. He criticizes those, including Sophists, who use arrangement only to make arguments effective without evaluating their veracity. Aristotle recommended a four-part arrangement: introduction, statement of facts, proofs, and conclusion. Cicero followed this rigid, temporal pattern but added a section for refutation: "say something before addressing the case, then set forth the case, after that prove it by establishing our own arguments and refuting those of our opponents, then conclude the speech" (*De Oratore* 2.307). Quintilian's adaptation of five parts reverberates through primary and secondary school pedagogy in the United States, especially in the ubiquitous five-paragraph essay. Modern interpretations of classical forms, no matter how narrow, continue to have a powerful influence on writing pedagogy and on generation after generation of what is seen as the "common sense" arrangement of essays. It is the "common sense" and basic elements of writing and arrangement as well as assumptions of linearity or sequential ordering that Stein embraces and reinvents even as she invokes, for example, a traditional arrangement of a composition handbook as in *How to Write* or a largely linear argument in "Composition as Explanation" even though its central premise is the necessity of "beginning again and again and again" (220).

Quintilian's discussion of arrangement, however, actually suggests something more than a formulaic ordering; it suggests an ancient dynamism in arrangement theory that the moderns (Stein and other modern artists aside) by and large failed to carry forward: "But just as it is not sufficient for those who are erecting a building merely to collect stone and timber and other building materials, but skilled masons are required to arrange and place them, so in speaking, however abundant the matter may be, it will merely form a confused heap unless arrangement be employed to reduce it to order and to give it connexion and firmness of structure" (*Institutio Oratoria* Book VII. preface. 1–2).

To have effective arguments, generating materials is not enough. Rather, as Quintilian suggests, "skilled masons are required" to construct, following the architectural metaphor, effective oratory. If it were "possible to lay down general rules which would suit all subjects," the canon of arrangement would be quite simple, but it is not. Quintilian devotes a whole book (VII) of *Institutio Oratoria* to arrangement. Skillful arrangement requires "the pleader must rely upon his sagacity, keep his eyes open, exercise his power of invention and judgment and look to himself for advice" (VII, preface, 4–5).[7]

The ancient canon of arrangement depended to some degree on what the particular rhetorical situation required. "While ancient discussions of arrangement were formal and prescriptive to some extent, ancient rhetors paid much more attention to rhetorical situations than to formal rules" (Crowley and Hawhee 198). Ancient conceptions of arrangement oscillated between arrangement as prescriptive and arrangement as an aid to invention. *Rhetorica ad Herennium* presents these two options: (1) adhering to six precepts of rhetoric or (2) allowing the arrangement to be dictated by the specifics of particular situations. Richard Leo Enos makes a similar case in "The Emergence of Literate Rhetoric in Greece." Enos traces the shift from oral discourse to written composition through the lens of paragraphing and finds that "the paragraph is not merely a formulaic convention but rather a conceptual notion in the inventive process of composition" (238). Although paragraphs "aid in the arrangement of oral discourse," they also "serve an inventional function . . ." (236). Stein's interest in sentences and paragraphs can be read through a similar lens as an exploration of the tensions between the formulaic or the conventional, as in the formal features of genre, and the inventive dynamism of arrangement as a heuristic that orients further thought and composition. The experience of disjuncture, of syntactic lacunae for example, between the parts of the whole in a Steinian arrangement require a practice of reading as invention, of finding rhetorical or aesthetic resources not previously available.

Largely due to the influence of eighteenth-century discourse theorists, modern rhetoric all but eliminated classical invention from the rhetorical process, as was previously discussed. Eighteenth-century rhetorical theory, which grounded nineteenth-century thinking about rhetoric, dismissed invention in favor of managing or arranging arguments. James Berlin notes that by the nineteenth century rhetoric was predominately defined as managing, not discovering material; this in effect reduced rhetorical invention to arrangement (*Rhetoric and Reality* 64). Sharon Crowley suggests that this shift in rhetorical invention also collapsed the canons of arrangement and style: "because language had only one function—to mirror thought—the function of arrangement came to be very like that of style in current traditional rhetoric" (*Methodical* 121). Invention was reduced to or subsumed by arrangement. Proper arrangement simply mirrors clear thinking. This line of analysis resonates with a brief turn to rhetorical history in the work of Michel Foucault amid his analysis of Western philosophy when he cites the banishment of the Sophists as the moment when discourse was seen to simply convey preexisting meaning: "Western thought has seen to it that discourse be permitted as little room as possible between thought and words" (x).[8] If an argument is thoroughly and clearly thought through, then the arrangement of the argument need only mirror this thinking. Because all minds are ostensibly structured in the same way, the arguments will be effective. Arrangement is not a heuristic. It is, instead, reified as a structure of thought and expression, both strongly inflected with moral significance.

Hugh Blair's influential *Lectures on Rhetoric and Belles Lettres* teaches the management of arguments, not their discovery or creation, and lays the groundwork for collapsing the canons of arrangement and style. Blair's *Lectures* rarely discuss arrangement as a canon or as central feature of rhetoric. Rather, he emphasizes close attention to style, nearly at the expense of arrangement. Good style means the text is arranged properly and effectively. This is nowhere more apparent than in the index to the second edition of the *Lectures* (1785), prepared by Blair himself, which includes more than thirty subcategories under the heading "style" and no entry on arrangement, with only a single mention of the word under "argument." Here, Blair acknowledges that effective arguments "in some measure, depend on the right arrangement of them" (358). He offers four brief pieces of advice. First, to avoid confusion and dilution of persuasive effect, avoid blending arguments. The second rule is to move from weak to strongest arguments, though this rule is "not to be always followed" depending upon the arguments available and the rhetor's trust or distrust in his cause (359). Third, if one's arguments are "strong and satisfactory," then they ought to be "distinguished and treated apart from each other," but if the arguments are "doubtful" or "presumptive," then "it is safer to throw them in a crowd, and to run one into another" (359). Finally, Blair warns against "extending Arguments too far, and multiplying them too much" (360).[9] Although he does briefly address arrangement in Lecture XXXI, "Conduct of a Discourse in All Its Parts—Introduction—Division—Narration and Explication," this scheme for arrangement, in its inevitable sequencing, requires little discussion. Rather, Blair turns his attention to style, devoting nearly a third of his *Lectures* to its discussions.

The modern approach to arrangement as a textual auxiliary to reason derives rhetorical theory from a model of the well-ordered mind and the ostensible precise self-containment of thought in transit from sender to receiver. Quantifying, classifying, and defining systems of arrangement included dictionaries and encyclopedias and extended to understandings of the human mind.[10] Faculty psychology, influenced by Locke and popularized by the Common Sense Realists, conceived of the human mind as arranged into separate faculties, each with a specific mental task. Locke's epistemology assumed all human minds operate in the same way. The senses gather information from the external world, which the mind processes and stores. Arguments do not need to be invented; rather, rhetors must carefully review their own thought processes and then arrange their arguments following a similar sequence, which will allow the idea to move from the mind of the rhetor to her audience. If language were simply a presentational means, then proper order would clearly follow from clear thinking. Rhetoricians, if they addressed arrangement at all, taught it as the management of arguments, ordering them logically to make a persuasive case to a rational audience whose minds purportedly processed information in the same way regardless of the topic or social context.

Although Locke's epistemology was premised on a universal human mind, it was George Campbell's *Philosophy of Rhetoric* (1776) that incorporated Locke's philosophy into rhetorical theory. A Scottish Enlightenment philosopher and Presbyterian minister and educator, Campbell hierarchized the arrangement of the human mind, adding the imagination and the passions to Locke's categories of understanding and will. To be effective, or eloquent as Campbell has it, discourse must be "adapted to its end"—"to enlighten the understanding, to please the imagination, to move the passions, or to influence the will" (1). Effectively adapting discourse to its end means that the rhetor has successfully transferred the idea in her mind to her audience. Campbell admits that while we might have conclusive arguments, we must also have a way of conveying them persuasively. Not only must the arguments be understood, they must be "felt": "in order to persuade me by them to any particular action or conduct, it is further requisite, that by interesting me in the subject, they may, as it were, be felt. It is not therefore the understanding alone that is here concerned. If the orator would prove successful, it is necessary that he engage in his service all these different powers of the mind, the imagination, the memory, and the passions" (72). Aware that his inclusion of the imagination and passions might be read as an assault on reason and logic, Campbell underscores that "these are not the supplanters of reason, or even rivals in her sway; they are her handmaids, by whose ministry she is enabled to usher truth into the heart, and procure it there a favourable reception" (72). Although they are rendered "handmaidens," the feminine and subservient to the rule of reason, imagination and the passions are given a place in the process of argumentation because of their persuasive potential with the audience. The gendered figures Campbell employs to describe the relationship of reason and the passions in the well-ordered mind suggest how the patriarchal dictates of social "order" were inscribed as theory in a modern dispensation.

If modernist aesthetics were overcommitted to formal innovation as an achievement in itself, modern rhetorical theory erred even more egregiously in its pedagogy of unobtrusive form. Modern rhetoricians oriented their craft to the very same principles of Enlightenment reason whose limitations were explored and rejected by literary modernists. Stein was one among many literary discontents working out the contradictions of traditional literary form, and the sensational iconoclasm of this high modernism tends to obscure her investigation of the rhetorical canons of invention and arrangement. Stein's reception of two traditions of arrangement, the literary and the rhetorical histories, collapsed into one another. Responding to both traditions, Stein's writing investigates how compositional practices and practices of arrangement forward or resist larger ideological and cognitive arrangements.

Stein Arranging Experience

Stein's acute and much-commented-upon focus on form, a quintessentially modernist approach, was not only literary innovation or an illustration of Pound's dictum to "make it new," but also a response to a narrowing in thinking about compositional practices in literary modernism and modern rhetorical theory. Her broad, interdisciplinary, and cultural interest in linguistic innovation has always exceeded literary and formal concerns. More than working within or even breaking and revising traditional literary forms, Stein made a telling mess of each, refusing to follow conventions and yet refusing to do away with conventional form altogether. Troubling traditional arrangement was a matter of acting in the continuous present by exercising a critical intelligence at the crossroads of centuries. As easy as it may be to see Stein as waving a banner for formal novelty fit for the emerging century, which clearly excited her imagination, her iconoclasm was not doctrinaire. Just as she refused to reject grammar or clarity, she did not completely reject linearity in time and arrangement; rather, she reclaims these categories as invented and inventive.

In an interview with Donald Sutherland late in her life, Stein reflected on language and the sentence as a frame for our experience of the world. "But any sentence is in itself an organization of experience." If "any sentence," as Stein says, is "an organization of experience," then our sentences, the ways in which we talk and write, give order to experience even when they confound understanding (183–184). In this textual form, Stein's paratactic arrangements are not particularly orderly or clear as understood in modern rhetorical theory; nor are they complete chaos, lacking in all order and arrangement. Her sentences often lack punctuation, repeat words and phrases, call attention to themselves and rely on unattached pronouns, syntactic alterations, and linguistic recreation. They can also be remarkably straightforward, quotable quips: her renowned "a rose is a rose is a rose is a rose"; the instructive last line of her portrait of Picasso, "Let me recite what history teaches. History teaches"; her pronouncement in *The Making of Americans* that "I am writing for myself and strangers"; and the witty acknowledgment that "It takes a lot of time to be a genius, you have to sit around so much doing nothing, really doing nothing." Whether immediately comprehensible or extraordinarily confounding, Stein's arrangements refuse finitude, calling to question, into play, the conventions themselves.

Lyn Hejinian, purveyor of the open text, underscores the importance of form to Stein's writing and thinking: "For Stein, the container was from the start an interesting problem. To regard description—or the page of writing—as a container was to betray the nature of the thing described, the flow of its existence, and the flow of the consciousness perceiving it" (104).[11] New thinking and new formal arrangements were co-extensive, mutually productive, and dynamically in flux temporally. What some treat as essential frameworks or first principles, Stein treats as method and process. She did not deviate from so much as re-inhabit discursive, cognitive, and ideological arrangements, the textual sequence, a chain of premises, and a set of affect-rich assumptions. Throughout Stein's canon, arrangement becomes not an ordering system or even an odious abstraction; rather, it becomes a heuristic, productive art that creates the possibility for new forms and ways of thinking to be created, challenged, or ignored.

In testing the productive potential of arrangement, Stein joined a growing number of modernists discontented with the formal order of modernity. By the time Stein began her formal experimentation in writing just after the turn of the century, the idea of arrangement was changing, shifting from one century to the next. A still life was no longer a tableau. Portraits become increasingly disarranged, paradoxical snapshots of multiple, simultaneous moments in the manner of Duchamp's *Nude Descending a Staircase.* Picasso's famous 1906 portrait of Stein is one of his last to retain static, ordered resemblance from a single point of view; the following year Picasso's *Les Demoiselles d'Avignon* rendered angular, disjointed bodies, a rearrangement Stein endorsed. Commenting on her travels across the United States during her lecture tour, Stein said that from the airplane window: "I saw there on the earth the mingling lines of Picasso, coming and going, developing and destroying themselves . . . yes I saw and once more I knew that a creator is contemporary, he understands what is contemporary when the contemporaries do not yet know it, but he is contemporary and as the twentieth century is a century which sees the earth as no one has ever seen it" (88). The frame has shifted, one century to the next, opening up new perceptual possibilities. Although Picasso had not seen the earth from an airplane, he, according to Stein, "inevitably knew that the earth is not the same as in the nineteenth century . . ." (88). Similarly, Stein's writing often connects geography and grammar. Jennifer Ashton notes, "how Stein imagines the paragraph is how she imagines America itself, . . . a bounded our boundaried whole" (292). In the movement of one century to the next, Stein saw Cubist abstractions in the land and a shift in representational arrangement in words.[12]

As Picasso began to rearrange his subjects, Stein began her early experiments with arrangement. *The Making of Americans*, which she started in 1903, followed the traditional novelistic form of a family history. Stein drew the curtain back on her own production of narrative form, interjecting meditations on the process of writing and the making of *The Making of Americans.* Rearranging form even further, *Tender Buttons* (1914) takes inventory of the domestic material worlds in three sections: "Objects," "Food," and "Rooms." At the same time, the divisions in *Tender Buttons* demonstrate how trenchantly Stein remained focused on making order and arranging text even as her writing moves beyond the conventions of literary genre for models of arrangement. Stein opens the work referencing the arrangement of objects: "A kind in glass and a cousin, a spectacle and nothing strange a single hurt color and an arrangement in a system to pointing. All this and not ordinary, not unordered in not resembling" (9). Arrangements are, in fact, frameworks, though they may not provide clarity or even order. Order does not necessarily lead to mimetic resemblance with familiar patterns or stable genres, indicating a neat correspondence between words and objects, between content and form. At the same time, Stein makes clear that this kind of arrangement is "not unordered." Stein's "perfectly unprecedented arrangement," as she says later in "Objects," reflects the way in which we perceive and experience the world before we put it into order, the ways in which we come to a gradual understanding—or not—of what we see and experience (24). In one sense, *Tender Buttons* is a record of an experience of arranging.

Focusing specifically on Stein's sentence arrangement, Ron Silliman notes, "The syllogistic move above the sentence level to an exterior reference is possible but the nature of the book reverses the direction of this movement. Rather than making the shift in an automatic and gestalt sort of way, the reader is forced to deduce it from the partial views and associations posited in each sentence" (*The New Sentence* 84). Stein's arrangements implicate the reader on the level of the sentence, as Silliman points out. The arrangements in *Tender Buttons* are particularly challenging; they are partial, seemingly arbitrary, and full of questions without answers and pronouns without referent. "Question and pronoun," says Neil Schmitz, "...dominate the discourse, so much so you could say *Tender Buttons* is about the pause it must give readers, about their question, their desire for the referent."[13] Stein herself offers advice for what readers might do in the pause before proceeding with the text: "Act so that there is no use in a centre" (63). Stein's recommendation neither confirms nor denies a center. She sets the issue aside instead directing readers to take action, to do something with her words, to make our own arrangements.

Reading *Tender Buttons* creates the experience of scanning a room, the eye catching certain "objects," noticing patterns of light, image, color, and words. Charles Bernstein points out, "Poems are stuck in black and white, which means that every color connected to a poem is proof of the inner life of words" (*Recalculating* 173). One way to "arrange" a reading of *Tender Buttons* is to follow a thread of color. The opening stanza tenders "a single hurt color. . . . The change in that is that red weakens an hour. . . . The change of color is likely and a difference a very little difference is prepared. . . . Light blue and the same red with purple makes a change. . . ." (9–10). The still life has changed right before our eyes. Stein has set it in motion. Discussing *Tender Buttons*, she explains, "I began to do this thing, I tried to include color and movement . . ." ("Portraits" 189). She shifts attention from the color to its function with adjectives that perhaps function metaphorically or literally: "a single hurt color." This is still "a system to pointing" but the objects are not still. Prepositional confusion draws attention to "to." Wouldn't we generally have a system *for* or a system *of* or, perhaps, a system *to point* with? Stein's use of the gerund *pointing* makes the word a verb; this follows the rule that gerunds must be used when the verb comes after a preposition. Perhaps more to the point, Stein uses a present participle, the form of a verb ending in *-ing*. Grammatically speaking, this form is used in forming continuous tenses, which describe an action that is ongoing. Stein has arranged it so that we have an opportunity to participate in the continuous present/tense of her writing.

Tender Buttons overflows with objects to be arranged. In the first section, "Objects," Stein's organizing principle entails section headings such as: "A Carafe, That Is a Blind Glass"; "Glazed Glitter"; "A Piece of Coffee"; "Nothing Elegant" "A Plate"; "A Seltzer Bottle"; "A Long Dress"; and "A Red Hat." The following section, "Food," begins with an inventory of the contents of the section: "Roastbeef; Mutton; Breakfast; Sugar; Cranberries; Milk; Eggs; Apple . . ." and so on. Stein seems to address the predicament of arrangement, offering some direction in the section "A Box": "Out of kindness comes redness and out of rudeness comes rapid same question, out of an eye comes research, out of selection comes painful cattle. So then the order is that a white way of being round is something suggesting a pin and is it disappointing, it is not, it is so rudimentary to be analysed and see a fine substance strangely, it is so earnest to have a green point not to red but to point again" (11). The arrangement of these sentences gives a reader pause and leaves work to be done. One imagines the "rapid same question" might be the reader's "What? What? What?" in response to Stein's text. In a poem otherwise saturated with color, white stands out. What is a "white way" or a "white way of being round"? Perhaps the phrase "being round is something suggesting a pin" is simply a prima facie statement. But it is just a suggestion, not a solution. Stein's "So then" indicates that we have covered certain points and what follows ought to clarify. The beginning of the sentence is promising: "So then the order is that . . ." and although we return to a color (or is it colorless, "a white way of being"), we are led around in a circle: "round is something suggesting a pin." What is the point? It might be disappointing says Stein, but we are told definitively "it is not." This is, Stein suggests, a rudimentary endeavor, existing only in its basic form, waiting to be developed. What is the point? In Stein's return to color, the complementary red and green, we find a lesson in pointing, not from color to color but simply "to point again," to keep the text in motion, the mind at work, the experience at play, the arrangement rearranging.

Stein's discussion of the visual arts in *Everybody's Autobiography* explains the "prison of framing" and the challenge of creating art with "a feeling of movement inside" (322, 321). Art, suggests Stein, provides literal and figurative frames, "pictures have been imprisoned in frames, quite naturally and now when people are all all peoples are asking to be imprisoned in organization it is quite natural that pictures are trying to escape from the prison the prison of framing" (322). She contemplates how, then, might one not "live in its frame." Frames that organize to a point of imprisonment shut down "a feeling of movement inside the painting" (321). While Stein hopes "to have it happen the picture to be alive inside in it" (322), she draws a distinction between a "painting of a thing moving" and "the thing painted having inside it the existence of moving" (321). Stein explores the logic of the frame, the space between context and content, the literal and metaphorical framing of words on the page.

Although Stein explicitly discussed Cubist painting vis-à-vis her writing, she also implicitly considers acts of reading and the relationship between the work of art, its potential "feeling of movement inside," and efforts of imagination required by the reader or viewer to see more than the object and to experience the movement. She addresses the problem of the literal and conceptual frames in her lecture "Pictures": "I have passionately hoped that some picture would remain out of its frame, I think it can even while it does not, even while it remains there" (*Lectures* 86). The painting like the words in Stein's portraits potentially exceed the content represented, spilling over conceptually, even as the painting remains framed. Stein, the writer, shares "the first hope of a painter . . . that the painting will move, that it will live outside its frame" (87). A literal frame of the painting or the generic frames of literary convention can become conceptual. In her discussion of twentieth-century aesthetic autonomy and politics, Lisa Siraganian connects the function of frames to Stein's grammar: "Literal frames, according to Stein, suffer from the same flaws as commas and quotation marks: they impinge on the beholder's pleasure by telling you when the painting begins and ends instead of requiring you to work out the distinction yourself" (36).[14] More than beholders, readers of Stein have work to do, their own arrangements to make. Not only does she leave us to ponder, as she says in her primer on composition, *How to Write*, "A sentence says you know what I mean," we must next consider, "Now what is the difference between a sentence and I mean" (31). Furthermore, she also hopes that we enjoy the process: "Happy is to find what it does" (33). Although we may be used to a sentence that "Pleases by its sense," Stein asks readers to ponder, "What is a sentence mostly what is a sentence" (34). We are not required to figure it all out; "mostly" will do.

Making Arrangements

Written after her successful lecture tour, *Everybody's Autobiography* is a chronological accounting of Stein's life beginning as requested with "What Happened After *The Autobiography of Alice B. Toklas*," which is the title of chapter one.[15] Following the form of a traditional autobiography and narrating events in her life chronologically, Stein also applies pressure to its generic norms even in the opening line: "Alice B. Toklas did hers and now anybody will do theirs" (1). Where we might have expected Stein to finally identify herself as the subject and author of her own life story, we get instead "anybody."[16] *Everybody's Autobiography* is a day-to-day accounting in which Stein addresses the potential problem of organization: "The world is completely covered with people and these people would like to be completely organized to live" (105). "But," says Stein optimistically, "anybody can get tired of anything, except living, and perhaps they will get tired of organizing" (105). Here, she draws a tension between "living" and "organizing." While anybody might like organization, it also becomes problematic. To be completely organized, to put everything in its place, leaves little to do.

In "Composition as Explanation," Stein discusses the "time-sense" of the "modern composition" and the changing understanding of the "time of composition" and "time in the composition" (225). She connects how "one finds oneself interesting oneself" with making arrangements: "And so now one finds oneself interesting oneself in an equilibration, that of course means words as well as things and distribution as well as between themselves between the words and themselves and the things and themselves, a distribution as distribution. This makes what follows what follows and now there is every reason why there should be an arrangement made" (224). Words on the page are inevitably received as objects of arrangement. We arrange them even as they arrange our perception and experience. Stein's interest in how we know, what we know, and how we convey what we know also includes an exploration of how that knowing is limited or made possible by our arrangements. Different arrangements constrain or make possible different ways of knowing, being and living. As a writer interested in the continuous present, the pleasure of words, and the necessity of thoughtful acts of composition, Stein turns her attention to sentences and not to the linguistic structures of language alone. Stein's investigation was not Sausurrean but an exploration of the ways in which arrangements of language underscore what already exists—tacit agreements we have about our worlds and the words we use to describe and create them.

How to Write offers Stein's most ambitious rethinking of the canon of arrangement by mapping the intersections and cofunctionality of grammatical, geographical, historical, and theoretical assumptions about form. She points out that we can have "Arrangement by grammar" and that "Arrangement [can be] a noun" (64, 130). Countries like the United States also have arrangements geographically and linguistically: "In the oldest country the United States of America there is the oldest arrangement of lines and words" (72). In "Sentences," a hundred-page chapter in *How to Write,* Stein explores the boundaries and functions of sentences, asking repeatedly, more than fifty times, "What is a sentence." She offers many proclamations in response: "A sentence is made by coupling"; "Sentences may be alike"; "A sentence is why they find it"; "A sentence comes to be for use"; and "This is a sentence as arrangement" (115, 117, 117, 125, 138). Because sentences function in a variety of ways, Stein asks, "With which arrangement are they in agreement" (136). Stein's "they" oscillates between those who have much to gain by learning to "Think and think and think a sentence" and those who understand that "A sentence is made for *their* use" (146, 126, emphasis added). For "them," the unspecified third-person plural, Stein suggests a kind of self-serving utility: "A sentence is an interval during which if there is a difficulty they will do away with it. A sentence is a part of the way when they wish to be secure. A sentence is their politeness in asking for a cessation" (133). "They" follow the prescribed arrangement, making sentences "for their use" and fulfilling their desire for security or at least a summative break in the flux of signification and thought.

This security, however, comes at a price, one Stein cautions against. Although their actions may appear polite, their arrangement implicitly asks for "cessation" (133). In the previous chapter, "A Grammarian," Stein alerts "you" to the danger of making arrangements that lead to closure: "It stops because you stop. Think of that. You stop because you have made other arrangements" (111). Certain arrangements shut down the possibility of change and bind words and thought within static structures. In "Sentences," Stein imagines and models a way to "Think of a sentence"—a directive she offers nearly forty times—without stopping. We might, Stein suggests, choose to be in agreement with certain arrangements that are generative and leave open opportunities to continue. This approach, according to Stein, "is very well done because it does not stop" (27).

In "History of Messages from History," Stein hypothesizes "a difference between history and description," marking a distinction between "history" and "messages from history" that makes possible different arrangements. History leaves messages for recipients who cannot be contacted directly or that readers receive after the fact. Therefore, recipients of messages from history must learn to "Manage changes" within narratives or "Read it for changes" (263,

264). Messages from history are often *his* stories. If "he" or "They make history," then it might make it "difficult to remember her" (267, 262). Patriarchal descriptions are not history. Stein asks that we "Think what history is" noting that "Intention is not history nor finality finality is not history" (267). There is work to be done and changes to manage. Stein's exploration of the anchoring of historical knowledge in the arrangements of narrative and its reception were at the heart of her self-consciously modernist compositional practice. History becomes permeable, open for discussion and rearrangement. History is not over. It does not stop.

In an interview by Donald Sutherland, Stein explains the shift in composition in "life and literature" from the nineteenth to the twentieth century, noting that "we are more comfortable in the composition of nineteenth century life and literature" because "a mentioned cup of tea was part of an hour which was part of a day which was part of a week, month, season, or year, which was part of say the annals of Britain, which were part of the general onward evolution of something that was part of a cosmic order" (193–194). The arrangement follows a similar trajectory in the literary realm: "A sentence was part of a paragraph which was part of a chapter which was part of a book which was part of a shelf of books which was part of England or America or France and so on" (194). In the twentieth century, the arrangement changed to the point that "nothing now is really convincingly part of anything else" (194). The composition of life and literature is no longer a linear sequencing, or if it is, it no longer reflects, as Stein says, "the way life is conducted" (194). Looking back on her early work, she was "amused ... to find that her early arrangements and abstractions, which had seemed to be highly acrobatic and gratuitous if refined formal exercises, were turning out to be literal transcriptions of the most evident realities, that is the same abstractions and arrangements on which life is more and more consciously conducted by people at large" (194). As Stein makes clear, we are always in medias res, no longer within a linear sequence with a beginning and an end, as the nineteenth-century model assumes. We can compose our living even as it is happening, not by stepping out of or ignoring the past, but by seeking opportune moments for, in Stein's often repeated phrase, "being living."[17] "Nothing is worse," says Stein, "than to have somebody telling you step by step where you are on the map" (186). When all the arrangements are made, when grammar does not suppose or use invention, we simply follow the map, connect the dots, and adhere to the rules or the confines of genre. Stein, however, hopes we remain in a "perpetual state of discovery," constantly finding the available means, where our arrangements function at most as an outline, "where the very small percentage of information it carries is a mere courtesy" (186, 184). We must do the rest.

For Stein, arrangements are agreements that can solidify, break, or reinvent habits. They can be a kairotic choreography on the space of the page and across time, organizing language dynamically, sequencing toward particular ends, sounds, or repetitions to achieve immediate effects in the words and on the reader. Arrangement in Stein's hands becomes an inventive style. In this chapter, I have taken pains to confine the conversation to arrangement as distinct from style. But for Stein, as we will see, questions of formal structure are always also questions of style.

4
An Exacting Style

> A thing that seems very clear, seems very clear but is it.
>
> Stein, *Lectures in America*

> There is another thing that one has to think about, that is about thinking clearly and about confusion. That is something about which I have almost as much to say as I have about anything.
>
> Stein, *Lectures in America*

> Think of how do you do as very necessary.
>
> Stein, *How to Write*

The final rule in Edwin A. Abbott's *How to Write Clearly*, a grammar book widely used at Stein's alma mater, Harvard University, throughout the nineteenth century, offers advice in the form of a warning about the requirements for an effective style of composition: "56. Caution: let clearness be the first consideration" (40). When Stein began to write in earnest around the turn of the twentieth century, an emphasis on style flourished so much so that those in the field of rhetorical studies lamented the reduction of the realm of rhetoric to a narrow sense of style as perspicuity, the rhetorical term for clarity. Although Abbott's entire work offers rules and exercises for writing clearly, his 56th rule underscores how this clarity might be achieved through an effective, "forcible" style:

> Forcible style springs from (1) vividness and (2) exactness of thought, and from a corresponding (1) vividness and (2) exactness in the use of words.
>
> 1. When you are describing anything, endeavor to *see* it and describe it as you see it. If you are writing about a man who was killed, *see* the man before you, and ask, was he *executed, cut down, run through the body, butchered, shot*, or *hanged?* . . .
> 2. Exactness in the use of words requires an exact knowledge of their meanings and differences. This is a study by itself, and cannot be discussed here. (40)

While Abbott stayed true to his word and did not comment further on what he meant by "exactness in the use of words," Stein did just that.[1] In *How Writ-*

ing is Written, Stein says, "While I was writing I didn't want, when I used one word, to make it carry with it too many associations. I wanted as far as possible to make it exact, as exact as mathematics" (157). Discussing *Tender Buttons* in her lecture "Portraits and Repetition," she explains, "And the thing that excited me so much at that time and still does is that the words or words that make what I looked at be itself were always words that to me very exactly related themselves to that thing the thing at which I was looking" (191–192). Written in 1913, Stein's *Tender Buttons* is a tour-de-force in the study of exactitude: rooms, food, and objects are looked at, seen, named, and described with meticulous, perplexing, and playful precision. "A mind under is exact," contends Stein, "and so it is necessary to have a mouth and eye glasses" (45). What the mind is under is not quite clear, perhaps the pressure to find and articulate clarity, which requires precision in speaking and seeing. Eyeglasses may be required to sharpen the focus, to see the words clearly. But with Stein, "The teasing is tender and trying and thoughtful" (45). When working with Stein's words, the teaching and learning require practice. Stein recommends, "Lecture, lecture and repeat instruction" (41).

Although it would be easy enough to read Stein's writing as dealing a deathblow to the concept of clarity and ushering in a modern or postmodern stylistics, Stein, in fact, shares the nineteenth-century obsession with perspicuity. The vividness and exactness of Stein's writing, however, performs very different conclusions, with, I would argue, a greater degree of exactness than her literary Realist precursors or her analytic philosophical forefathers could have imagined. In "If I Told Him, A Completed Portrait of Picasso," written in 1923 and published in *Vanity Fair* in 1924, Stein surely gains the status of a master stylist of exactness. Stein's written reciprocation for Picasso's oil likeness of her offers another demonstration of her fascination with exactness: "Exact resemblance *to* exact resemblance *the* exact resemblance *as* exact as *a* resemblance, exactly *as* resembling, exactly resembling, exactly *in* resemblance exactly *a* resemblance, exactly and resemblance" (190 emphasis added). The precision of exactitude, as Stein indicates in this passage, rests on the relation among words and the smallest grammatical units (prepositions, articles, and suffixes): *to, the, as, in, a, -ly.* Like Abbott, Stein's exactness entails the precision of seeing a man before her and describing him as he is seen; by expressing positionality, extent, inclusion, specificity, and degree, respectively. Stein's decades-long commitment to what Abbott calls "forcible style" refuses to extricate complexity, instead underscoring and confronting Abbott's requirement "to *see* it and describe it as you see it."

In an instance like this it may be easy to see how Stein's style of writing places her too unequivocally in the canonical literary tradition of modernism. Inspired by Ezra Pound's command to "Make it new!" it seems as if literary modernism does away with an emphasis on clarity opting instead to focus on aesthetic innovation. The master stylists of modernism, including Stein, Ezra Pound, T. S. Eliot, William Carlos Williams, Wallace Stevens, and H.D., certainly questioned and reinvented conventions of literary and poetic form often through stylistic innovation.[2] However, even central tenets of literary modernism share an explicit focus on clarity. For example, the Imagist's directive to "use no superfluous word" and "to produce poetry that is hard and clear, never blurred or indefinite," is strikingly similar to the rhetorical focus on perspicuity. Stein's writing similarly forgoes a grand style with its rhetorical and figurative excess, though, some might argue, her repetitive writing lacks the "economy of words" deemed necessary for clarity and proper artful expression.[3] In spite of claims to the contrary, Gertrude Stein is a no nonsense kind of writer. She tells "it" like "it" is, without demanding that we lock "it" down, explain "it" away, or even understand "it" in a manner apart from the kind of thinking we equate with the event of understanding. In the entry "Breakfast," in *Tender Button's* second section, "Food," Stein offers an early articulation of what remains a central concern throughout her decades-long compositional investigations: "What language," she asks, "can instruct any fellow" (41). Her formulations of language move beyond formulaic representations of genre, and her instruction comes at an exacting price: "A long complicated sentence *should* force itself upon you, make you know yourself knowing it . . ." ("Poetry and Grammar" 221, emphasis added). To know is not enough for Stein; one must also "know yourself knowing," an experience that may require addressing the weight of the words and the pressures of persuasion. To do so requires, as Stein states in *How to Write*, thinking "of *how* do you do as very necessary" (28 emphasis added). Rather than following the conventions of a particular style or even creating a new style, one must make a rhetorical move and work to understand *how*.

Even though Stein worked in and with a variety of literary and artistic forms, including novels, plays, portraits, valentines, autobiographies, sketches, letters, and operas, genre was secondary to her primary interest in language, or, more specifically, in written language, in *how* to write. Nonetheless, Stein does not dismiss form; she clarifies her relationship with it, noting that she "let[s] it come" rather than using it to frame, shape, or structure her composition and its meaning (Preston 194). In a 1935 *Atlantic Monthly* interview, Stein clarified the critical miscalculation of the function of form to her writing: "It is the critics who have really thought about form always and I have thought about—writing!" (Preston 194). Stein's distinction between "writing" and its forms establishes the core of her *ars rhetorica.* She refuses to separate form from content or exactness from indeterminacy, conceptualizing style instead as a heuristic for exploring the available means of the moment. Discovering the available means is more than determining *what* to say; rather, *what* and *how* arise simultaneously for Stein because rhetorical invention and style are inextricably linked. Stein's writing explores the tensions and dynamics between innovations in literary form and rhetorical invention where style becomes a vital force in a rhetorical situation that neither exceeds nor is reducible to the event itself. Perhaps Malcolm Cowley's somewhat dismissive assessment of Stein's style is more apt than intended: "Her style is like a chemical useless in its pure state but powerful when added to other mixtures" (1).

To set the stage for this reading of Stein, I turn to the ancient rhetorical canon of style as a way to expand our thinking about style beyond the disciplinary frame provided by literary studies and literary history.[4] Connecting the reduction of style to clarity of content with the rhetorical and poetic culture in which Stein came of age—an age of perspicuity—demonstrates how Stein's writing refuses to divide belles lettres from perspicuity, rhetoric from composition, genre from writing, and confusion from clarity. John Muckelbauer's notion of an "affirmative style of engagement" helps to explain Stein's stylistics as a reinvention of the rhetorical canon of style. For Stein, style functions not just as a key element of *literary* writing but of composition itself.

Ancient Rhetorical Canon and Modern Stylistics

Since its designation in antiquity as one of the five canons, style or elocution has been a central category of rhetoric, though its prominence has waxed and waned. Early accounts of the canon of style in the *Rhetorica ad Herennium* (c. 80 BCE), the oldest complete Latin textbook on rhetoric, position style as a bridge across form and content. Style is the "adaptation of suitable words and sentences to the matter devised."[5] In other words, as the third canon, style comes after the argument has been discovered (*inventio*) and arranged (*dispositio*). Even now, this is a familiar schedule of events for an ostensible process of composition.

The influence of the *Rhetorica ad Herennium* spans centuries, particularly its division of style into three levels: grand, middle, and plain or low. Following the *ad Herennium's* categories, Stein's "ordinary" language might be cast as a kind of "plain" style.[6] Given the seeming complexity of Stein's writing, her diction is astonishingly simple, arising from "daily life" as she says. She theorizes and addresses the omnipresence of "daily life" in her first *Narration* lecture, delivered at the University of Chicago in 1935: "I can say it enough but I can say it more than enough that the daily life is a daily life if at any moment of the daily life that daily life is all there is of life" (10). Reading Stein does not require a dictionary or vast knowledge of the history of literary figures, allusions, and tropes. Unlike Eliot's iconic "Wasteland," Stein's writing requires no footnotes. When she began to publish her own works in the early 1930s with the help of Alice B. Toklas, she named her press the Plain Edition, a title chosen because, as

Stein says, it allows us "'to realize two meanings in one word'—plain as simple or clear and plain as commonplace" (Dydo 417).[7] In both senses of the word, Stein's style is "plain,"—the domestic tableaux in *Tender Buttons* and the "daily living" during war in *Wars I Have Seen* and *Narration* —without elevated diction or excessive ornamentation and, as the *ad Herennium's* definition suggests, appropriate for instruction.

Since its inception and well into the nineteenth century, the virtues of style have centered on clarity, correctness of language (diction, syntax, and grammar), and propriety (appropriateness). In the *Rhetoric*, Aristotle's definition of style emphasizes clarity: "Style to be good must be clear, as it proved by the fact that speech which fails to convey plain meaning will fail to do just what speech has to do" (1404b). For Cicero, who was once thought to have authored the *ad Herennium*, "embellishment of discourse" requires "in the first place, pure and correct Latin, secondly with simple lucidity, thirdly with elegance, lastly in a manner befitting the dignity of our topics and with a certain grace" (309). Correct usage and clarity are required *before* "elegance" and *before* selecting an appropriate "manner" in which to present already clearly and properly defined ideas. Thus, one's "meaning" is established, the content determined, and then style is added. Ornamentation comes after, when figures of speech or other rhetorical flourishes might be added to attain rhetorical ends (persuasion, action, delight, and admiration).

In modern stylistics, elocution or style must be clear, straightforward, and logically argued, an imperative made clear in John Locke's *Essay Concerning Human Understanding*, where he accuses rhetoric of being an "instrument of error and deceit" because it interferes with rational thinking and clear communication (Book II, 34). While figurative language might be acceptable in a literary realm, non-literary modes of discourse must be free of rhetorical ornamentation to insure clarity. Although Stein inherited from the nineteenth century a narrow sense of belletristic style as ornamentation, in which elevated diction and figures are used to adorn already formulated ideas, her extensive explorations of style go far beyond both mere embellishment and literary modernism's command to innovate. Stein does not simply turn away from nineteenth-century conceptions of the rhetorical canon of style out of which she wrote or its investment in perspicuity; she does, in fact, heed Edwin Abbott's caution to "let clearness be the first consideration" no matter the form, genre, purpose, or method. For Stein, "thinking of how do you do," of how writing is written, does not jettison nineteenth-century belletristic concerns; it maintains a rhetorical emphasis on perspicuity but always through the lens of invention.

Stein came of age intellectually under the tutelage of William James, George Santayana, and Hugo Munsterberg during her time at Radcliffe College. In her writing, she often sets herself amid distinguished men of letters, including, as she says in *Narration,* "Emerson, Hawthorne Walt Whitman Mark Twain Henry James myself Sherwood Anderson Thornton Wilder and Dashiell Hammett" (10). She also positions herself as a not-so-silent fifth among the exemplary men in *Four in America* (Ulysses S. Grant, Wilbur Wright, Henry James, and George Washington).[8] Generatively enacting a similar set of ironies and tensions, we can situate Stein among the men of modern rhetoric, alongside, for example, Hugh Blair, whose landmark *Lectures on Rhetoric and Belles Lettres* (1789) defined the study of rhetoric for nearly a century, particularly in the United States.

For Blair, the study of rhetoric was the study of managing, not inventing arguments. The canon of invention, which Stein refuses to relinquish, gave way to an almost exclusive focus on arrangement and style, also of central interest to Stein. Like Abbott, Blair stresses the importance of beginning with a focus on clarity: "our first object must be to make our meaning clearly and fully understood, and understood without the least difficulty" (100). Blair, who claims that style "has always some reference to an author's manner of thinking"—a point with which Stein might agree—requires two things of authors: clear and distinct ideas and "exact and full comprehension of the force of those words which he employs" (107–108). These requirements must be met *prior* to writing, according to Blair, so that the writing transmits the author's ideas and intent clearly to the audience. "This, then, we may be assured, is a capital rule as to Style, to think closely of the subject, till we have attained a full and distinct view of the matter which we are to clothe in words . . . ; then and not till then, shall we find expression begin to flow" (215).

Stein's theory of style takes Blair's to task on two points. First, she rejects Blair's assumption that a sovereign authorial mind can contemplate ideas and reach a point of clarity and then, as Blair suggests, "clothe [them] in words" (215). She also challenges his requirement that an author be "fully understood . . . without the least difficulty" (100). Stein's writing begs the question of what "fully" understanding something might be. She calls attention to the fact that the line between clarity and confusion is much less clear than Blair suggests: "A great many think that they know confusion when they know or see it or hear it, but do they. A thing that seems very clear, seems very clear but is it" ("Portraits and Repetition" 173). Our sense of clarity is caught up in our ways of thinking; on this point, Stein and Blair agree. Furthermore, attaining any understanding, complete or partial, may prove to be demanding, particularly when, as Stein suggests, coming to understand requires thinking "about how do you do"—not just following a given style, a cultural trend, an institutional imperative, or a grammatical rule. Style is never neutral. Stein's style does not interfere with perspicuity; it requires the reader or audience to recognize its rhetorical force, its ability to frame ideas and their reception, and its ability to neutralize or animate a rhetorical situation.

Playing with Perspicuity

Stein's conception of style moves beyond the economy of more or less, adorned or unadorned, plain or fancy. She returns belles lettres to perspicuity, redefining clarity in more conceptual than grammatical terms. Although many have characterized Stein's style of writing as nonsense or gibberish, others have used kinder descriptive terms—disjunctive, fragmented, dissociative, and paratactic—yet they too suggest a lack of clarity. In his pioneering *Disjunctive Poetics*, Peter Quartermain reads Stein's writing as assaulting "clarity by suggesting that clarity is itself an assault upon and hence violation of the sheer complexity and richness of a sensory world... (21). At the same time, Stein does not obliterate clarity; rather, she reinvents it and asks her readers to do the same. Her style becomes a cue for readers, for clarity, toward meaning, not, of course, in an immediately referential way, but clarity nonetheless. Often concerned with communicating effectively with her audience, Stein insists, "It does mean something I do assure you it does mean something although it is very difficult to say it in any way except in the way that I said it then" ("Portraits and Repetition" 204). In other words, Stein says what she means carefully and precisely, and further, *what* it means is inextricably connected with "the way I said it *then*," the precise moment it was said (204 emphasis added). Stein's "then" is not only a rhetorical moment—an inventive moment in Aristotle's sense of finding the available means—but also a singular, kairotic moment, responsive to and appropriate for its particular time, to the demands and possibilities of what Stein calls the continuous present, a sense of time that refuses to settle into chronology. In other words, "the way I said it then" may not be the way to say it now or the way it needs to be or can be said at another time.

To better understand the theoretical and rhetorical complexity in Stein's sense of style as more than a literary technique, I turn to John Muckelbauer's *The Future of Invention: Rhetoric, Postmodernism, and the Problem of Change* (2008), in which he addresses the problem of change, critiques the idea that "change is always and everywhere the effect overcoming and negation," and offers an "affirmative style of engagement" that hinges on the occurrence of repetition (x). Muckelbauer reiterates postmodern scholarship's reliance on three styles of engagement that repeat the oppositional structures of negation and, in the end, offer little change. First, advocacy emphasizes the traditionally privileged term of the binary, which does not result in change but instead "conserves, or rather, reproduces long-established power differences" (6). The second approach, critique, advocates for the traditionally underprivileged term, inverting the dyad "to overcome its hegemony by supporting the concepts that have been historically derided" (7). Change does indeed accompany this approach but in the end simply reproduces the same oppositional structure. The third approach refuses to side with or privilege either term, opting instead to "valorize the indeterminate 'in-between'" as a "generative, ambiguous space" (8, 9). Even here little changes because, as Muckelbauer points out, the oppositional structure remains intact. Although there is change in the third approach, "the content only changes by repeating the same negative relational structure" (9). At stake for Muckelbauer are not the oppositional terms themselves but the *ways* in which the oppositions are generated and maintained.

In his discussions of postmodernism, when using analytic philosophical terms, Muckelbauer's argument remains in a rhetorical realm: "the content or the 'what' of the proposition . . . may be of less importance than the 'how' of the movement through those propositions" (xii). The "may be" in his statement is not equivocation but a space for supposition and rhetorical invention. Muckelbauer turns to rhetorical studies to theorize a connection between invention and style that calls into question "the entire 'Hegelian framework' of dialectical negation" (5). Although he remains rooted in the history of continental philosophy, Muckelbauer incorporates shifting conceptions of rhetoric's first canon, invention, alongside so-called postmodern questions.[9] He finds that this history of invention generates the possibility of an "affirmative style of engagement" that neither breaks from nor merely repeats dialectical negation. Because efforts to change remain "trapped in the complex repetition of dialectical change," Muckelbauer seeks to develop and to demonstrate an affirmative style (11). In order to do so and because we cannot simply remove the dialectical structure or the history of negative dialectics, Muckelbauer argues that "everything hinges on *how* one repeats" (13). And where there is repetition, there is, or ought to be, Gertrude Stein.

Repetition is a central feature of Stein's style, as is perennially argued by literary critics.[10] From her earliest writing to her most famous and often-repeated or ridiculed quip, "A rose is a rose is a rose is a rose," Stein's writing explores the syntactic, semantic, and philosophical properties of repetition. Marianne DeKoven underscores the centrality of repetition to Stein's early experiments with writing: "It is undoubtedly safe to assert that no other writer has ever used repetition as extensively as Gertrude Stein did," particularly between 1906 and 1911 (*A Different Language* 40). Her repetition opens up a "new possibility," as Janice Doane notes, by breaking "the linear sequence of the plot" and offering "the possibility of a new style" (*Silence and Narrative* 80–81). Stein's use of repetition, according to Harriett Chessman, "Draws attention away from its status as a referential sign," and multiple appearances of a word "renews its immediacy and liveliness" (82). Peter Quartermain finds that through repetition, Stein's "pronouns begin to acquire concreteness" so that the "repetition enhances rather than diminishes meaning or detaches the word from its meaning" (38). At the same time, however, Stein acknowledges that repetition can be problematic. Repetition can acclimate readers to ideas, offering repeated opportunities to make sense or to come to a gradual understanding, but it can also form and maintain habits that keep readers stuck in the past or bound to particular logics and concepts of clarity.[11] Stein's repetition offers a pedagogical imperative, inviting readers again and again into a potential process of meaning making and also, perhaps more so, toward an understanding that the engagement itself might be pleasurable regardless of its results.

In "Portraits and Repetition," Stein addresses the operations of repetition and the way in which her style bears a primary rhetorical force that beckons the reader into the moment. Well aware that her repetitive patterning was often ridiculed or parodied, Stein told her audience "every time one of the hundreds of times a newspaper man makes fun of my writing and of my repetition he always has the same theme, always having the same theme, that is, if you like, repetition, that is if you like the repeating that is the same thing" (167). Acknowledging that she and her writing were targets of mockery, Stein turned the tables on those who mock by calling into question their limited understanding of her repetitive style. Their repeated theme was that Stein repeats; they offered no analysis of how, why, or to what end. Their caricature of her repetition performs the same criticism they level against her: they simply repeat their same claim over and over. Even in her criticism of the reporters' failure to see their own tautological argument, Stein's repetition functions differently.

While they might "like repeating . . . the same thing," Stein does not. She draws a distinction between repetition and insistence where insistence "in its emphasis can never be repeating, because insistence is always alive and if it is alive it is never saying anything in the same way because emphasis can never be the same not even when it is most the same that is when it has been taught" ("Portraits and Repetition" 171). Stein anticipates Derrida's assertion that repetition can be at once rhetorical and ethical, warning that repetition done "in a mechanical way" is "just repeating, not animating" (10).[12] Thus, with Derrida in mind, the critics were not inventing new ways to address Stein, they were merely repeating the same claims over and over; repetition is not insistence. Insistence, demanding something forcefully, insures for Stein that the style of repetition is more than mechanical reproduction. Rather, it becomes "alive," to use Stein's word, and it becomes inventive. To insist is an assertion, a belief that something can or should be done. In other words, one who repeats can play a role, however limited, in how the repetition happens and how it is received. A journalist commenting on one of Stein's lectures explains his experience of her use of repetition: "To hear Miss Stein read her own work is to understand it—I speak for myself—for the first time . . . you see why she writes as she does; you see how from sentence to sentence, which seems so much alike, she introduces differences in tone, or perhaps accent. And then when you think she has been saying the same thing four or five times, you suddenly know that she has carefully, link by link, been leading you to a new thing"[13] Repetition is the performance of multiplicity toward clarity, a performative moment that opens singular opportunities for understanding and invention. How one repeats makes an enormous difference, so much so that Muckelbauer claims, "everything hinges on how one repeats" (13). Stein would agree, although she extends Muckelbauer's how, as we shall see, more fully into the realm of poesis.

An Elucidation: Stein's Sophistic Pedagogical Style

In analyzing "An Elucidation," Ulla Dydo establishes Stein's role as a "school teacher who elucidates step by methodical step" (*A Stein Reader* 429). She also notes that Stein invites her students, readers of her texts—including critics—to "enter, look, listen, and participate, not to wait for paraphrase and principles" (*A Stein Reader* 429). While the poem certainly does invite readers to participate, I would argue, in fact, that it *does* offer readers an opportunity to paraphrase and note principles.[14] Stein's pedagogy is less Dydo's schoolmarm and more Gorgias's Sophist. She offers lessons in language, examples of argumentation and persuasion, and amusing exhibitions of her skill.

While Stein often puts on a good show whether she is teaching readers *How to Write,* lecturing in America, making Americans, or writing geographical history, style for Stein is, as "An Elucidation" suggests, more than performative. Turning to one of ancient Greece's most famous Sophists, Isocrates, we find an early instance of performativity combined with rhetorical invention, though Stein adapts her version for her twentieth-century audiences. Isocrates's "art of discourse" relies on a kairotic creativity that arises from and within the moment.[15] In "Against the Sophists," Isocrates acknowledges the "bad repute" earned by some Sophists: "If all who are engaged in the profession of education were willing to state the facts instead of making greater promises than they can possibly fulfill, they would not be in such bad repute with the lay-public" (163). Although some Sophists might deserve criticism, as Isocrates admits, not all do, most especially Isocrates himself, who is presented as the primary example of a "good" Sophist. The problem, he says, is that these "instructors of youth" apply "the analogy of an art with hard and fast rules to a creative process" (171). Isocrates differentiates between the art of using letters, which "remains fixed and unchanged," and the art of discourse, which requires invention, creativity, and responsiveness to the particular moment. Students cannot simply study and mimic what others have done because "what has been said by one speaker is not equally useful for the speaker who comes after him" (171). Not all repetition is equal; *how* one repeats makes a difference and depends on timing and context. Stein acknowledges a similar point, as I have discussed, when she says, "the way that I said it then" may not be appropriate for the way it needs to be said now, at another time, or in another context ("Portraits and Repetition" 204). The art of discourse, according to Isocrates, is "good only if it has the qualities of fitness for the occasion, propriety of style, and originality of treatment" (171).[16] Much of Stein's writing, "An Elucidation" in particular, fulfills Isocrates's requirements for a good art of discourse.

"An Elucidation" is a Sophistic lesson in style. If the ancient Greek Sophists armed their students with lessons in public speaking so that they could participate in civic life, defend themselves in court, arbitrate disputes with neighbors, or respond to the immediate demands of their communities, Stein's lessons shift, at least initially, to the words on the page. On that page, they test Descartes's *cogito ergo sum*, the central statement of modern epistemology that assumes individual minds are a source or the only source of certain knowledge communicated in a syllogistic logic that presumes stylistic clarity. If we take Stein at her word, the title, "An Elucidation," suggests clarification and explanation; to elucidate is, etymologically, to make clear. Throughout the work she offers a great deal of evidence that this piece is, in fact, making numerous gestures toward clarity: "I have an explanation of this in this way. . . . I will now give more examples. . . . I will give other examples to you. . . . Let me explain properly. . . ." (174–178). In addition, the speaker is ever reassuring to readers: "You understand. / You do understand. . . . Let me lead you to find this. . . . Do you all understand if you please. / Do you all understand why I explain. / Do you all understand elucidation. . . ." (177–181).[17] These continual interjections by the writer keep the reader in the continuous present, aware of the words, and mindful of the singular demands of the text. Stein positions her first-person speaker as a kind teacher lapsing in and out of the lecture, the lesson, to check in with her students, the readers, who she knows are struggling with a difficult text. Although not easy, she wants her lesson to be clear.

Immediately following the title, Stein offers the first lesson, "Halve Rivers and Harbors"—a title when spoken aloud doubles into the homonym—halve/have—not to a point of ambiguity, but a simple doubling, suggesting that elucidation happens in words on a page and in their sound in an ear. What we have or what is halved are "rivers and harbors"—water in motion and at rest. Harbors, plural, are places of shelter, protected from rough water, although we may also harbor doubts, keeping them hidden in our mind. If, as Stein suggests, elucidations "have rivers and harbors," then we as readers and students can follow the current wherever it takes us or seek refuge—elucidations have both. The title, however, claims to offer one: *an* elucidation, within which, perhaps, we find rivers and harbors, movement and shelter.

The poem's opening lines appear to be an outline, particularly if numbers are added to the lines:

> Elucidation.
> (1) First as Explanation.
> (2) Elucidate the problem of halve.
> (3) Halve and have.
> (4) Halve Rivers and Harbors,
> (5) Have rivers and harbors.

Not only are her key points exceptionally clear, she also indicates how her argument will progress: first, as explanation, perhaps the outline itself and next, as an elucidation of the problem of halve, which has three steps from halve/have, to halve rivers and harbors, to have rivers and harbors. This is a gradual, difficult lesson. Stein's first-person speaker immediately checks in: "You do see . . . you do see . . . you do see, you do see . . ." (174). The repeated comment asks readers to pay attention to what is happening in the text, to avoid settling into automatic habits of reading, and to consider whether they "see." The repetition makes the point or, perhaps, introduces the possibility that the student is confused and doesn't follow. Slowing down, the teacher offers a lesson in the first person based on personal experiences with rivers and harbors: "I refuse rivers and harbors I have refused. I do refuse" (174). This lesson can be, and has been for our speaker, challenging to the point of refusal. But the lesson continues: "I receive . . . , I accept" (174). The logic of this repeated refusal, reception, and acceptance is not syllogistic. Its knowledge, if it is received or accepted at all, occurs gradually, over time. But this speaker has only "elucidated the pretence . . . and the acceptation." This lesson is, at best, about making something appear to be true or arriving at a generally accepted and recognized meaning. This is a Sophist's lesson, an exercise in playing with clarity, rejecting the simplicity of syllogistic logic, and recognizing and shifting how words perform their meaning.

However, Stein warns, "This is a new preparation. / Do not share"—readers must do it on their own. "He will not bestow" (174). Elucidation takes repetition, though the form is different. Sometimes it looks like lines of poetry:

This is a new preparation.
Do not share
He will not bestow
They can meditate
I am going to do so. (174)

And then a new way, "an explanation of this in this way," where Stein repeats the statement but in the form of a sentence: "If we say, Do not share he will not bestow they can meditate I am going to do so, we have organised an irregular commonplace and we have made excess return to rambling" (174). Here, Stein calls attention to the positioning of words on the page and to the significance of both repeating and changing the form. Patterns are revealed. Readers are offered multiple opportunities for coming to a gradual understanding. "I will now give more examples" (175). This is a general lesson. "I always like the use of these, but not particularly" (174). Other sections follow a similar pattern: a title followed by poetry and prose and a first-person explanation; it is the same lesson presented in different ways. Stein admits that this approach may not work: "In this way you see that I have not succeeded" (185). Although success may not be imminent, Stein offers encouragement in the form of a witty aphorism: "If at first you don't succeed try try again" (185). Additionally, she calls into question what might count as success, "Suppose for an instance suppose as an instance we mention success. I succeed and you succeed" (186). The success of "You" and "I" appears interdependent. To "know yourself knowing" when working through complicated sentences requires, as Stein explains, that one "disentangle rather than cut the knot" ("Poetry and Grammar" 221). Style becomes a heuristic, a manner of interaction among reader, writer, and audience about their relationships and attempts at communication. Successful communication embraces elucidation, repetition, confusion, uncertainty, patience, and a willingness to engage. "How pleasantly I feel contented with that" ("An Elucidation" 186).

An Ethic of Style

While the speaker of "An Elucidation" may feel contented with its epistemological rejection of closure, issues of clarity continue to persist. These issues are rather contentious in the case of contemporary philosophic discourse.[18] Here I would like to review briefly Jacques Derrida's debate with John Searle in the late 1970s, which though typically discussed as an early confrontation between continental and analytic philosophy, can also be understood as a debate about the political and disciplinary stakes of clarity and style. In "Afterword: Toward an Ethic of Discussion," a letter written in response to questions posed by Gerald

Graff nearly a decade after the debate, Derrida begins by highlighting the necessity of considering *how* ideas are discussed. He asks, "Am I right to insist . . . on the debate itself, its possibility, its necessity, its style, its 'ethics,' its 'politics'?" (111). The "*way* we discuss," says Derrida, even "'among ourselves,' in the academic world," encompasses questions of style as well as questions of ethics and politics that arise along with the possibility and necessity of the debate itself.[19] Derrida singled out academic discourse because it was the specific context for his discussion with Searle and also because Searle moved the debate to a different audience when he accused Derrida in the pages of the *New York Review of Books* of engaging in a "low level of philosophical argumentation" and a "deliberate obscurantism of the prose"—a common and persistent claim against continental philosophy.[20] Essentially, he faults Derrida's style for its lack of clarity.

Making a similar and more recent critique about continental philosophy's lack of clarity, Gary Gutting, a philosophy professor, addressed "Bridging the Analytic-Continental Divide" in the pages of the *New York Times* (February 2012). Although he offers a useful history of twentieth-century analytic and continental philosophy, Gutting condemns the writing of continental philosophers for being unnecessarily difficult, so much so that he advises "most analytic philosophers" to forgo reading these primary texts and opt instead for "reliable and much more accessible secondary sources." He valorizes the writing of analytic philosophers for "its commitment to clarity" and recommends to continental philosophers "training in analytic philosophy . . [to] greatly improve [their] writing." Gutting concludes that the gap between analytic and continental philosophy "will begin to be bridged only when seminal thinkers of the Continent begin to write more clearly." The assumption that our ideas can be expressed logically, precisely, and style-free and, further, that these skills can be learned and applied equally to all communicative events, extends from Locke and is precisely the sense of clarity Stein calls into question. The *ways* we write, argue, and communicate with one another matter. "Style-free" is also a style that reflects and refracts particular points of view, epistemological assumptions, and ways of thinking, revealing some, concealing others. Gutting assumes not only that meaning can be detached from the writing itself, but also that a particular kind of writing better serves the ideas presented. Clarity remains a gatekeeper, a disciplinary mechanism that ensures that writing does not get in the way of thinking. "Supposing a sentence is clear," Stein asks incisively in *How to Write*, "whose is it" (148).

Stein maintains a commitment to clarity, but not at the expense of thinking about it stylistically and exploring the manner in which it succeeds or fails, communicates intended meanings, and, as Derrida says, structures absence, or in other words what is not said or what is impossible to say. Stein calls into question assumptions about clarity: "A great many think that they know confusion when they know or see it or hear it, but do they. A thing that seems very clear, seems very clear but is it" ("Portraits and Repetition" 173). What is dismissed as confusing or obfuscating may after all be clear or may become clear gradually and slowly, *clarifying* in process if not *clear* on the face of things. In a sense, Stein suggests that there is more clarity to be found if we could only find ways to see it. For Stein writing and thinking are intimately entwined. Her style is a performance of the logics, illogics, and nonlogics of articulation, constantly emphasizing *how* the articulation might occur, under what circumstances, with whom and toward what end. She challenges prevailing habits, ways of thinking, and the idea of structure itself, relying instead on suppositions about articulation, grammar as invention, and the challenge and cost of achieving clarity. In other words, Stein believes one's style, including one's approach to clarity, makes possible—or not—certain realities, ways of thinking, and ways of being.

Although Muckelbauer alters the scope of rhetorical invention, he, like Sharon Crowley, perpetuates a version of rhetorical theory that borders on but ultimately elides the poetic. Although Crowley defines a postmodern sophistic model of rhetorical invention as privileging "movement, flexibility, contingency, and difference," her definition of rhetorical invention emphasizes generating all "*argumentative* possibilities . . . that are available and articulable in any given moment and situation" (56 emphasis added). While Crowley's definition remains deeply rooted in argumentation and persuasion even as she critiques their modernist logics, Muckelbauer's focus on style begins to move toward what I would call a poetics of invention or a poetics of rhetorical theory. Muckelbauer's "art of invention" opens the possibility of an asignifying, contingent, and generative compositional practice. "If, through this generative approach, rhetoric is rendered indistinguishable from a broadly conceived art of invention, then this art of invention, in turn, becomes indistinguishable from the massive, interdisciplinary effort to rethink the basic principles that engineer western conceptions of truth, knowledge, and inquiry" (25). Muckelbauer's critical project examines the generative intersubjective dynamics of style. His definition of rhetoric as an art of invention borders on the poetic not due to his focus on style, the canon most closely associated with literature, but because he connects style to invention.

Like Muckelbauer, Stein shares an affirmative model, refusing what we would now call negative dialectics or a negative relational structure, opting instead for an inventive singularity of repetition (44). Here, too, Stein breaks with philosophical and literary modernists who lament the loss of order and certainty or rage against a fragmented world. Stein forges different ground. Her landscape is not Eliot's wasteland; her interactions with identity are not Kafkaesque dystopic nightmares. For Stein, a lack of certainty is not only a philosophical crisis, it is an opportunity. She does not seek, finally, to privilege one term over another (for example, human nature or the human mind, identity or entity, male or female, self or other, true or false, or clarity or opacity) or even to navigate between them, which, as Muckelbauer makes clear, simply reinscribes the categories rather than opening up new possibilities. Style, then, becomes key. Much more than an addendum to predetermined content, style is a complex theoretical and rhetorical approach to language use. Style, as line-by-line rhetorical practice, is the core of Stein's rhetorical theory.

The ideas, worlds, and grammars we negotiate are convoluted, confusing, and complex. It is difficult to understand, clarify, resist, and revise them. Elucidation often requires repeated explanation, as Stein's style of repetition shows, along with the careful reading of primary sources Gutting recommends eschewing. What is clear is that dealing with the complexities of our world and words is difficult. "Thinking of how do you do" is, indeed, very necessary. By articulating and questioning clarity in all its complexity, Stein does not shun the category, but she does question *how* clarity is achieved, what makes it possible, and what falls out of focus in the ostensibly clearly formed statement. For Stein, style is an interactive, affirmative, and inventive register in which readers and writers access the continuous present, a rhetorical and kairotic space that requires continual negotiation of one's available means, a poesis of engagement. That the ongoing negotiations are difficult, may not yield immediate conclusions or clarity, and exceed, are contained within, and make possible the rhetorical situation is, for Stein, clearly a necessity and an ethic of style.

5
Troubling Memory

> How can I rightly narrate? . . . Like the poets, I ought to commence my relations with an invocation to Memory.
>
> Socrates in Plato's *Euthydemus*

> I gradually and slowly found out there were two things I had to think about; the fact that knowledge is acquired, so to speak, by memory; but that when you know anything, memory doesn't come in.
>
> Stein, "How Writing is Written"

> She is the anticipation of conviction of remembering being existing. She is the anticipating of a new one having been an old one. . . . She is the convocation of anticipation and acceptation. . . . She is the complication of receiving, she is the articulation of forgetting. . . .
>
> Stein, *Two*

In *Euthydemus*, Plato's witty critique of Sophistic trickery, Socrates puts Memory center stage, a condition for narrating or, at least, narrating "rightly." The assertion of Socrates's *ought*, that he *ought* to commence his narrative by calling upon memory, might indicate a duty one has or even a desirable state toward which one should aspire when commencing to narrate. But invoking memory poses a challenge for any writer interested in time, particularly if interested in cultivating a "continuous present," as Gertrude Stein claimed to be. Calling on Memory seems to require immediately turning back toward the past, away from the present, even as one begins. Memory can access the external world we seem to confront objectively, the internal processes of cognition, and a recalcitrant linguistic realm where "memories" are generated, preserved, and transmitted. In "How Writing is Written," Stein sets the task before us to work, as she did, "gradually and slowly," in our thinking about memory, a complicated and contradictory terrain with roots in the world, the mind, and the word (155). Stein's exploration of memory, including its cultural, temporal, or narrative functions, is also a pedagogical project, both an act of memory in itself and also a lesson, however insightful or misguided, in remembering and articulating what is forgotten.

However, for Stein, this past is not necessarily recounted in description or traditional narrative, perhaps with the arguable exception of *The Autobiography of Alice B. Toklas*, where she retrieves and retells events from her past, although even here the memories are told at the remove of Toklas's perspective. More often, Stein uses writing to explore and theorize memory, not to show or display her memories, but to demonstrate how memory works or might work, particularly when attempting to live and write in the continuous present—a temporal space of the now and a site of rhetorical invention. In the continuous present, memory and forgetting coexist in the space and time of writing where the "articulation of forgetting" occurs and becomes the central function of memory (*Two* 108). For Stein, there is still no escaping the past or its temporal pull on the present. This is a particular problem for the writer who, as Stein says, is "always just under the shadow of the thing that is just past" ("How Writing is Written" 154). Like the Sophists who recognized a rhetor's ability to work with ever-changing circumstances and contingency, Stein's continuous present can be read as an ongoing articulation of forgetting, a space to address failures of memory, and a moment to develop a craft that explores what has been with what is, antecedents within a continuous present.

If, as Stein claims in "Portraits and Repetition," "Remembering is repetition anybody can know that," then the "articulation of forgetting" is something else, something other than simply repeating what has come before (178). More than the retrieval of a static past, Stein's articulation of forgetting is kairotic, an ancient Greek conception of time that demands attunement with the present moment even as it considers the past as a possible and productive resource. Kairos does not do away with history; rather, kairos, according to John Poulakos, recognizes "that speech exists in time and is uttered both as a spontaneous formulation of and a barely constituted response to a new situation unfolding in the immediate present" (*Sophistical Rhetoric* 61). Stein draws attention to the limitations and inadequacies of the chronological presumptions that structure what we know and how we say what we know. Refusing this received conception of time along with its reliable ordering is a rejection of the assumptions about temporality undergirding the classical canons. Stein pursued how this interrogation of a sequential beginning-middle-end applies to narrative, time, history, and memory.

In the same way Stein makes grammar matter, not by eliminating it or railing against its prescriptive conventions, but by supposing "a grammar uses invention," Stein's art of memory accrues "gradually and slowly" across many of her works where she shows it to be necessary, problematic, foundational, and generative. In an early portrait, Stein says, "she was one not forgetting that she was remembering that anyone should remember . . . she was one believing in remembering" (*Two* 156). Stein's art of memory is an articulation of forgetting, a repeated reminder that what appears natural, even the linearity of time, is bound up in habits we have forgotten and in words that continually recollect.[1] By locating Stein's thinking about memory within the historical and philosophical shifts in the study of language at the turn of the twentieth century, we can begin to examine how memory in Stein's hands becomes a function of composition, a kairotic and inventive engagement with the moment.

Troubling Mnemonics: Remembering the Forgotten Canon

Memory is often called rhetoric's forgotten canon. As communicators we no longer rely on the same kind of mnemonic and memory devices used in the days before paper, computers, flash drives, and the cloud. Rhetoricians are just beginning to reconsider the canon of memory, due in part to recent cross-disciplinary scholarship from memory studies, an emerging field that examines the shift from what we know to how and why we remember it, a distinction not lost on Stein. Even in the early twentieth century, Stein recognized memory's connection to writing and its cultural function as much more than an individual's power of recall because "remembering *in itself* is not really an important enough thing to really need recalling" (*Narration* 59, emphasis added). She warns against an understanding of memory as mimesis, a mere reiteration of the past, suggesting instead that what is important is the articulation of forgetting, understanding the ways in which memory articulates the contemporary and frames what is possible in the continuous present.

Forgotten amid the disciplinary shuffle around the turn of the twentieth century and fundamentally interdisciplinary from its inception, rhetorical studies failed to find a solid home in the modern university particularly at the onset of the twentieth century. Stein's experience at Radcliffe, the women's college at Harvard University, in the mid-1890s makes clear how limited the study of rhetoric had become, which left the study of memory to the newly formed disciplines of psychology and philosophy. By the mid-twentieth century, when interest in classical rhetoric began to stir, Edward P. J. Corbett published *Classical Rhetoric for the Modern Student*, a text Richard Leo Enos called "one of the most important contributions to rhetoric and composition of this century" (395). Although Corbett initiated a place for rhetorical studies and rhetorical history within the teaching of composition, the canon of memory did not fare well in his conception of classical rhetoric: "Of all the five parts [canons] of rhetoric, *memoria* [memory] was the one that received the least attention in the rhetoric books. The reason for the neglect of this aspect of rhetoric is probably that not much can be said, in a theoretical way, about the process of memorizing" (38). Here Corbett reduces the concept of memory to *memorization,* a purpose it served but also exceeded, particularly in rhetoric's earliest incarnations as Socrates's invocation to narrate rightly makes clear.

Greek and Roman rhetoricians would have been puzzled by Corbett's dismissal of the possibilities of memory. The anonymous author of the influential treatise on rhetoric *Rhetorica ad Herennium* (c. 80 BCE), perhaps the most thorough ancient text on memory, calls memory a "treasure-house of the ideas supplied by Invention" and the "guardian of all the parts of rhetoric" (205).[2] The *ad Herennium* elevates the role of memory to guardian, responsible for looking after, defending, and protecting all the canons.[3]

Even Plato famously venerated the essential work of memory in his dialogue *Phaedrus*, in which Socrates speaks "in honor of memory" because it is memory that allows for "communion . . . with those things the communion with which causes God to be divine" (481, 483). Plato writes against forgetting, ironically rejecting writing in his written dialogue and claiming "this invention [of writing] will produce forgetfulness in the minds of those who learn to use it, because they will not practice their memory" (563). At best, writing might, in Plato's conception, give "the appearance of wisdom"; it will fail to lead to recollection of Ideal forms.[4] For Plato, what must be remembered is outside the individual mind, existing in a Universal Form. Acts of retrieval for Plato are not a technical task to aid recall or a mnemonic device working from topoi; instead memory takes on metaphysical importance, becoming a means for discovering what was lost when the soul became embodied. While Plato shuns writing, Stein finds it an ideal means for working through the problem of memory and the articulation of forgetting.

The Roman statesman, Cicero, explicitly addressed memory in his widely read treatise *De Oratore*. Both of these influential writings are heavily influenced by Greek rhetoric, a debt he often acknowledged. *De Oratore* offers lessons in memorizing that use images attached to specific places to aid recall: "persons desiring to train this faculty of memory must select places and form mental images of the things they wish to remember and store those images in the places, so that the order of the places will preserve the order of the things."[5] Memory functions as a storage facility full of information to be accessed at appropriate times and in the appropriate order. Jocelyn Penny Small points out that Cicero's mnemonic lessons bind words to vivid mental images "as if inscribing letters into wax" and reads Aristotle's topoi as memory storage "bins" (88). Both Cicero and Quintilian offer an architectural metaphor for storing and retrieving memories.

Not unlike Stein's spatial lessons in *The Geographical History of America or The Relation of Human Nature to the Human Mind*, Quintilian describes memory as an "animating principle," which relies on architectural arrangement of thought in order for effective recall:

> These symbols are then arranged as follows. The first thought is placed, as it were, in the forecourt; the second, let us say, in the living-room; the remainder are placed in due order all round the *impluvium* [center of the

> atrium] and entrusted not merely to bedrooms and parlours, but even to the care of statues and the like. This done, as soon as the memory of the facts requires to be revived, all these places are visited in turn and the various deposits are demanded from their custodians, as the sight of each recalls the respective details. (trans. Butler XI.ii.20–21)[6]

Memory can be envisioned as a storage container readily accessed through metaphorical connections of architecture, journeys, or pictures. However, Quintilian considers this system of memory-as-container limited because it overlooks what has happened in the spaces remembered: "For when we return to a place after considerable absence, we not merely recognize the place itself, but remember things that we did there, and recall the persons whom we met and even the unuttered thoughts which passed through our minds when we were there before" (XI.ii.17–18). Memory for Quintilian cannot be separate from place, nor can it be separate from time. While architectural spaces function mnemonically, the spaces carry within them other memories and, even, "unuttered thoughts," which reflection may recall. We cannot, therefore, simply use an architectural space or a public place as a memory container, because we cannot take it out of time. The spaces one remembers, if only used as mnemonic devices, are preloaded with memory, carrying with them their own pasts. Stein explores similar spatial mnemonics in *The Geographical History of America*, where America functions as a topoi, a commonplace for discovering suitable proofs, for delineating the relation, as the title says, between human nature and the human mind. "America" becomes for Stein a spatial and temporal site of generative memory where relations necessarily invoke the complexities of time and place.

Although Aristotle's *Rhetoric* offers no sustained discussion of memory, his influential *On Memory* develops a psychological theory of memory, putting forward one of the first explications of memory as a temporally troubled cognitive capacity. Here, Aristotle offers a vivid, if ancient, explanation of Stein's trouble with memory vis-a-vis the continuous present:

> there is no such thing as memory of the present while present, for the present is object only of perception, and the future, of expectation, but the object of memory is the past. All memory, therefore, implies a time elapsed; consequently only those animals which perceive time remember, and the organ whereby they perceive time is also that whereby they remember. (*On Memory* 449b 24–25)

Aristotle suggests that our perception of time enables us to remember. Memory is locked not just in time but in past time; it requires by necessity elapsed time. It cannot, seemingly, exist in a continuous present because "there is no such thing as memory of the present *while* present" (emphasis added). Aristotle speaks to the tensions between the two senses of time identified in ancient Greece as *chronos,* or chronological, linear, and measurable time, and *kairos,* or opportune moments within specific situations. Kairos is qualitative, not quantitative; it is Stein's continuous present, a window of opportunity for invention, for exploring and creating ideas.[7] However, it is not atemporal because opportune moments might require awareness of past moments. Although Stein grapples with this issue of being aware of time in memory as early as *The Making of Americans*, her most sustained meditation on the composition of memory existing in the continuous present is in *Stanzas in Meditation* —a text to which I will return—where, as Joan Retallack suggests, "the act of composition is . . . an act of presentness" that does not "leave history behind" (*Poethical* 11).

Although a brief history of the ancient rhetorical canon of memory helps to ground our understanding of Stein's sense of memory, it is the move toward modernity that offers a fuller sense of the centrality of memory to Stein's thinking and writing. In the nineteenth century, "new rhetoricians," combined classical rhetoric with modern philosophical theories of knowledge and psychological theories of the mind. The Scottish Common Sense Realists Hugh Blair, George Campbell, and Richard Whately redefined the theory and practice of discourse, particularly in North America.[8] The so-called new rhetoric incorporated elements of faculty psychology and modern theories of the mind into their rhetorical theories. In *The Philosophy of Rhetoric* (1776), for example, George Campbell drew on faculty psychology, specifically, assumptions about the ability of individuals to examine their own mental states. He assumes that the aims of discourse arise not from common wisdom of the community but from within the mind of the rhetor.[9] According to Campbell, memory is one faculty of the mind, a "repository of all the stores from which our experience is collected" that can aid in effective communication (80).[10]

Rhetorical conceptions of memory veered away from ancient community-based conceptions, became "methodical," and were located within a sovereign authorial individual mind, according to Sharon Crowley.[11] Crowley points out that eighteenth-century discourse theorists made certain assumptions about the human mind: not only could it investigate and verify its own workings (Descartes's *cogito*), the human mind worked in "an organized linear sequence," where these "sequential workings were accurately inscribed in memory and could be accurately reproduced upon demand" (12). Memory became not kairotic, but methodical, structured, logical, organized, and reproducible, a kind of memory that is settled, not troubled, one that has forgotten the articulation of forgetting.

As modern rhetoric became increasingly focused on precise and perspicacious argumentation, memory fell out of the canons, paving the way for Corbett's dismissal. In the same way rhetoric became focused on the rules of correct usage, memory became a scientific and quantifiable entity. Although interest in the rhetorical canon of memory waned, interest in memory grew across the newly forming disciplines in institutions of higher education particularly toward the end of the nineteenth century when research universities and graduate schools became prevalent in the United States. Philosophy and psychology, fields of great interest to Stein, vied for institutional ground in the university, and the study of memory was caught up in the split. Formerly located within the field of philosophy, the "new psychology" became empirical and scientific, leaving behind metaphysical questions in favor of data gathered in psychology laboratories. Thinkers like Stein's undergraduate teacher, William James, rejected the exclusion of philosophical and metaphysical concerns in the study of psychology; James conducted this work in the 1890s when Stein was his student.[12]

Stein found herself in the midst of this disciplinary struggle as she conducted experiments, including one called "Unconscious Memory and Invention," with Leon Solomon in the Harvard Psychological Laboratory. At this same time, her professor Hugo Munsterberg oversaw a number of studies on the psychology of memory including "The Place of Repetition in Memory."[13] Although Stein's initial curiosity about memory may have begun in the Psychology Lab, her ongoing interest in memory expanded well beyond the scientific and quantifiable concerns of the laboratory. She claims to have enjoyed the laboratory work and research during her first two years of medical school at Johns Hopkins School of Medicine. However, she attributes her dropping out after four years to boredom: "she was so bored she could not remember the things that of course the dullest medical student could not forget" (*Autobiography* 101).[14] Following in James's footsteps, Stein maintains philosophical and metaphysical concerns in the study of psychology embracing the fluidity of memory without reducing its complexities to quantifiable data.

In the same way writing instruction was reduced to following or memorizing the rules of correct usage, memory often became reduced to rote data retrieval in the nineteenth century. If the mnemonist's task was to increase one's power of recall to enable effective speaking, lecturing, or preaching, then the critique of the model of memory as static data retrieval might hold, and we might accept Corbett's dismissal of the canon as lacking any theoretical ground. However, the early twentieth century proves an interesting time for theories of memory, offering more nuanced concepts that include theories of temporality, the mind, psychology, narrative, and history along with epistemological challenges to how knowledge is formed, shared, recorded, and remembered. Memory becomes a complex process where acts of remembering, whether individual or communal, are constructed, selective, and partial.[15]

Although the work of French philosopher Henri Bergson was tremendously influential in the early twentieth century, scholars are divided about Stein's connection with him. Malcolm Brinnin recounts Mabel Dodge's claim that Stein was not a "disciple of Henri Bergson" (185). However, in 1911, Mina Loy visited Stein in Italy and commented on the pervasiveness of Bergson's thinking on time: "This was when Bergson was in the air, and his beads of Time strung on the continuous flux of Being, seemed to have found a literary conclusion in the austere verity of Gertrude Stein's theme—'Being' as the absolute occupation" (Curnutt 178). Stein biographer Linda Wagner-Martin notes that Stein "would have known of Bergson's groundbreaking work through philosophical and literary circles, as well as artistic ones" (322).

Bergson's influential *Matter and Memory: Essays on the Relation of Body and Spirit,* published in 1896 when Stein was an undergraduate studying with James and Munsterberg, defines memory as more than material, as the subtitle suggests. Bergson theorizes two kinds of memory: memory as habit, which simply repeats a past action, and pure memory, which is dynamic, moving from the contemplation of images toward action. For Bergson, memory is "placed at the confluence of mind and matter" (320). This dynamic memory, according to Bergson, allows "us to grasp in a single intuition multiple moments of duration, it frees us from the movement of the flow of things, that is to say, from the rhythm of necessity" (303). While Stein's modernist sense of time might be construed as Bergsonian, her conception of habit and movement differ. Rather than freeing "us from the movement of the flow of things," Stein seeks to break habits by putting ideas, conventions, and rules in motion. Discussing *The Making of Americans*, Stein identifies as "strictly American . . . a space that is filled with moving, a space of time that is filled always filled with moving" ("Gradual" 161). Where Bergson follows the movement of memory at the intersection of mind and matter, Stein works to keep that motion at play in language.

"she is the articulation of forgetting": Stein's Memory Lessons

Nearly all of Stein's major works, including *How to Write*, *The Autobiography of Alice B. Toklas*, *Making of Americans*, *Geography and Plays*, *The Geographical History of America*, and *Stanzas in Meditation* address memory, remembering, and forgetting. Memory was, as Richard Bridgman acknowledges, "a matter of perpetual interest to Gertrude Stein" (8). Others have read Stein as dismissing memory merely as a problem to overcome. Preeminent Stein scholar Ulla Dydo notes "Reminiscences have to do with histories and identities outside the playscape before us . . . and memory is about the logic of developing plots, which Stein shuns" (*Language* 276). John Whittier-Ferguson identifies Stein as "one of our century's most skeptical and thorough students of memory" (122).

He agrees that Stein "like any number of modernists" is concerned "centrally with the faculty of memory," but he describes her relationship with memory as hostile: "the way she writes, the way she moves through successive versions of a text, constitutes the methodological foundation of her assault against the reign of memory, the tyrannies of time" (133). Because memory is, by definition, about something in the past, Whittier-Ferguson finds that Stein's skepticism centers on the ways in which we and the subjects we remember are positioned in time. Claudia Franken also find memory to be problematic because it forces "undesirable contents upon the poetic process" (68).[16] "Writing about memory," as Franken suggests, leads Stein to reject "the emotional interference of remembrance with creative expression" (68).

Although Stein certainly problematizes a sense of memory limited to a storage container full of static objects from the past that can be accessed and written *about,* she models a contradictory and complex sense of writing *with* and *through*—not just about or against—both memory and forgetting. As many of her key texts show, memory is not an insurmountable problem or simply something to get out of the way in order to occupy and write the continuous present. She does much more than attack, dismiss, or subordinate memory. More than a skeptical student, Stein is an astute teacher of the art of memory and the refusal of forgetting, drawing lessons from the nineteenth century's obsession with memory and the mind. Stein theorizes memory as a central and inescapable category of her thinking and writing. Although the continuous present may appear timeless, for Gertrude Stein, it is not a moment without memory or forgetting.

However, memory *is* troubling for Stein. She chides those who reduce memory to mimesis, a mere resemblance of the past because "a resemblance was something that presupposed remembering" ("Portraits and Repetition" 175). In "Portraits and Repetition," a text to which I return, Stein defines "the trouble with a great many so called intelligent people" as a problem with memory: "they mix up remembering with talking and listening" (171–180). Reflecting on "The Gradual Making of The Making of Americans," she underscores the vitality and necessity of "listening and hearing and feeling the rhythm of each human being" (145). In other words, these people who mix things up mistake remembering as *equivalent* to talking and listening when it is removed from the present, merely mimics the past, and offers nothing new. Stein's earliest portraits, often identified as a kind of literary cubism that put into words what Picasso put on canvas, continually explore the ways in which talking and listening are bound up in memory and forgetting, making it difficult to understand our own activity in remembering and our ability, or lack thereof, to find critical distance from the ostensible objects of memory.

In "What Are Masterpieces," Stein comments that for some people "memory is necessary to make them exist" (90). These people, according to Stein, cannot create masterpieces because their identity is bound to and defined by the past. If, she asks, "you know who you are because you and others remember anything about yourself," then you run the risk of being overdetermined by memory, perhaps in the same way the rules of grammar can restrict how we write, what we know, and how we know (84). But by supposing "a grammar uses invention," as I previously discussed, the rules of grammar contain possibilities beyond restriction. If we are defined by how we are remembered along with how we remember ourselves, then the present becomes not continuous but dictated by the past. Stein has other plans for memory.

Memory and how we remember can be more than tyrannical. Stein concludes "Reread Another," a play written in 1921 and originally published in *Operas and Plays* in 1932, with a declaration about memory: "My memory does not tell me how and what to remember and so what do / I do. I remember everything." Here, memory is decidedly not prescriptive, nor is it rendered unimportant. Stein posits the question "what do I do," even as she answers it: "I remember everything." Rather than a photographic memory or an ability to recall with precision, Stein suggests memory is not a thing to be retrieved but an activity one does, that "I do," a creative process in itself.

Memory and History in *The Making of Americans*

Stein struggled with the problem of memory even in her earliest writing. In *The Making of Americans*, her articulation of forgetting is also an articulation of thinking about the narrative function of memory. Her changing understanding of modernist conventions of narration includes a new way of understanding memory, the temporality of words, and the past in the present. This novel, which she began to write shortly before moving to Paris in 1903, after leaving medical school at Johns Hopkins just two years before, invokes and complicates the notion of memory as a container of the past or as a storehouse of ideas to draw on for the present. Stein calls this work "not just an ordinary kind of novel with a plot and conversations . . ." but "a record of decent family progress" (33).[17] On the face of it, narrative is a repository of history, an archive, a record of the past. It is also more. *The Making of Americans* is a book, at least in part, about narrative repetition, about, as Stein says, "escaping from the inevitable narrative of anything" (*Narration* 25).

The Making of Americans tells the story of an immigrant family, ostensibly from and about the past, though its style of telling marks it as one of literary modernism's premier works. Stein herself, not uncharacteristically boastful, identifies the novel as a "monumental work," calling it "the beginning, really the beginning of modern writing" (*Autobiography* 215). Charles Bernstein comments that although this novel may introduce modern writing, Stein "moved into the twentieth century grounded in the nineteenth," a century where "the use of the family as a microcosm for the state or church or world" was a recurring structure that "dramatized, and hence declared, the dialectic struggle between our inner lives and the external world" ("Inventing" 58–59).

Although Stein credits *The Making of Americans* with the beginning of modern writing, literary modernism's inception remains debatable. Virginia Woolf famously declared that human character changed "on or about December 1910"—the same year T. S. Eliot began "The Love Song of J. Alfred Prufrock," though it was not published until 1915. James Joyce published *Dubliners* in 1906 but did not begin work on *Ulysses* until 1914; it took eight years before it was published in 1922. *The Making of Americans* was not, initially, the monument Stein had hoped. In 1908, she discarded the original manuscript, what Ulla Dydo identified as "a fairly conventional nineteenth-century family novel" (*A Stein Reader* 17). Beginning again, Stein's narration became a radical departure not just because it broke from traditional novelistic conventions but because of Stein's reworking of history and memory. The novel's subtitle, "Being a History of a Family's Progress," indicates that the novel was a study of past events, even as Stein began to rethink the discursive possibilities of memory.

Perhaps ironically, perhaps didactically, Stein opens *The Making of Americans* with the word "Once": "Once an angry man dragged his father along the ground through his own orchard. 'Stop!' cried the groaning old man at last, 'Stop! I did not drag my father beyond this tree.'"[18] Still on his own land, a father is being dragged forward by his son, the next generation, in an act of repetition that is also, perhaps, a progression. History is repeating. But the child is reprimanded by the past. Angry and adamant, the father warns the child not to move beyond his tradition. How is a family to progress if the past—our memories of and stories about the past—are destined to merely repeat, thereby dictating the parameters of the present? Stein addresses the complication of repetition with the opening word *once,* which denotes both one occasion and one time only as well as some point in the past, a memory. *Once,* in Stein's opening, marks an occasion not of singularity but of a repetition, something happening twice, or perhaps with each generation, an invocation of memory, a repetition of the past, and yet a singularity in relation to time.

Stein offers a lesson in memory, in how to remember and why memory is so central to "being existing," as she says repeatedly in *The Making of Americans*, even as she troubles efforts to identify, control, or resist the dynamic processes of memory. Immediately following the epigraph, Stein addresses the burden of memory: "We need only realise our parents, remember our grandparents and know ourselves and our history is complete" (3). We might "realise our parents" by becoming fully aware of them in the present even as we "remember our grandparents," the generation that has passed. Connecting this awareness in the present with what has come before, Stein seems to suggest the potential of narrative to capture but not be bound by the past. In this sense, what is continuous about the present is a reworking of the past, a constant ordering and reordering of how one generation moves into the next. Reworking memories is a kind of articulation of forgetting. Rather than ignoring or overlooking the past, what is forgotten are its dictates, its patterns, its habits, which confine rather than open up possibility.

Perhaps the major contribution of *The Making of Americans* is Stein's theorization of the art of memory as an articulation of forgetting, a craft that explores what has been (or might have been) in the context of what is. During the first decade of the twentieth century while she worked on *The Making of Americans* (1903–1911), William James published his initial treatise on pragmatism, generally referred to by its shortened title, *Pragmatism.* As a student of James in the 1890s during the period in which he was formulating key ideas for this work, not only would Stein have been familiar with James's definition of pragmatism, she also would have known the full title: *Pragmatism: A New Name for Some Old Ways of Thinking.*[19] In defining "What Pragmatism Means," James also considers how old ways of thinking affect new ones: "The new idea . . . preserves the older stock of truths with minimum of modification, stretching them just enough to make them admit the novelty" (50). "New truths thus are resultants of new experiences and of old truths combined and mutually modifying one another" according to James (113). Stein, too, tells stories about history where the new does not simply replace the old; rather, they interact and mutually modify. What goes on in the present, even in the presentness of writing, is a continual reordering of a temporal continuum.

For Stein, writing out of the nineteenth century entailed more than acknowledging or rejecting discursive habits of the past. As an astute reader of discursive culture, Stein remained interested in why these changes were happening and also how they were happening. She begins the novel by pointing to connections between the "old" and the "new": "The old people in a new world, the new people made out of the old, that is the story that I mean to tell, for that is what really is and what I really know" (3). This is a problem of memory, of how we remember the past, of how we live in the present. Although the world may be new, it continues to include "old people," as Stein says, and while it also includes "new people," they have been "made out of the old" (3). The old and new as well as the past and present cannot be separated, particularly when trying to tell stories, particularly in acts of composition. Narrative inevitably, at least partially, takes the form of a history of remembering and the articulation of forgetting.

"This is the way to have memory": Memory without Certainty

Whether Stein traces the history of family progress in *The Making of Americans*, explores the mnemonic memoryscapes of *The Geographical History of America or The Relation of Human Nature to the Human Mind*, or meditates on mindfulness in *Stanzas in Meditation*, she troubles memory, transforming it into what William James calls "the art of remembering," an imaginative skill that he equates with "the art of *thinking*" (*Talks* 143). She takes her art further, making it integral to "being existing." In "Two: Gertrude Stein and Her Brother," a long, early portrait written between 1910 and 1912 and not published until 1951, Stein invokes the necessity of memory through a litany of anticipation:

> She is the anticipation of conviction of remembering being existing. She is the anticipating of a new one having been an old one. She is the anticipation of expression having immaculate conception. She is the anticipation of crossing. She is the anticipation of regeneration. She is the anticipation of excelling obligation. She is the anticipation. She is the actualisation. She is the rising having been arisen. She is the convocation of anticipation and acceptation. She is the lamb and the lion. She is the leaven of reverberation. She is the complication of receiving, she is the articulation of forgetting, she is the expression of indication, she is the augmentation of condensing, she is the inroad of releasing. (107–108)

Written around the time that Alice B. Toklas was replacing Stein's brother Leo at 27 Rue de Fleurus, "Two: Gertrude Stein and Her Brother" is a lengthy proclamation of Stein and Leo parting ways. "She," who we might initially take to be the Gertrude Stein of the title of this portrait, is the anticipation of many things; Stein's prescience about the early twentieth century has become true many times over.[20] The repetition of "anticipation" suggests a sense of expectation. One imagines much anticipation around the event, the final parting of brother and sister.

The repetition of "She is" in this passage constructs a memory of her, recording who "she" is, even as it brings her into being so that "remembering being existing" is not a static event but a dynamic, immediate articulation of who she is becoming in the present tense. What "she" anticipates in this passage begins and ends with remembering and releasing. In between, "she" or her anticipation take on religious overtones from "immaculate conception" to "crossing" to "regeneration" to "actualisation," and then, shifting to past tense, "having been risen" (107–108).[21] Stein recalls and complicates a central transitional event in the history of Western civilization, the Crucifixion. This story of birth, death, and resurrection becomes complicated in its reception, however. In fact, it is "She"—the subject of each sentence—who "is the complication of receiving" perhaps because "she is the articulation of forgetting" even in a moment of remembering (108).[22] What is forgotten? What is Stein articulating? Earlier we are told "She was not forgetting what she was not remembering" (92).

Midway through the passage, "she" shifts, becoming Alice, Stein's "expression of indication," a preference for a desirable course of action. Although Toklas had been living with Stein and her brother for several years, Leo officially departed 27 rue de Fleurus in 1912. Leo leaves, a brother crucified. Toklas arrives, a lover ascended, and the transfiguration complete. "She is the rising having been arisen." Stein's narration locates memory in the telling, in the repetition, in the acts of remembering and recording. The portrait is not a flashback as much as it is memory at play, memory in motion—a kind of memory that is "not forgetting" and "not remembering" (93). Stein puts the conundrum this way: "She was not forgetting that which she was not remembering. In not forgetting what she was not remembering she was saying all she was saying . . . she was not forgetting what she was not remembering, she was not forgetting anything in not remembering anything, she was not remembering and she was not forgetting and she was saying what she did say" (92–93). To articulate forgetting, for Stein, is to give voice to a failure to remember and to theorize memory as an inescapable category of thinking and writing. If it were not articulated, would it still be memory or would it remain forgotten?

That memory's complexity is more than a problem to be dismissed occurred to Stein in another early portrait, the often overlooked group portrait, "Jenny, Helen, Hannah, Paul and Peter," written between 1910 and 1912. Remembering, a central concern of the portrait, causes problems between Jenny and Helen who are both "being living" but also "not completing being living" (168). Stein juxtaposes Jenny, "who is moving in the direction of continually remembering," with Helen, who "was not like the other one [Jenny]" (151, 160). While this is a portrait of people, mostly Jenny and Helen, being and living together, they have more to do; their lives are not complete. Whereas Jenny is "one not forgetting that she was remembering that anyone should remember . . . she was one believing in remembering," Helen seems to struggle with memory by neutralizing it: "She was knowing that remembering is nothing. She was knowing that not remembering is nothing" (156, 161). We might read Helen's understanding of memory as unimportant. To remember or not to remember are equivalent; neither matter. They are both "nothing." Alternatively we might read Helen's comment more literally to say that remembering and not remembering are not any single *thing*. Remembering is not an object to be retrieved, nor is not remembering.

Coming to understand remembering is gradual, complicated, and varied for different people; it is also connected to knowing. Jenny and Helen's trouble with memory is, in part, epistemological. Eventually, "both of them were not remembering that anything is something. They both of them were not remembering very much of that thing that anything is something" (169). Is not remembering equivalent to forgetting? Can we articulate forgetting not by locking down memories and referents but through some other means? What is that means? And what if we do not remember that anything is something? That is precisely Jenny and Helen's problem: they do not remember that "anything is something," nor do they recall that remembering can be inventive.

Stein complicates the problem further by noting that even if we might come to know or believe something, like Jenny and Helen, we cannot "be certain that anything is something" (169). Stein continues to explore their relationship until "There was no use to say more," at which point Hannah is introduced and remembering falls away for nearly the remainder of the portrait. Stein returns briefly to memory in the penultimate paragraph with a declarative statement: "This is the way to have memory. This is the way" (234). Stein's ambiguous pronoun seeks a referent but finds nothing except seeming non sequiturs. If we apply "this" to the portrait itself, Stein's way of having memory is to engage with it, to explore it gradually, perhaps to acquire knowledge by it or even to forget it. The way to have memory does not require certainty. Certainty is not a requirement for remembering or for being living.

More than two decades later, Stein's playful and instructive musings on memory in "Portraits and Repetition," one of her *Lectures in America*, brings some clarity to the seeming contradictions in her thinking and writing about memory. She seems to suggest that she attempts to write portraits without repetition and memory: "I say that there is no repetition because, and this is absolutely true, that the exciting thing inside in any one if it is really inside in them is not *a remembered thing*" (183 emphasis added). The "exciting thing"—whatever it might be—is precisely *not* some *thing* retrieved and remembered. One is tempted to read Stein's aside, the claim to absolute truth, as both exaggerated and humorous. She goes on to say that she worked to "make a portrait of that inside them without any description of what they are doing and what they are saying" because that way, Stein claims, "I too was neither repeating, nor remembering nor being in confusion" (184). But, in fact, Stein found it difficult to avoid repeating, remembering, and being in confusion in her portraiture.

Stein opens the lecture "Portraits and Repetition" with a reference to "Composition as Explanation" and goes on to reference by title or by excerpt nearly thirty of her works, including more than a dozen portraits. Stein's citations offer a kind of repetition, a history and a textual memory, perhaps even a portrait of her oeuvre. The lecture functions as a kind of composition as explanation where Stein strives for clarity and understanding even as she attempts to craft more than "a remembered thing." Although she asserts that she wanted to conceive of herself "as completely talking and listening," remembering continually gets in the way just as it keeps appearing, again and again, throughout the lecture. In a paragraph that begins "I remember very well what happened," Stein introduces "the bother that has always been a bother" (175). The challenge, as Stein describes it, is what happens or might happen "at the same time" as talking and listening: "If listening was talking and talking was listening then and *at the same time* any little movement any little expression was a resemblance, and a resemblance was something that presupposed remembering" (174–175 emphasis added). A conceptual impasse or temporal complication becomes clear in the following paragraph when Stein claims, "Already then as you see there was a complication which was a bother to me in my conception of the rhythm of a personality. I have for so many years tried to get the better of that the better of this bother. The bother was simply that and one may say it is the bother that has always been a bother to anybody for anybody conceiving anything" (175). This bother is the problem of memory, a problem that cannot be avoided or, even, written away. While one might achieve "completely talking and listening," other things may be happening at the same time, things that may be remembered or forgotten. "Portraits and Repetition" is, in part, Stein coming to terms with how repetition, remembering, and confusion might aid rather than hinder acts of composition.

Writing about objects allowed Stein to "avoid this difficulty of suggesting remembering" (188). Stein attributes her shift from portraits of human beings to portraits of "rooms and food" to a problem of memory. However, the difficulty was not long avoided, and Stein discovered a way, as she said, to weaken "the strictness of not letting remembering mix itself with looking and listening and talking. . . . In the portraits that I did in that period of which I have just been speaking the later period considerably after the war the strictness of not letting remembering mix itself with looking and listening and talking which began with *The Making of Americans* and went on all through *Tender Buttons* and what came immediately after, all the period of *Geography and Plays* this strictness perhaps weakened a little weakened a little because and that in a way was an astonishment to me" (196). Prior to this point in the lecture, Stein has already demonstrated how memory can function pedagogically. She explicitly and repeatedly turned to memory by telling stories about her own gradual understanding of "this thing": "I remember very well first beginning to be conscious of this thing" and "I remember the first time I really realized this" (168). Several pages later she says: "I remember very well what happened" (174). What she remembers is "conceiving [herself] as completely talking and listening," a place allegedly free of remembering except when she, ironically, remembers it (174). Rather than recovering and recording pieces of the past, Stein looks, listens, and pulls things together. She gathers words, images, and things people have said and seen. She is an empiricist, who explores the multiplicities of possibilities in any given moment rather than getting mixed up in the conundrum of what is or is not *the* case.

After Stein acknowledges the loosening of "this strictness," memory and remembering disappear from the lecture, and the focus shifts to melody, repetition, portraits, and grammar. As is the case in other lectures, Stein works overtly with repetition and with memory. She repeats her key points, transitioning by noting "To go back to something I said" and "This time I do repeat; in going over this again" (179, 200). She also repeatedly checks in with her audience: "Do you see what I mean" (188, 200), "You do see why" (189), or "I hope you quite all see what I mean" (206). The fact Stein gave the lecture "Portraits and Repetition" before an audience foregrounded the challenge—if not the impossibility—of writing and now speaking, without repeating, remembering, and confusion. The lecture itself performs the contradictory and necessary elements of Stein's art of memory by skillfully juxtaposing what is remembered within the unfolding of the present.

Dynamic Places of Memory in *The Geographical History of America*

In her later works, Stein theorizes more fully different methods of remembering and the problem of what to forget and what has been forgotten. Where ancient Greek mnemonic devises were used for retaining and retrieving carefully and previously articulated thought, Stein's geographical mnemonic is an aid to thinking and articulating forgetting; it puts into words the complex, problematic, and generative category of memory. Written in 1935 after, and perhaps in response to, her celebrity status gained during her lecture tour in the United States, *The Geographical History of America or The Relation of Human Nature to the Human Mind* is an experimental and philosophical meditation that evades predictable logics, including the logic of memory and history ensconced in a genre of family history as in *The Making of Americans. The Geographical History* can be and has been read as a philosophical meditation on the nature—or composition—of knowledge, reality, and existence. To this list, I add memory as an articulation of forgetting.

Stein's central claim remains constant throughout: "To know what ideas are you have to think of geographical history and the relation of the human mind to human nature" (50). Indeed, Stein opens the work by invoking a memory in the form of geography and history: "In the month of February were born Washington Lincoln and I" (45). The narrator places herself within this historical narrative by calling to mind a particular month in which she and two prominent United States' presidents were born. "These," according to Stein, "are ordinary ideas" (45). Even in the opening line, Stein demonstrates how to think of geographical history by locating a particular moment and calling upon the past. To understand ideas requires memory; it requires looking back and locating oneself in time and place. In this sense, memory happens to an idea, to echo William James's sense of truth. James posits "the truth of an idea is not a stagnant property inherent to it. Truth *happens* to an idea. It *becomes* true, is *made* true by events. Its verity *is* in fact an event, a process, the process namely of its verifying itself, its veri*fication.* Its validity is the process of its valid*ation*" (*Pragmatism* 92). Likewise for Stein, memory, although it is located in time and place, is not stagnant; it is a heuristic, an articulation, a process.

The Geographical History of America, then, can be read as a performative meditation on the constructedness of memory, the ways in which memory happens to an idea. It explores the ideas of its own composition: geographical history, human mind, and human nature. Most scholars agree on the definitional distinction between the works' two key concepts—human nature and the human mind—as well as Stein's preference for the human mind. For example, Bruce Kellner identifies the work's "major premise" as Stein's "preference for the human mind over human nature" (34). The human mind or entity, as Stein calls it, is the site of genius and creation, a place of heightened attention and pure meditation that is removed from the constraints of time and memory. Human nature produces "identity writing" designed for an audience, written by an author located in time and working from memory. Richard Bridgman calls the human mind "pure and objective" and "in every way superior to human nature" (261–264). But the full title itself, *The Geographical History of America or The Relation of Human Nature to the Human Mind,* indicates that this work is more a consideration of the *relation* between these categories than an explication of, or strict insistence upon, their difference. Does Stein's conjunction indicate a linking of alternatives, a synonym, or an afterthought? Even if their relation is oppositional, the categories are mutually dependent, not mutually exclusive.

Throughout the text, the human mind and human nature continue to be defined with and against the other. Rather than simply privileging one term over the other, Stein explores the ways in which "entity" writing is contained within "identity" writing. She plays with the relation linguistically where *entity,* the fact of existence or being, is contained within the word *identity,* the collective characteristics that make something or someone known. However, this linguistic relation is defined *in* writing; it takes place through the act of writing.

Although this work explores philosophical aspects of identity, presence, composition, and geography, philosophical meditations pose their own troubles because, as Stein points out, "Philosophy tries to replace in the human mind what is not there that is time and beginning" (186). Philosophical inquiry by necessity occurs in time, operates on first principles, and works within systematic logics. Kellner comments on Stein's philosophical endeavor, calling *The Geographical History* "a meditative consideration of . . . the metaphysics of the writing process" (*A Gertrude Stein Companion* 33). It may well be but Stein's metaphysics never, finally, move beyond the "physics" in its broad scientific sense as an exploration of the physical properties and phenomena of some empirically verifiable object or idea, pen on page. Insofar as Stein has a metaphysics, it resists existence beyond the experiences of reading and writing. Here, again, she remains James's student.

Thus, although *The Geographical History of America* attempts to theorize the writing process through the seemingly privileged site of the human mind, the theory Stein writes and performs remains rooted in and on the earth; it is *geo*-graphical. Stein demonstrates how states of being are—and include—a continual reordering of states of memory. With the human mind, Stein writes, "There is no remembering and there is no forgetting because memory has to do with human nature and not with the human mind" (109). Memory relates to human nature; human nature relates to the human mind; the relation is inescapable. For Stein, memory retains its original etymological sense of being mindful or having a full mind, conditions which she sees as cultural, linguistic, and kairotic. Seizing opportune moments requires assessing the constraints of time and the possibilities available within the moment.

Instead of architectural mnemonics like Quintilian's, Stein adopts a more expansive geographic mnemonic of place, a topos, the very heart of classical rhetoric. If we take Stein at her word, *geography* includes not just *geo* or earth but also *graphia* or writing. It is a story of past events rooted in and on the earth, the surface of the page, our material world. Ulla Dydo explains more fully Stein's sense of geography and its connection with composition: "Geography is never simply about location, scenery, and the space of the earth, though it includes these. It is about the arrangement of words in compositional space, the disposition of elements from the inside" (*A Stein Reader* 467). Geography includes the surface of the page, the literal space of composition; it also includes states of being, a particular condition at a specific time in the territory of thinking and writing. More than an abstract theory of the writing process, Stein's meditation is from the beginning kairotic, located in place (the spaciousness of the American landscape) and time (historical time invoked in the opening line). The work itself seizes an opportune moment to meditate on the relation of the human mind to human nature, a relation constantly troubled by memory and forgetting, within the geographic space of America with its promise of democracy, open space, and celebration of the quotidian. We might read Stein's mediation on human nature and the human mind as language itself, with words themselves always caught in memory, history, and time even as they arise in the human mind, in our recollected pasts.

Stein's geography lessons remain grounded in a continuous ordering and reordering of states of memory. She claims, "It is better not to remember because there is no such thing no such thing as remember. Therefore there is not" (64). The repetition of "no such thing" is a hesitation and also a forceful declaration, underscoring the reason why it is better *not* to remember. Do we require repeated reminders? Might we forget? Is there irony in the repetition that reminds us not to forget that "there is no such thing no such thing as remember" (64)? Stein makes a comparative claim between not remembering and remembering: "It is better not to remember." Her reason: "there is no such thing as remember." But to make a comparative claim or to evaluate one thing against another requires forming an idea or opinion based on one's experience or previous knowledge. In other words, one must remember experiences or ideas in order to determine that one is better. Thus, the challenge brought to bear by Stein in this very sentence is that the sentence itself is premised on and comes from memory. So while it might be "better not to remember," it is also impossible *not* to remember, particularly when putting words on a page, perhaps even more so when reading words on a page. The seeming contradiction after the conjunction—"*because* there is no such thing"—reminds us that "remember" is never simply a "thing" or an object or bits of stored data to be retrieved. Even as it works with the past, the "articulation of forgetting" always invents something new, something out of one's place.

Stein may try to conceive a way to write from the human mind, from entity, but she makes clear that to read from this place is not possible. Here is a telling instance, a seeming non sequitur where Stein underscores the inevitable temporal tension between the writer and reader and the inevitable interruption of memory: "Because the human mind knows what it knows and knowing what it knows it has nothing to do with seeing what it remembers, remember how the country looked as we passed over it" (55). Stein references her astonishment of an aerial view of the American landscape as she traveled by plane across the United States to give her lectures in the mid-1930s. Because "the human mind knows what it knows" (in the present tense and present moment) not what it knew (past tense), at that moment there is no memory. "It has nothing to do with seeing what it remembers"; it simply knows. But Stein complicates with subtle humor how temporary, limited, and impossible this moment is. Even in her sentence, just as she is claiming that what the human mind knows "has nothing to do . . . with what it remembers," a reminder to remember appears just after the pause of a comma: "remember how the country looked as we passed over it" (55). The second-person imperative asks the reader to remember just after we have been told that the human mind in the act of knowing does not remember and has nothing to do with memory. Stein will not let us forget this conundrum. She will gradually make clear that geography, like memory, does not stay still; its topoi are dynamic places, heuristics that open up possibilities in the continuous present even as they include the past.

Just as Stein was writing *The Autobiography of Alice B. Toklas*, an uncharacteristically conventional work of autobiographical memory documenting contexts and characters in Stein's life in Paris, she also wrote *Stanzas in Meditation.*[23] Known as one of Stein's most challenging, unyielding, and hermetic texts, *Stanzas in Meditation* is a long poem between 150 and 225 pages depending on the edition; it is divided into five parts, the first four with 15 to 24 stanzas identified by Roman numerals. Part 5, the longest, has 83 stanzas.[24] Part of what makes the work so challenging, explains Ulla Dydo, is that by 1932, the year in which Stein filled six notebooks with the text of *Stanzas*, Stein's "way with words changes and contexts virtually vanish," a change that offered "new freedom, new ways with words ... as if her writing ... barely hinged anymore to whatever it is that generates it" (472).[25] *Stanzas* might be read, then, at least in part, as a meditation on the limitations and necessity of memory. Verging on complete abstraction from particular referents, *Stanzas in Meditation* moves beyond "things" and into a sustained practice of meditation to become mindful, to clear the mind and to empty words of referents. Dydo asks how text and context can relate when "her language virtually empties out of references?" (489).

Although *Stanzas* and *The Autobiography* are often seen as "alter egos," they share an abiding interest in memory. The *Autobiography*, written in Toklas's voice, self reflexively explores identity, personality, memory, and memory transmission. *Stanzas* explores active memory with an "I" remembering or wanting to be remembered, from "I wish to remain to remember that stanzas go on" to "This what I say makes me remember that" (112, 173). Saying leads to remembering; it points to particular times, places, and objects. Remembering happens at specific times: "It is the day when we remember two" (65). Here, too, memory is troubling, posing problems: "I could just as well remember what I saw / Or if not I could just as well remember / What I saw when I could" (177). Memory is faulty; one can only remember when one can. Some memories are lost, irretrievable, absent, and forgotten. But certain things require memory: "The only thing that helps with that / Is memory. / And sometimes I remember and sometimes I do not" (232). But what exactly does memory help with? The object of Stein's pronoun—"The only thing that helps with that"—remains unnamed even as memory is unequivocally identified as the "only thing" that helps. *Stanzas* will not allow us to leave the "now" of the meditations in our own recourse to memory.

Remembering and forgetting are inescapable, necessary, even imperative, at least as long as we are alive, according to Stein, "because if you are killed you do not remember no you do not, it is only on land where it is dangerous but where you were not killed that you remember" (57). Stein's insistence on the problem of memory is also a lesson on the danger of forgetting that our ways of writing, reading, and thinking are habits. Stein's writing gifts the reader with textual experience that opens the possibility of not forgetting. "To forget is not to remember but to remember is not to forget" (390).[26] Speaking and writing are invocations of memory. Writing is always an articulation of forgetting. To narrate rightly, as Socrates has it, we invoke memory as a heuristic that both recovers and critiques, even as it opens up, kairotically, an ever-changing moment, Stein's continuous present.

6

Gertrude Stein Delivers

> This has interested me very much . . . this enormous publicity business. . . . People now know the details of important people's daily life unlike they did in the Nineteenth Century. Then the novel supplied imagination where now you have it in publicity.
>
> Stein, "A Transatlantic Interview"

> You see what I mean by what I say. But I know you do.
>
> Stein, "Portraits and Repetition"

> All this is very important because it is important. . . . I hope I have been making it slowly clear to you.
>
> Stein, "Pictures"

> Do you understand. Do you any or all of you understand. . . . It makes an awful lot of difference to me.
>
> Stein, "Portraits and Repetition"

In the fall of 1934, Gertrude Stein arrived in America to much buzz about "Gertrude Stein." Her photo appeared on the cover of *Time* magazine on September 11, 1933, following the blockbuster success of her accessible and witty *The Autobiography of Alice B. Toklas* (1933). Journalists and a film crew waited at the dock to document Stein's arrival. Her name appeared in lights in Times Square. Receptions were held in her honor. She enjoyed tea at the White House with Eleanor Roosevelt and dinner in Beverly Hills with Charlie Chaplin. She received the key to her hometown city of San Francisco. A two-month lecture tour turned into seven. Fans and skeptics filled lectures halls across the United States to hear her *Lectures in America.* Everywhere she went Gertrude Stein made headline news.

After nearly three decades of living in France, where she wrote several demanding and enigmatic works now revered as modernist literary classics—including *Three Lives* (1909), *Tender Buttons* (1914), *The Making of Americans* (1925), and *How to Write* (1931)—and after entertaining some of the early twentieth century's most famous writers, artists, and critics, Stein published *The Autobiography of Alice B. Toklas*, a memoir written in the "voice" of her companion and lover, chronicling their lives and renowned salon at 27 rue de Fleurus in Paris. In a 1933 review of *The Autobiography,* Edmund Wilson notes, "though her influence has always been felt at the sources of literature and art, her direct communications with the public have been extremely blurred and broken" (247). Stein was, as *Time* magazine called her in 1933, "one of the least-read and most-publicized writers of the day." Not only did *The Autobiography's* success mend and extend her relationship with the public, its "easefully written," "plain style," according to Neil Schmitz, moved her "out of the marginality of a distant French avant-garde into American letters" (752). It also moved her firmly into the realm of celebrity, practically making "Gertrude Stein" a household name. Wanda Corn calls Stein "the people's modernist" because she was able to explain and perform the principles of modernism "in a plain, unaffected style [that] was keeping with what depression-era Americans wanted in their heroes" (249). Capitalizing on this fame, Stein, the expatriate, was persuaded to return to the United States to lecture about her writing and to bring with her the Parisian avant-garde.

A lecture tour meant Stein faced a shift in modes of delivery and of composition, from writing to speaking, from the philosophical and rhetorical explorations of *How to Write* to the public performance of *Lectures in America*. Because, as Stein asserted, "nobody writes as they talk," she found herself with reason to discover "how my writing would sound to others" and how to "make them [her audiences] understand" ("And Now" 63). Discovering her available means, what would be effective for her audiences, would entail careful orchestration of her arrival within a culture of communication increasingly structured by the rise of corporate public relations, mass media, and celebrity culture.[1] Stein used public relations strategies to capitalize on her celebrity and to introduce an American audience to her modernist compositional processes. These PR strategies helped Stein bring readers to a product that had proved a difficult sell. A media darling, however, she also managed to position herself as media critic, a quizzical interpreter of the culture from which, among writers, she herself had perhaps most to gain.

Even when Stein is ostensibly writing about writing in perplexing texts like *How to Write* or *The Geographical History of America*, she addresses the function of language in culture as a means of making oneself or one's ideas known—or present—to audiences, an issue that became even more urgent when she began to lecture publicly and her mode of delivery, the circulation of her composition, shifted from print to public speaking.[2] Stein's interest in the social and cultural functions of language is rhetorical and grounds the literary and poetic elements of her work, most especially during her lecture tour.

For Stein, there is nothing new, nothing invented, no genius in oration when its delivery is a mere transmission of data, reduced to recitation that does not account for kairotic specificities of speaker and audience. Stein's *Lectures in America* attempt to shift the public focus from a discussion of literary form to rhetorical theory, from genre—with lectures devoted to literature, pictures, plays, portraits, and poetry—to an exploration of how we communicate in various forms, venues, and times, particularly when situated in an age of spin. Approaching the delivery of her lectures within their historical context, Stein mediates between the nineteenth and twentieth centuries, taking into account the distinctions between speaking and writing. Her mode of delivery positions her more akin to the Sophists, not a "mere Sophist" as Aristotle has it or a purely deceitful trickster as Plato has it but an itinerant intellectual, wandering around teaching, questioning, giving public exhibitions of her skill, willing to privilege probability over truth, interested in exploring all things, all of Aristotle's categories, and all the while maintaining an investigation of language-in-culture. The Sophist's insistence on self improvement and on gaining facility with language challenged the established power structures by creating the possibility of a world not predicated on automatic, unquestioned deferral to authority and the wisdom of elders. And like the Sophists, Stein negotiates the tensions between Platonic shadow play and ideal forms, between spin and truth, between slick self-promotion and critical pedagogy, and asks her audience to do the same, to imagine their place in the delivery of her lectures.

Taking her celebrity on the road and addressing audiences directly entailed a fundamental reconsideration of her relations with the public and offered an opportunity to experiment with the aesthetics of delivery. Whether limiting the size of the audience to a maximum of 500, refusing to charge for tickets, requiring a desk and chair rather than a podium, or masterfully charming audiences during post-lecture question and answer sessions, Stein orchestrated nearly every aspect of her delivery. She used public relations strategies to fill the auditoriums and to attempt to persuade her audiences to read her work. The lecture tour became an occasion for engaging the public relations culture that dictated the terms of the circulation of her image and for re-theorizing delivery in an age of publicity and mass mediated celebrity. Stein's view of cultural production entailed more than an individual author creating and promoting texts. Her methods for managing her image identify her as an astute observer of an important shift in the material conditions under which rhetoric operated in the early twentieth century.

Although Timothy Galow suggests that Stein was "theoretically unequipped to challenge the many critics who were directly or indirectly cultivating a banal celebrity persona for her," her astute handling of the lecture tour itself is a theoretical performance of her art of inventive delivery—one that responds to and engages both her critics and her celebrity persona (111). Arriving in the United States in 1934, Stein emerged into a media landscape in which the purview of mass mediated messaging had recently expanded well beyond business and government. I begin this chapter by charting this communicative expanse, the setting of Stein's media success, and then consider Stein's relation to her celebrity, including her initial reluctance to tour and her skillful use of PR techniques as she capitalized on the popularity of her own brand, "Gertrude Stein." Finally, I examine Stein's delivery of her lectures through the lectures themselves along with Stein's efforts to negotiate the shift in the source of the public's imagination from the nineteenth-century novel to twentieth-century publicity. For Stein, the art of delivery became a central feature of the age of mass-mediated relations with the public.

The "Enormous publicity business"

By the time Stein landed in New York City in the fall of 1934, the age of mass mediated public relations was well underway. At the turn of the twentieth century, American corporations began to recognize the benefits of interacting differently with their various publics. Formerly, captains of industry often shared railroad magnate William H. Vanderbilt's "public be damned" stance, which led to widespread mistrust of the rapidly expanding corporations that were increasingly regarded by the public as "soulless."[3] Big business, along with the U.S. government, responded by developing more sophisticated strategies to relate with the public and to manage public opinion by branding their image and developing "personalities" for their corporations.[4] Due in large part to the success of widespread public opinion management during World War I, publicists began to better understand the potential reach of public relations in American culture. For example, in an effort to mobilize support for U.S. involvement in World War I, the federal government established the Committee on Public Information (CPI) one week after President Woodrow Wilson declared war on Germany. Director of the CPI, George Creel, expanded government publicity tactics well beyond the traditional press agent to include new forms of mass media and new modes of persuasion. Creel argued that "every possible media should be used to drive home the justice of America's cause" (157–158). To pave the way for the delivery of her lectures, Stein adopted many of these methods for her publicity. Although she initially planned to stay in the United States for two months, her publicity efforts were so successful and the lectures in such demand that she stayed almost seven months, giving nearly sixty lectures from coast to coast.[5]

During this same period Virginia Woolf published her experimental novel, what she called her "playpoem," *The Waves* (1931); T. S. Eliot converted from "The Wasteland" to *Ash Wednesday* (1930) and lectured at Harvard (1932) where he explained *The Use of Poetry and the Use of Criticism* (1933); James Joyce continued writing *Finnegan's Wake*, publishing it serially in several literary magazines; finally, poetry publishing split along aesthetic and political lines with *Poetry*, *Pagany*, and *Criterion* focusing on the poem (including Stein's) and leaving politics to *The Nation*, *The New Republic*, and *New Masses*.[6] Between the time of Creel's "House of Truth" (1917) and Stein's lecture tour in 1934, the United States went through an unprecedented economic crisis: the stock market crashed in 1929, followed by the bond market in 1931 and the mortgage market in 1932, the gross national product fell nearly 50 percent, and almost a quarter (approximately 15 million) of American workers were unemployed. Any remaining vestiges of hope in Enlightenment rationalism, scientific inquiry, or the progress of history were lost in the wasteland of political and economic instability that led to increasing hostility toward big business. At the same time, the field of public relations and public opinion management burgeoned.

Citizens of our paparazzi-saturated twenty-first century will take as given that mass mediated communications supply publics with an imagination of the social and our places within it. But, when Stein began her lecture tour in 1934, the idea of publicity as something to be managed by and cultivated for *individuals* was quite new. On the one hand, Stein participated in a long and ongoing tradition of lecturing across America begun in earnest with the completion of the transcontinental railroad in the 1860s and used by abolitionists, politicians, literary figures, women's rights advocates, and others who found national audiences for their causes. What changed after the turn of the twentieth century, particularly during the period during which Stein spoke, was the prevalence of mass mediated public relations and the role of the individual "personality." What Stein called the "enormous publicity business" was made possible through modern technology, which enabled people, according to Stein, to "now know the details of important people's daily life unlike they did in the Nineteenth Century" (*Primer* 22). *The Autobiography of Alice B. Toklas*, which gave readers access to the details of Stein's personal, daily life, transformed her into one of these "important people." Publicity for Stein's lecture tour reflected these changes, relying on nearly all outlets originally introduced by Creel's Committee on Public Information: "the printed word, the spoken word, motion pictures, the telegraph, the wireless, posters, [and] signboards" (Creel 157–158). Stein's popularity also prompted additional publicity outlets: advertisements in magazines, department store window displays, and dinners with other famous Americans from artists and film stars to university presidents to politicians, all covered by the press.[7]

Modes of persuasion were also shifting. Two decades before Stein's lecture tour, Creel discovered that emotional appeals were a more effective means of managing public opinion, much more so than providing factual data to a public conceived as rational, as had earlier been the case. Modern methods of persuasion began to rely heavily on the image transmitted through a rapidly expanding mass media. Stuart Ewen notes that "the modern pioneers of persuasion" found the image to be "an effective antidote to critical thought" due to "its apparent capacity to advance a worldview in a bedazzling moment, and to stun the public mind into submission" (212). Although Ewen specifically addresses visual images, Mark Wollaeger notes in *Modernism, Media, and Propaganda* that artists, because they were "engaged in acts of communication within a media ecology," had "to compete not only with increasingly pervasive new media but with organized efforts to use those media to manage the public" (3). Stein's long-time connection with visual artists and interest in collecting modern art made her well aware of both the power of the image and its relation to storytelling, personality, and persuasion.

In the 1927 *Vanity Fair* article, "Blazing Publicity: Why We Know So Much about 'Peaches' Browning, Valentino, Lindbergh and Queen Marie," Walter Lippmann describes the accelerating "publicity machine" as "a powerful lantern which plays somewhat capriciously upon the course of events, throwing now this and now that into bright relief, leaving the rest in comparative darkness" (121). Indeed, by the time Stein considered coming to America, public discourse in the United States was increasingly mediated by public relations messaging. Just five years prior to Stein's lecture tour, two of the definitive texts in public relations and public opinion management were published: Walter Lippmann's *The Phantom Public: A Sequel to Public Opinion* (1927) and Edward Bernays's *Propaganda* (1928). Observing that "virtually no important undertaking is now carried on without it," Bernays launched his own publicity campaign in which he argued for the necessity of a "public relations counsel," not just in business and government where it was increasingly common, but also in politics, "women's activities," education, social services, and the arts (54). If corporations and other organizations could develop personalities to sell to the public, individuals could do so as well. Thus, by the 1930s, individuals of note and means, like Stein, used government and corporate marketing strategies to brand themselves, shape their image, and sell their products.[8] According to her early biographer Malcolm Brinnin, Stein's celebrity had reached "such proportions that her eminence on the American scene was for a time shared only by gangsters, baseball players and movie stars" (307–308). The age of publicity had arrived and Gertrude Stein with it. And yet, the majority of her writing remained out of print or rarely purchased by the reading public.

Stein's writing and public speaking are recognizably enmeshed within shifting cultural perceptions of "the public"—who constitutes and defines the public and how the public can and should be addressed. During the lecture tour, Stein told *Chicago Tribune* reporter Fanny Butcher that she was thrilled to be in "close touch with the American public." She confessed to a *New York Herald Tribune* reporter that it was "highbrows" and not "ordinary people" who bored her. In *The Autobiography*, she called herself—through Toklas's narration—"democratic" and noted that "one person was as good as another" (176). But moving from her more personal and private Parisian salons to public lectures halls across America required expanding her relations with "the public." Participating in the business of her own publicity required Stein to craft ways to interact with the publicity machine, particularly when some thought, as Sherwood Anderson reported, that she might be "what we Americans call 'putting something across' . . . by a strange freakish performance . . . to attract attention to herself, get herself discussed in the newspapers" (5). Not only did newspapers cover her lectures with witty headlines like the *Chicago Herald's* "Understand Einstein? Just Try Stein-Stein," they also ridiculed her with parodies of her style in *Life Magazine* and cartoons in the *New Yorker*. Stein's famous tagline "a rose is a rose is a rose is a rose" and titles of her works were invoked to sell products via print ads and department store window displays.

Alyson Tischler explains that Stein's distinctive language made products fashionable, noting that Stein "also benefited from these ads, not only because they provided her publicity, but also because they helped to explain her most difficult prose to the public" (23–24). But Stein had been a critical agent in the business of her own publicity well before the lecture tour. In "Picturing Gertrude," the first story in *Seeing Gertrude Stein: Five Stories*, Wanda Corn charts Stein's growing understanding of "the power of imagery to shape her reputation and public identity," which began as early as 1906 when Picasso painted his famous portrait of Stein (5). Typical of male portraiture, Stein appears seated, dressed in dark, solid colors, hands on knees, filling the plane of the picture and looking forward with a determined gaze. Corn notes, "In hindsight, we can see that Picasso caught Stein in the process of inventing a bohemian look" and creating "a new persona of une hommesse, a mannish woman," which "began to push at gender boundaries in public ways" (31, 28).[9] Sitting for a painting by Picasso or Vallotton, a photograph by Man Ray, or a sculpture by Lipchitz allowed Stein to orchestrate her image from the privacy of her own home or a friend's art studio; lecturing publicly entailed a different kind of image management in the mass mediated public sphere.[10]

Participating in the process of celebrity construction and the circulation of her image, Stein worked to shape public opinion. Modernist innovation could use the same techniques as the "special pleaders" or "the public relations counsel," as Edward Bernays originally dubbed them less than a decade before Stein's tour. Might these same public relations techniques bring her audiences to the lecture halls as well as to the challenges and pleasures of her writing and speaking? Although she engaged in multiple, at times perhaps irreconcilable, rhetorical projects, including manipulating PR messaging to her own professional advantage and strategizing her modes of delivery in an age of publicity, Stein approached the delivery of her lectures as an opportunity to "stay with the language . . . that has come to be spoken and written" (*Lectures* 238). But staying with the language of the mid-1930s required participating in a mass mediated, celebrity culture.

Gertrude Stein Mediates "Gertrude Stein"

In a 1933 review of *The Autobiography of Alice B. Toklas*, Louis Bromfield notes that Stein had "an extraordinary power of personality," which led him to "suspect that Gertrude Stein the writer has been plagued by being Gertrude Stein the individual, Gertrude Stein the person" (1). Bromfield's suspicions were correct. Stein was a reluctant public speaker. Initially she turned down the American lecture tour just as she initially turned down earlier requests to lecture at Cambridge and Oxford Universities in the mid-1920s. Edith Sitwell, who arranged the Cambridge and Oxford invitations and eventually convinced Stein to speak, told Stein, "It is quite undoubted that a personality does help to convince half-intelligent people" (qtd. in Mellow 293). The lectures in England provided an opportunity for Stein to develop her public personality and practice speaking publicly. In the next decade, she became skillful at deploying her personality to win over audiences across the United States. Although nervous about addressing a large audience, Stein delivered "Composition as Explanation" at Cambridge in 1926 and then at Oxford to a standing-room only audience. Mellow describes Stein's nervousness about lecturing, noting her "plain-spoken" delivery style and her adept handling of hecklers during the question period following the lecture, a skill she used later to charm skeptical audiences, including journalists, during the lecture tour (292–296). More confident by the time she came to lecture in America, Stein calmed her nerves by insisting on having a light meal alone with Toklas before her lectures.[11]

When Bennett Cerf, Stein's publisher at Random House, and Carl Van Vechten arrived at the dock to meet Stein and Toklas in the fall of 1934, they found they were not alone. Reporters from all of New York's major papers awaited Stein's arrival, which became front page news. Stein continued to receive extensive press coverage for nearly seven months of public engagements. Surprised by Stein's handling of "that bunch of fresh photographers and newsmen" from the moment she stepped from the boat, Cerf called Stein "the publicity hound of the world" who "talked as plain as a banker" and came across as "a very direct, brilliant woman" who "disarmed everybody" (102, 103). Although Stein claimed to "never [have] imagined that [celebrity] would happen to me," her masterful handling of the press and success at winning over her audiences resulted from more than her magnetic personality. Gertrude Stein knew how to deliver "Gertrude Stein" (*Everybody's Autobiography* 2).

For years Stein kept track of the circulation and reception of her image. Like many public figures, she used clipping bureaus such as Romeike's to monitor her press coverage.[12] In reference to the publication of *Three Lives* (1909), Stein comments, "It is rather astonishing the number of newspapers that noticed this book" (*Autobiography* 137–38). Initially resistant to the idea of returning to the United States and lecturing, Stein dismissed her literary agent, William Bradley, for booking a tour without her approval, telling him, "you must understand me well enough to know that putting myself in other people's hands is a thing that for me is quite and entirely impossible" (qtd. in Dydo 597). Later, after reconsidering and realizing that a tour would entail a concerted public relations' effort, she consulted William G. Rogers, a journalist, whom she felt "was more in touch with American popular sentiment" (Rice 333). In addition, Cerf encouraged her to lecture and offered to do publicity in the United States prior to her arrival. Stein agreed and began to prepare for the challenge of lecturing in America. Due to the American public's tendency to be more interested in the image of "Gertrude Stein" than her work, Stein, the lecturer, had to craft her delivery carefully.

Once stateside, Stein used numerous newspaper and radio interviews as opportunities to influence her relations with the public and the public's relationship with her writing. In the fall of 1934, in an article entitled "Not an Admirer of G. Stein," the *Chicago Daily Tribune* questioned not just the opacity of Stein's work but also her "admirers," who "are trying to kid themselves into thinking they are superintelligent and can make sense out of the mess. No intelligent person is fooled by either Stein or her admirers" (14). In various interviews to promote her lecture tour, Stein stressed the requirements—her requirements—of intelligibility. As a point of clarification during a radio interview in the fall of 1934, Stein challenged the NBC reporter's assumption that "to be successful [Stein's work] must be at least understandable":

> Look here, being intelligible is not what it seems, after all these things are a matter of habit. . . . You mean by understanding that you can talk about it in the way that you have the habit of talking . . . putting it in

> other words . . . but I mean by understanding enjoyment. If you go to a football game you don't have to understand it in any way except the football way and all you have to do with *Four Saints* [an opera in collaboration with Virgil Thomson] is to enjoy it in the *Four Saints* way. . . . Don't you see what I mean? If you enjoy it you understand it, and lots of people have enjoyed it so lots of people have understood it. You see that is what my lectures are to be. They are to be a simple way of telling everybody this thing, that if you enjoy it you understand it. (Lundell 88–89)

Stein describes the interviewer's assumptions about intelligibility and his simplistic expectation of clarity in delivery as a "matter of habit," a cultural tendency implicit in our ways of talking that may or may not have something to do with the process of understanding. How we know, according to Stein, is "a matter of habit," a matter that takes form in our talking. Whether one is watching a football game or listening to a Steinian opera, understanding is not about getting "it" but rather about enjoying and making or finding meaning during the process. Walter Cronkite, then a young reporter for *The Daily Texan* and aware of Stein's negative press, concurred with this view when he interviewed Stein prior to her lecture in Dallas. Cronkite called her "genuine—the real thing in person," and described her thinking and speaking as "straightforward," noting that any "writer that had interviewed Miss Gertrude Stein, that had chatted with her for any length of time over two minutes, would never again write such an inane review of the works of one of the most publicized of modern writers." Cronkite found that Stein's enthusiasm "spreads to anyone with whom she comes in contact." The enigmatic author and the famous celebrity became during interviews (such as the one with Cronkite), an approachable, charming, intelligent woman—a "Gertrude Stein" anyone might like, a "Gertrude Stein" for everyone.

However, the lecture tour was not Stein's first attempt at formulating her mode of delivery of her work or her image. *The Autobiography* itself can be read as a rhetorical act of public relations and self-advertisement—the beginning of the expansion of her brand or, as Helga Lenart-Cheng argues, "a perfect occasion to stage an advertising campaign for her own writing and public image" (120).[13] Reviewing correspondence with Stein's agent, Catherine Turner finds that Stein intended to cultivate a broader audience by securing a mainstream publisher for *The Autobiography* and to use it as "bait for a publisher and for consumers" in the hopes of solidifying her place within modernism and creating interest in her other books. Building on her success and growing popularity, Stein's public relations' efforts took the form of what we would now call a branding campaign. This campaign included a logo and tagline imprinted with "a rose is a rose is a rose is a rose," which appeared in a circle—a never ending sentence—at the top of her personal stationary. In *The Autobiography,* Stein uses the word "device" to describe her tagline: "Speaking of the device of a rose is a rose is a rose is a rose, it was I [Toklas] who found it in one of Gertrude Stein's manuscripts and insisted upon putting it as a device on the letter paper, on the table linen and anywhere that she would permit that I would put it" (169).[14] Stein, in other words, invokes Toklas as a partner in delivery, where delivery becomes more than proper enunciation and effective gesticulation; it becomes a textual and inventional process. Delivery, in Stein's hands, moves beyond voice and body to include the materiality of the branded identity as it circulates domestically, textually, and culturally.[15]

Initially, in relation to the age of publicity, Stein represents herself as a curious participant. In *Everybody's Autobiography* written after the lecture tour, she claims, "I was very much interested to know just what they know about what is good publicity and what is not" (6). She also admitted to liking her celebrity: "It was very nice being a celebrity a real celebrity who can decide who they want to meet and say so and they come or do not come as you want them. I never imagined that would happen to me to be a celebrity like that but it did and when it did I liked it" (2). Although Stein acknowledges liking the celebrity perk of deciding "who they want to meet," her use of "they" and "them," rather than the first-person "we" and "us," suggests an ambivalence about being included in the category. The third-person pronouns seemingly position Stein outside the category of "celebrity." Stein's analysis of celebrity culture was specific to the United States: "It always did bother me that the American public were more interested in me than in my work" (51). She preferred France's approach to publicity because "publicity in France is really not important, tradition and their private life and the soil which always produces something, that is what counts" (*Paris France* 10). Even before the success of *The Autobiography of Alice B. Toklas*, Gertrude Stein wanted "readers not collectors"; she wanted "her books read not owned" (301). Stein, however, wanted to achieve more than simply enticing people to attend her lectures or convincing them to purchase her books. Alissa Karl notes: "Although Stein uses the marketplace to publicize her own version of modernism, she is critically aware of the possibilities for misapprehension in that marketplace and is very clear about how she wants to be read" (92). Reading Stein's work required more than being enthralled with Stein the celebrity; it required grappling with the challenge of Stein's words on the page.

Recognizing that her particular rhetorical situation was informed by her celebrity and the American popular culture that created and reflected that celebrity, Stein saw both challenges and opportunities. Kirk Curnutt explores how

"Stein's mid-1930's work also characterizes a unique moment in the development of celebrity discourse." Celebrity discourse for Stein became part of a much larger shift in rhetorical culture defined by the rise of public relations and public opinion management in the early twentieth century.[16] Even in her discussions of her celebrity, Stein theorizes communication more generally and delivery more specifically as circulating within complex temporal and cultural environments and with audiences increasingly disciplined by sophisticated and widespread methods of public relations. Always interested in how discursive shifts connect to writing, culture, and history, Stein notes:

> This has interested me very much. I think that is the reason why the novel as a form has not been successful in the Twentieth Century. That is why biographies have been more successful than novels. This is due in part to this enormous publicity business. . . . People now know the details of important people's daily life unlike they did in the Nineteenth Century. Then the novel supplied imagination where now you have it in publicity. ("A Transatlantic Interview" 22)

In Stein's analysis, publicity takes the communicative place of the novel. Attention given by the media to the details of the lives of "real" people, not fictionalized characters, superseded the novel as the site of the imagination. Fiction becomes displaced by "reality," so much so that, according to Stein, the Duchess of Windsor "was a more real person to the public and while the divorce was going on was a more actual person than anyone could create" (22).[17] But in the age of publicity, the novel, and by extension literary writing generally, no longer supplies the public's imagination or, in rhetorical parlance, the commonplaces of discourse. Stein laments:

> And since there is so much publicity so many characters are being created every minute of every day that nobody is really interested in personality enough to dream about personalities. . . . But now well now how can you dream about a personality when it is always being created for you by a publicity, how can you believe what you make up when publicity makes them up to be so much realer than you can dream. (*Everybody's Autobiography* 71)

These shifts in mass mediated culture leave the audience inundated with so much publicity that it takes the place of the imagination, rendering audiences passive and with a limited ability to be creative. In this communicative environment, audiences, including readers, have little imaginative work to do. The lecture tour promised an opportunity to use publicity to draw audiences away from "Gertrude Stein" toward the challenges and pleasures of her writing.

Stein Delivers

Mindful of the weight of the image of "Gertrude Stein," Stein drew on the fame she gained from the blockbuster success of *The Autobiography of Alice B. Toklas*, a novel that marks a transition from one century to the next. Although *The Autobiography* retains a predominantly nineteenth-century genre—the novel—Stein adopts a twentieth-century mode of storytelling that offers "details of important people's daily lives" in the form of a biography, which, as she noted, "have been more successful than novels" in the twentieth century (22). She documents her famous Parisian salons in a conversational, witty tone. She reflects and invokes her own personality and celebrity through stories and anecdotes of some of the early twentieth century's most famous artists and writers, including Henri Matisse, Pablo Picasso, Ernest Hemingway, Sherwood Anderson, Guillaume Apollinaire, and Isadora Duncan. Gertrude Stein claimed to find "very interesting" the changing means of communicative circulation from one century to the next, noting that after the turn of the century, "everybody talks as the newspapers and movies and radios tell them to talk" (*Everybody's Autobiography* 13). These new, omnipresent modes of mass communication, "newspapers and movies and radios," dominated ways of talking in the early decades of the twentieth century, dazzling audiences with new forms, idiomatic styles, and lexical resources provided by mass media.[18]

For all her interest in shaping her own celebrity within an emerging public relations culture, Stein offers a circumspect description of a process for communicative degradation in which mass media diminished the inventive potential of spoken language: "spoken language is no longer interesting and so gradually the written language says something and says it differently than the spoken language" (*Everybody's Autobiography* 13). Stein pointed to this tension between written and spoken language at the beginning of her lecture, "The Gradual Making of the Making of Americans." Telling the audience that "I am going to read what I have written to read," she asks later in the book, "Will you see it as clearly when I read you … [what] I have written" (135, 184). The delivery of her lectures entailed more than simply shifting from writing to speaking. Attempting to write as someone talks in the midst of new technologies changed the function of writing and complicated the act of speaking before an audience. For Stein, written language "knows" and written language "says something differently"—written language is capable of action, not just a representation of how "anybody talked"; in other words it is not simply a transmission of data in the Lockean sense from one mind to another. Spoken language offers its own opportunities, but an effective art of delivery must be developed. Stein developed an art of delivery that negotiated a mass-mediated culture that both circumscribed the terms of her circulating image and the ways in which "everyone talks."

Throughout the lecture tour, Stein performed the role of an intelligent, approachable but serious teacher who wanted to be accessible to her audiences. She maintained her celebrity presence through well-publicized interviews, which kept her name in print, filled lecture halls, and won over skeptical journalists and their readers. She also carefully orchestrated the parameters of the event and the space of the lecture hall: no more than 500 attendees, no charge for tickets, no introductions, no moderator, and no public events the night before a lecture—just a quiet dinner with Toklas. Considering the physical space of the lecture hall and her presence in it, Stein "tested the carrying power of her voice," according to James Mellow, "asking if she could be heard at the rear of the room," then she read "evenly and slowly" (384). Joseph Alsop, reporter for the *New York Herald Tribune,* described Stein's voice as "'the same slightly monotonous voice that mothers use to read to sick children" and reported that Stein's audience was "'variously pleased, mystified and infuriated,'" giving her "'rounds of delighted applause over and over again all through the performance" (qtd. in Mellow 386).[19]

For Stein, the oratorical event encompassed the performative elements of public appearance: how she looked and sounded, the conditions under which the speech was delivered, how she was perceived within and prior to the event, and how she wanted to be perceived. More than simply a "matter of how the voice should be used in expressing each emotion," as Aristotle has it, Stein's sense of delivery is more akin to, but goes beyond, Cicero's "language of the body."[20] Stein, the lecturer, embodied the craft of delivery, the rhetor circulating transnationally, a public relations event in a didactic mode. She entered the lecture hall dressed in dark lecture robes specially made for the tour. She was a short, stout woman with dramatic, short-cropped hair, the signature look for which she is remembered, though it was not adopted until 1926 at the age of 52 shortly before she began to lecture publicly. Although many venues commanded more, Stein limited the size of her audiences because she was concerned with holding the attention of her audience, particularly as the content of the lectures became challenging. Stein says, "I have written these lectures they are hard lectures to read and it will be hard to listen to them, anybody not used to lecturing cannot hold the attention of more than a roomful" (*Everybody's Autobiography* 181). Beyond the rhetor or the speaker's interest in attracting and maintaining the audience's attention, Stein's delivery explores how the relation between the audience and speaker addresses the theoretical core of writing—and now speaking—as Stein says in *The Making of Americans*, "for myself and strangers" (289). Where the ease of reading *The Autobiography* may have contributed to bringing audiences to her lectures, Stein crafted the lectures to be clear but not "too easy," like reading a newspaper (*Narration* 37).

At the end of a lecture, Stein told the audience, "All this is very important because it is important. . . . I hope I have been making it slowly clear to you" ("Pictures" 90). Stein underscored the importance of her lectures by calling attention to the fact that making sense of her lecture is a slow process that unfolds throughout the talk, a process similar to reading her seemingly unyielding written texts. One audience member who attended the Amherst College lecture claimed, "I was dead against her and I just went to see what she looked like" (Burns 374). Although curiosity about the celebrity "Gertrude Stein" brought this initially skeptical student to the auditorium, at the lecture he found that "she took the door of my mind right off its hinges and now it's wide open" (10). In an effort to help audiences understand her lectures and more generally the challenges of modernism, Stein responded to questions from the audience following each address. One reporter noted, "It is Miss Stein's interpolations in the course of her reading of her lectures that her audience seems to relish most. When she takes off her glasses and lays down her manuscript, her hearers edge forward in the seat and listen even more attentively than before" (qtd in Corn 242). Whether audience members came to encounter the celebrity or the writer, Stein delivered.

Stein's dilemma is illustrated by Dilip Gaonkar's provocative argument that a monologic communicative model grounded in a speaker and hearer "severely" limits how we read and participate in our mediated world. Gaonkar argues, "Even a renovated Ciceronian/Aristotelian theory of rhetoric, so long as it remains committed to the view of the speaker/author as the origin of discourse, is severely handicapped in reading discursive formations of not only modern science, but also modern polity" (344). That the "origin of discourse" might simply reside with an individual speaker or an author who transmitted knowledge to a receptive audience was not a mode of delivery accepted or practiced by Stein. Facing the lecture circuit brought home the pervasiveness of a linear model of communication and its concomitant mode of delivery where the speaker or writer prepared her ideas in advance and then performed the finished piece before a passive audience. Just as Stein wanted to "think of the writing in terms of discovery, which is to say the creation must take place between the pen and the paper, not before in a thought or afterwards in a recasting," so too might the occasion for public speaking offer a kairotic opportunity for invention (Preston 188).

In the lecture "The Gradual Making of The Making of Americans," Stein translates the narrative from *The Making of Americans* as rhetorical theory that explicates her shifting sense of working with an audience. She calls the audience's attention to the delivery of the lecture itself along with their role. Stein opens by recalling the days of her youth when she was "full of convictions," when her desire was twofold: "to hear what each one was saying in every way everybody has of saying it" and to help "to change them and to help them change themselves" (136).[21] She creates an image of herself as an active listener who works "to hear" not just what "everybody" says, but the ways—"every way"—in which it is said. Second, she is clear about her position as a teacher who offers "help." Stein is careful to note that these invoked changes are more than persuasion and "should of course be dependent upon my ideas and theirs *theirs as much as mine*" (136 emphasis added). Stein seeks parity with her audience, underscored by the repetition of the word *theirs*, without negating her authorial role. At the same time she invites, if not instructs, the audience to participate. In the lecture "Portraits and Repetition," she asks repeatedly, "Do you understand. Do you any or all of you understand. . . . It makes an awful lot of difference to me" ("Portraits and Repetition" 180–181).

Even as she reads what is already written, delivering an iteration of the past, Stein's self-referential delivery attempts to move the audience toward "what has not been written," calling attention to "the inevitable problem of anybody living in the composition of the present time" ("Plays" 104). In the lecture "Plays," Stein analyzes the complicated interrelation of the audience, speaker, time, and text. She plays with the ways in which delivering a lecture before a live audience mimics a theater performance. Both events place the speaker and audience in real time, sharing the same moment, opening a kairotic encounter, an opportune moment to do more than deliver an argument. Delivering a lecture also gives both the speaker and audience the opportunity to adapt to and take advantage of changing and contingent circumstances. As a public speaker, Stein faced the same stumbling blocks that she identifies for stage actors: "clothes, voices, what the actors said, how they were dressed and how that related itself to their moving around" (115). Commenting on the difference between seeing and hearing and the shift from reading to watching (a shift that can occur with written plays that are performed just as with written speeches that are delivered), Stein asks her audience, "Is the thing seen or the thing heard the thing that makes most of its impression upon you" (101). How can a speaker best reach her audience? The interrogative asks the audience to consider for themselves what makes the most impression on them. In another lecture, she equivocates between statement and interrogative: "You see what I mean by what I say. But I know you do" ("Portraits and Repetition" 184).

To demonstrate a way of interacting with narrative, Stein uses the lecture "Plays" to perform an example of "living in the composition of the present time." She does this even as she recalls the textual past, specifically her textual past through references to several of her earlier works, including *How to Write*, *The Making of Americans*, and *Geography and Plays.* Stein asks, "what's the use of telling another story . . . since there are *so many* and everybody knows so many and tells *so many*" (118–119 emphasis added). Stein directs the question to herself and her audience, calling attention to the current, mass mediated culture in which so many stories circulate—stories about products, corporations, causes, "important people," and celebrities. Rather than simply reiterating the past, telling the audience what they already know, or reporting journalistically on events, Stein struggles to find a way "to say what you nor I nor nobody knows"—a challenge that requires audience participation or, at the very least, an awareness of knowing what they know and recognizing that the boundaries of knowing are flexible, just like the identities of public speakers (121). Stein draws audience attention less to what happened—a mimetic repetition of the past—and more to "what made what happened be what it was" (122). Understanding what made something "be" requires not just "finding out how you know what you know" but also an understanding of the contexts within which knowing occurs (114).[22] The context includes, as Stein has already demonstrated, texts from one's past and the current embodied, kairotic moment of addressing an audience.

If knowledge of one's audience has always been a central rhetorical concern, Stein's contribution to modern rhetoric was her recognition of the ways in which the public's habits of reading and storytelling were caught up in early twentieth-century mass-mediated culture that focused on celebrity and image management. Stein insisted on staying "with the language" even as its context of celebrity and pervasive public relations messaging increasingly shaped what it said, what could be said, and how it can be said—a point she makes clear by never allowing her content to stray too far from language and the performance of how it works.

Following the lecture tour, Stein continued to contemplate audience: "When you are writing before there is an audience anything written is as important as any other thing and you cherish anything and everything that you have written. After the audience begins, naturally they create something that is they create you, and so not everything is so important" ("What are Masterpieces" 318). Here her focus shifts from the oratorical performance to the writing but still with the role and function of the audience and speaker in mind. Working with—speaking to or writing for—an audience enacts more than collaboration: it enacts invention. The inventive potential of delivery becomes kairotic where the speaker herself is created within the event even as she creates the audience.

This invention is a particular challenge for an author whose celebrity personality preceded her, as was the case with Stein. For Stein, a lecture is more than merely an individual's performance of a finished text. Delivery in Stein's hands becomes inventive, the circulation of heuristics for mediating ideas and identities circulating in rhetorical situations. Stein approaches delivery as more than a technical performance, a supplement to a finished text; the art of delivery for Stein becomes an inventive extension of her relations with the public.

7

Supposing Stein

Toward a Conclusion

> I like the feeling of words doing as they want to do and as they have to do when they live where they have to live.
>
> Stein, *Narration*

> Language as a real thing is not imitation either of sounds or colors or emotions it is an intellectual recreation and there is no possible doubt about it and it is going to go on being that as long as humanity is anything. So every one must stay with the language their language that has come to be spoken and written and which has in it all the history of its intellectual recreation.
>
> Stein, "Poetry and Grammar"

The epigraphs with which I begin this conclusion have as strong a claim as any in Gertrude Stein's voluminous archive to at least provisional *ars rhetorica* status or just as likely *ars poetica.* The distinctions blur. Arriving at this conventional space of concluding, summative comment might best be made by thinking a bit more about the inconclusive definitional division between rhetoric and poetics, an issue implicit in the preceding chapters. An inconclusive stopping point may well be most appropriate here, another opening in lieu of a closing, for during the time in which this book was written, Stein's celebrity enjoyed a resurgence. Although her theoretical legacy did not feature prominently in this resurgence, we can here consider its trajectory going forward.

To be sure, Gertrude Stein's allure never seems to go out of fashion. In the spring of 2011, Stein reappeared in the United States in grand style with two major exhibits premiering in San Francisco: "Seeing Gertrude Stein: Five Stories" and "The Steins Collect: Matisse, Picasso and the Parisian Avant-Garde." At the same time, a major studio film release, Woody Allen's Oscar-winning *Midnight in Paris,* featured many scenes set in Stein's salon at 27 Rue de Fleurus. Roger Ebert remarks that Kathy Bates's portrayal of Stein is just as he imagined: "an American, practical, no-nonsense, possessed with a nose for talent, kind, patient. . . . something like the Stein evoked by Hemingway in *A Moveable*

Feast." Stein and her charmed circle continue to draw attention and, increasingly, controversy as was the case with the art exhibits, which garnered sensationalist mainstream media coverage that alleged Stein's sympathy for, even support of, the Nazis.[1] As a lesbian, a Jew, and a collector of "degenerate art" living in occupied France, Stein is a survivor whose wartime politics, or lack thereof, have certainly been found to be disappointing or objectionable by many critics. These allegations have received careful consideration, particularly in a dossier of essays collected by Charles Bernstein, *Gertrude Stein's War Years: Setting the Record Straight*, and in Steven Gould Axelrod's "*Mrs. Reynolds*: Stein's Anti-Nazi Novel."[2]

I have chosen to conclude with Stein's war writing as a way to emphasize the ethical precepts underpinning her inventive canons. The first epigraph above construes "words" as being simultaneously grounded and evasive. The second epigraph takes a long view of "humanity" within an undisclosed historical movement. Both suggest the ethical bent of Stein's theory, which seems the right place to address, as a final word on her canonical interventions, the cofunctionality of rhetoric and poetics. In the context of World War II, the aesthetic openness of Stein's writing and her poetics of invention, as well as its radical embrace of rhetoric as a theory of contingency—what I will call her rhetoric of supposition—take on sharp and at times stark definition.

Stein spent the last decade of her life living, literally, in the midst of the World War II, forced to leave Paris early in the war. She later lived in the Vichy-occupied French countryside in a small village outside of Lyon where she spent her days writing, walking many kilometers to find bread, and visiting with neighbors. The focus of her writing shifted, slightly, away from the sophistic pedagogy and performance of *How to Write* toward an investigation of her experience of war. Stein was preoccupied with war, or as she said about *Mrs. Reynolds*, with showing "the way anybody could *feel* these years" (331 emphasis added). This preoccupation is demonstrated in texts such as *Mrs. Reynolds*, an allegorical novel about Stalin and Hitler written between 1940 and 1943, *Wars I Have Seen* (1945), a diary-like account of Stein's day-to-day experience living through war, and *Brewsie and Willie* (1946), which contains Brewsie and Willie's musing about postwar America. When the composition of daily life becomes occupied by war, how does one live and compose a life? How does one "stay with language"?

During the war years, the egocentric, trickster genius of *The Autobiography of Alice B. Toklas* gave way to the conversational ethnographer in *Wars I Have Seen*, who wandered the French countryside and recorded the stories of those she met: "I listened to so many stories in those days. . . . There were so many stories" (x, 108). Often, the amiable and well-liked Stein found the stories sustaining: "Such pleasant stories. . . . There is another nice story that always pleases me" (79). But as the war dragged the stories began to invoke fear and confusion: "There are so many more stories so many stories and so much confusion. . . . These days you keep hearing rather worse stories about German atrocities against the civil population" (171, 180). By early 1944, in the midst of tremendous uncertainty, Stein remarked, "we hear stories and do not know whether they are true, we do not know what is happening . . . nobody knows why, nobody can think of any reason for it, nobody knows, nobody knows. Why. Nobody knows" (145). The uncertainty is palpable in Stein's professions, a record of weariness, fatigue, and fear. Anyone familiar with accounts of occupations and war zones will recognize this preoccupation with the vacuum of reliable information about missing friends and family members. Stein, a writer who had focused on the grammatical, theoretical, disjunctive, and performative pleasures of language and narrative for more than four decades, seems in these lines to have reached an impasse in her inventiveness. Assertions like these in *Wars I Have Seen* are striking for the closed form of their logic and syntax and for the gaps or lacunae in the multiple discursive, cognitive, and historical trajectories that Stein perpetually charted as the site of meaning making for writers and readers. War, in all its social, technological, psychic, and emotional elaborations, disrupts thought, memory, and communication, the core compositional components of living in the continuous present.

In 1946, the year Stein died, she made a statement on the war in which she offered a view of writing that took the destruction of war as a conceptual touchpoint. Following the World War II, amid the great ceremonies of public memory making in which many nations were engaged, Stein considered the stakes of war memories. In her "Reflection on the Atomic Bomb," a title selected by the editors of the *Yale Poetry Review* when it was published in 1947, Stein performs a central element of her poetics of invention by asking "What is the use" of remembering the destruction that destroys everything so "there is nothing left"—literally obliterating all, leaving "nothing to be interested about."[3] Conversely, Stein says if "they"—presumably the bombs or the people who drop them—do not destroy everything, "then they are just a little more or less destructive than other things." The destruction remains, and we are left to sort through the degree of this destruction.

Although we might read Stein's claim that "really nobody else can do anything about it" as a kind of resignation in the face of a weapon of mass destruction, Stein's primary interest is, as she says, in "the living" and "not the way of killing them." Indeed, she acknowledges, "there is so much to be scared of." Fear interferes with sound judgment, with our ability to make considered decisions, with our compositional practices, with our ability to live. Stein ends "Reflection on the Atomic Bomb" by noting that "Everybody gets so much information all day long that they lose their common sense." And surely common sense would never dictate dropping atomic bombs on cities densely populated by civilians.

Stein's professed disinterest in the atomic bomb is consistent with her more general theory of kairotic rhetorical invention, her insistently open-ended rhetoric of supposition. The bomb threatens space and time as well as the existential ground of memory and communication. The ambiguous final line of "Reflection on the Atomic Bomb" reads: "This is a nice story." It is anything but that, as Stein well knew. "This" could refer to Stein's own story, a lesson in choosing what captures one's attention, "the living," or "ways of killing." Alternatively, the ambiguity of "this" may be a sarcastic exasperation with "they" who not only drop bombs but also foster fear in a way that limits cultural imagination, induces submission, and destroys the inventive potential of language and the composition of living. War and its terrors eclipse the necessary creative space of supposition that fosters new and deeply felt forms of thought and rhetoric.

Throughout the preceding chapters, I have grounded Stein's rhetorical theory—not primarily or unequivocally—in the ongoing Anglo-American reception of the Greco-Roman rhetorical tradition. While there is no direct line from Aristotle to Stein, Aristotle's famous definition of rhetoric, often shortened to "discovering the available means of persuasion," is perhaps more open to a generative theory of rhetorical production than the popular translation suggests, the kind of rhetorical invention reinvented by Stein. George Kennedy offers a translation that reads: "Let rhetoric be [defined as] an ability, in each [particular] case, to see the available means of persuasion" (Book 1, chapter 2.1, brackets in the original). What is often excluded from the definition is the supposition, the opening words, "Let rhetoric be." To suppose is to begin with an assumption that something is the case based not on proof or certainty but on probability. Thus, Kennedy's translation is phrased less as a strict definition and more as a "working hypothesis" (36, note 34). This construction, "let rhetoric be" is, in itself, rhetorical in that it asks audiences to grant or acknowledge conceptual possibility, specifically, the possibility of rhetoric as invention. Rather than postulating that rhetoric is or is not definitively something, it asks us to suppose, to allow, or to permit that this is, at least for now, at this moment, and in this particular case, possible. This locution calls attention to itself as positioned right from the beginning. Further, it asks something of readers: to proceed *as if* rhetoric were invention, *as if* there were work to be done, ideas to discover, assertions to assess, actions to take, compositions to craft.

Distinct from the rhetorical habits of mind we inherit from the moderns, Stein among the moderns offers us a rhetoric of supposition that works productively, not destructively, by opening rather than closing possibilities, by multiplying rather than trying to eliminate probabilities in both reading and writing. Stein's continuous present offers, necessarily, an open text, a world of probability, not certainty, and a language full of possibility. Although "There is," as she says in *Tender Buttons*, "no certainty," there are across many of Stein's major works repeated suppositions. For example, in *How to Write*, as I have shown, Stein supposes "a grammar uses invention" (64); in *Tender Buttons*, she asks readers to "Suppose they are put together, suppose that there is an interruption, supposing that beginning again . . . suppose all this" (41); in *The Making of Americans*, she writes, "These then are such ones as would have it in them to be to themselves supposing" (502).

Although in the preceding chapters I have worked to locate Stein outside literary history, her rhetoric of supposition emerges at the crossroads of poetics and rhetorical invention. Her rhetorical theory investigates the intersections of writing, memory, history, and probable knowledge—the inventive processes excised from modernist elaborations of rhetoric. The ideas, worlds, wars, and grammars we negotiate on a daily basis are convoluted, confusing, and complex often in spite of our efforts to clarify or make sense of them. It can be difficult to understand, elucidate, resist, and/or remember them. What is clear is that dealing with the complexities of our world and words in every given case is demanding, an imperfect and ongoing process at best. As Joan Retallack acknowledges, there are consequences of not taking up the challenge: "Acts of responsible consciousness are difficult, but the refusal of difficulty is never benign" (19). Stein continually embraced difficulty, asking her readers again and again to "Now think. . . . Think well of this. . . . Think of the difference. . . . Think of that" (*How to Write* 109–111) even, as she reiterates in *Tender Buttons*, it can be a nuisance or make no sense:

> A no, a no since, a no since when, a no since when since, a no since when since a no since when since, a no since, a no since when since, a no since, a no, a no since a no since, a no since, a no since. (58)

Sense or no sense? Since when? It remains to be seen or made. Stein acknowledges difficulty as welcome and necessary:

> Now this is a difficult sentence and they will like it because if it is necessary they will be obliged and after a little it was pay-day. . . . A difficult sentence can make a letter. Nouns and verbs mingle in a difficult sentence because they will hope that they think so. . . . If they have no-

> ticed it this is what they feel when they see a difficult sentence which is to them such an appeal. . . . A difficult sentence is one that is welcome. (*How to Write* 204–205)

Stein's "they" implicates us, her readers, with an obligation to heed "such an appeal" posed by a difficult sentence. Stein frames "the difficult sentence" as "an appeal," a serious and urgent request, and a welcome one at that. "A difficult sentence is one that is welcome" (205).

By recasting the canons of rhetoric in a radically changed and communicatively complex intellectual environment, Stein avoids the impasses of modern rhetorical theory and mass communication that claimed the great majority of her contemporaries as writing subjects. The multifaceted and historically variable field of rhetorical studies was, and perhaps remains, an important, if underused, resource in our understanding of the cultural functions of language, the effective use of communication, the connections between language and power, and the ethical stakes of our communicative practices. Whether we reject these traditions of import or take them up critically and creatively, as is the case with Stein, rhetorical theories from their historical conceptions retain a connection to craft and utility in time and place. Through arrangement, style, memory, and delivery—all tied to invention—Stein's writing seeks ways to maintain the ground on which we can continue to live, write, and know even in the midst of war, uncertainty, ambiguity, and probability.

Stein, the eccentric aunt of the rhetorical tradition, is a rhetorical theorist of the probable, inventing a poetics of supposition grounded in situational practices of writing and reading. For Stein, as for the Sophists, rhetoric is an asignifying practice where it matters less what a statement is and more what it does or can do. It matters less if the proposition is true and more if it is effective in and responsive to its particular circumstance. Staying "with the language their language that has come to be spoken and written" offers or, perhaps, demands moments of articulation and, as Stein notes, opportunities for "intellectual recreation," not predetermined, but arising from and responsive to particular situations (238). Charles Bernstein's definition of poetics appears kairotically rhetorical: "Poetics is an activity, an informed response to emerging circumstances" (*Attack* 78). The continuous present continuously emerges, providing multiple moments to assess one's available means, to inventively explore probable suppositions, and to intellectually recreate rhetorically and poetically. In Stein's rhetorical theory, suppositions collapse a distinction between rhetoric and poetics, keeping open the possibility that their relation is yet to be written, emerging as we speak.

Now this is a new paragraph. The ending tell them how to finish makes
it an importance. . . .
This sentence has hope as origin.
A tapestry made easy by being seen.
Think of all these sentences and not to be annoyed.
After all what is the difference between it and you. (*How to Write* 28)

Notes

Chapter 1

1. These quotations from Stein's primary works correspond to the focus of chapters 2 through 6: Invention (*How to Write* 64), Arrangement (*How to Write* 136), Style (*How to Write* 28), Memory (*Two* 108), and Delivery (*Gradual Making of Americans* 180–181).

2. In the mid-1980s, when scholars of composition studies became interested in the history of their field, revisionary historians of rhetoric entered into a historiographical debate about rhetorical historiography. Sharon Crowley characterizes this debate as "essentialist" and "constructionist" because essentialist historians assume "history is a force that stands outside of history" as a stable, chronological category, and constructionist historians argue that rhetoric, like its history, is an invention tied to and implicated within the social practices and relations that produce it ("Let Me" 10). A decade later, historical investigations expanded to include rhetoric. See, for example, the collection of essays in Victor Vitanza's *Writing Histories of Rhetoric*, which trace in detail the epistemological and ideological grounds of various approaches to rhetorical history.

3. See Poulakos "Toward a Sophistic Definition of Rhetoric" 35–48. The Sophists enjoyed a revival in the late twentieth century when rhetorical historiographers revised their place in the canon. See Crowley, Jarratt, and McComiskey. The third volume of W. K. C. Guthrie's definitive *History of Greek Philosophy* is devoted to *The Sophists*. In "Plato's Pharmacy," Derrida demonstrates how Plato's strong distinction between philosopher and sophist cannot be maintained.

4. The history of rhetoric offers other divisions as well. For example, in his

Rhetoric, Aristotle identifies three branches of rhetoric: deliberative (legislative), judicial (forensic), and epideictic (ceremonial). See book I.3. While it may also be interesting to think about Stein and her writing through the medieval trivium—a designation for the lower division of the seven liberal arts, logic, grammar, and rhetoric—the five canons of rhetoric allow a fuller exploration of the interdisciplinary elements of Stein's writing.

5. Stein plays with the phrases "being existing" as early as *Making of Americans* and returns to it again and again. See, among others, "Many Many Women," "Italians," and "Orta or One Dancing."

6. Stein took three classes with James. The first, in 1893, was an introductory course on philosophy in which James lectured on psychology. Stein went to medical school at James's advice and considered a career in psychology. Stein dropped out of medical school in her final year but maintained occasional contact with James throughout her years in Paris. See Hoffman. Others have examined James's influence on Stein, including Meyer's *Irresistible Dictation*, 207–289; Ruddick's *Reading Gertrude Stein*, 12–41; Olson's "Gertrude Stein, William James, and Habit in the Shadow of War," 328–360. Schoenbach's *Pragmatic Modernism* further examines "habit" in relations to Stein and James.

7. In 1935 and 1936, Stein wrote a series of essays about America and money. See *How Writing is Written*.

8. The coauthors of *Seeing Gertrude Stein* and cocurators of an exhibit of the same name, Wanda Corn and Tirza True Latimer, identify Stein as more than a literary modernist or famous art collector. By scrutinizing art, photographs, and objects buried in the archive, they render a complex "visual" Stein and demonstrate her extraordinary reach across the arts.

9. See Perloff, *Wittgenstein's Ladder*.

10. Rainey's *Institutions of Modernism* examines the place of modernism in public culture, specifically institutional and economic settings of modernism and the methods for reaching audiences—the economy culture that gave rise to literary modernism. Although Rainey does not mention Stein, much Stein scholarship has explored Stein's complicated relationship to mass culture. Liesl Olson argues that Stein had specific strategies for dealing with different audiences and "high" and "low" versions of modernism. See Olson "'An Invincible Force Meets an Immovable Object': Gertrude Stein Comes to Chicago."

11. Three dissertations, two recent, consider Stein's connection to rhetoric. See Brazier, O'Sullivan, and Shaw.

12. Special issues of *Rhetoric Society Quarterly* include "Feminist Rereadings in the History of Rhetoric" in 1992 and "Feminist Historiography in Rhetoric" in 2002. For a comprehensive list of book-length studies, see Lundsford and Ede, 13–16. For anthologies, see Ritchie and Ronald's *Available Means*, Donawerth's *Rheto-*

rical Theory by Women Before 1900, and the second edition of Bizzell and Herzberg's *The Rhetorical Tradition*. For analysis of edited collections in women's rhetorics, see Ryan.

13. Both Ritchie and Ronald's and Donawerth's anthologies address the issue of recognizing or understanding women writers and speakers as rhetorical theorists by calling for a reconceptualization of what constitutes rhetorical theory. Ritchie and Ronald identify "the intersection of theory and practice" as "a central feature of women's rhetorical stances" (xxviii). Donawerth finds that rhetorical theories put forward by women "take conversation rather than public speaking as a model, seeing all communication as collaborative or dialogic" (xxxviii).

14. See Marianne DeKoven's *A Different Language* (1983). For an overview of trends in Stein scholarship, see DeKoven's "Introduction: Transformations of Gertrude Stein" and Lisa Ruddick's "Stein and Cultural Criticism in the Nineties."

15. Within the field of rhetorical studies, efforts to foster discussions across communication studies and English began in earnest in 2000. See Mailloux and Leff. For more recent assessments of rhetoric across the disciplines, see John Lyne and Carolyn R. Miller's "Introduction: Rhetoric, Disciplinarity, and Fields of Knowledge" and Don Bialostosky's "Rhetoric in Literary Criticism and Theory." James Berlin's *Rhetoric, Poetics, and Cultures* explores the historical and reciprocal relation between the domains of rhetoric and poetic. I refer to continental theory, postwar French and German philosophy written by seminal figures including Jacques Derrida, Michel Foucault, Gilles Deleuze, Jean-Francois Lyotard, the second-generation Frankfurt School, the rise of psychoanalytic criticism, and poststructuralist feminist criticism. For an historical overview of theory in the humanities, see Osborne.

16. Here are just a few of the founders and editorial board members: M. H. Abrams, Louis Althusser, Charles Altieri, Homi Bhabha, Wayne Booth, Kenneth Burke, Jonathan Culler, Paul De Man, Gilles Deleuze, Jacques Derrida, Stanley Fish, Northrup Frye, Fredric Jameson, Hans-Georg Gadamer, Julia Kristeva, Emmanuel Levinas, Edward Said, Gayatri Spivak, and Slavoj Zizek.

17. The University of Chicago's obituary for Booth calls him "one of the 20th century's most prominent and influential literary critics"; the *New York Times* uses a similar description: "one of the pre-eminent literary critics of the second half of the 20th century." However, in 1987 Booth gave the prestigious annual Ryerson lecture at the University of Chicago, which he titled, "The Idea of a University as Seen by a Rhetorician." In addition to many other works, Booth devoted several books to rhetoric: *The Rhetoric of Fiction* (1962), *The Rhetoric of Irony* (1974), *Modern Dogma and the Rhetoric of Assent* (1974). In 2004, he returned to rhetoric with the meta-manifesto, *The Rhetoric of Rhetoric*, in which he argued for the importance of and need for rhetorical studies, or in James Phelan's words, "the centrality of rhetoric to human inquiry and human interaction" (back cover).

18. The authors, Anne H. Stevens and Jay Williams, were also at the time of publication the journal's editors.

19. See Stevens and Williams. What is, perhaps, most surprising is how shocked the editors are by the lack of women in their list of theorists cited in *Critical Inquiry*. While the editors register their shock at this disparity, they do not address the important issue of *why* the field of theory and its representation in *Critical Inquiry* includes so few women.

20. The first formal English department founded in United States was at the University of Rochester in 1847. The study of literature was not institutionalized in England until the 1890s at Cambridge and nearly forty years later in 1930 at Oxford. Gerald Graff's *Professing Literature* offers an institutional history of intellectual trends in the university. Richard Ohmann's *English in America* historicizes the politics of education and examines the influence of capitalism on the study of English in the university.

21. See W. J. T. Mitchell, editor, *Critical Inquiry* homepage, http://www.journals.uchicago.edu/page/ci/brief.html. Date accessed: May 1, 2012.

22. See McKeon. Wayne Booth identifies McKeon as one of his "rescuers of rhetoric."

23. Even in the early twentieth century, Steven Mailloux notes that the disciplinary fragmentation of rhetoric continues to limit discussion even among rhetorical studies' scholars in English, composition and speech communication who "for the most part, still do not talk to each other" (32). Mailloux's *Disciplinary Identities* offers a critical history of the historical relations among academic disciplines while demonstrating what he calls "rhetorical hermeneutics" defined as "the use of rhetoric to practice theory by doing history" (42). Although I share Mailloux's desire to rethink the place of rhetorical theory and practice in English studies, I aim to recognize more fully the contribution of literary studies—through Stein's writing—to our understanding of rhetorical invention.

24. Blair's *Lectures on Rhetoric and Belles Lettres* (1783) is credited for identifying historical, philosophical, epistolary, fictive, poetic, and dramatic modes of writing as rhetorical, thereby collapsing distinctions between rhetoric and critical analysis. See Nan Johnson. In addition, the *Lectures* went through 130 editions between 1783 and 1911; it was the most widely taught text in American colleges throughout the nineteenth century.

25. In *Nineteenth-Century Scottish Rhetoric*, Winifred Horner connects the rise of literary studies and composition courses in the United States with Scottish rhetoric deeply influenced by Blair.

26. See Keith for a detailed history of institutional and pedagogical origins of speech communication. See also Mailloux's *Disciplinary Identities*.

27. Two notable exceptions include Hudson and Wichlen.

28. For example, John Franklin Genung's "The Study of Rhetoric in the College Course" emphasizes the need for students to develop an ability to express themselves clearly because "It is humiliating to be tantalized with rebellious pronouns, mixed metaphors, and absurdly collocated clauses, when the writer's whole energy should flow unvexed and unimpeded in the current of a powerfully conceived thought" (136, qtd in Brereton's *The Origins of Composition Studies.*) Genung's is just one example of "current-traditional rhetoric." See Sharon Crowley's *The Methodical Memory* and James Berlin's "Richard Whately and Current-Traditional Rhetoric."

29. Only since the early 1980s have graduate students had the opportunity to purse doctorates in composition and rhetoric. The journal *Rhetoric Review* has a series of articles tracing the developments in these programs. See Brown, Jackson, and Enos; Brown; Enos, Reamer, and Thompson; and Carlo and Enos.

30. Miller calls the composition course developed at the end of the nineteenth century with its arduous reading and weekly compositions a "gatekeeper" course that would allow an elite university education to a growing number of Americans but only after eliminating "nonstandard" community and familial dialects. See Miller's *Textual Carnivals*, 47–58.

Chapter 2

1. Stein's famous repetition appears for the first time in "Sacred Emily." Variations of or comments on the phrase appear in many of Stein's works including *The World is Round, Stanzas in Meditation, Alphabets and Birthdays*, "Poetry and Grammar," *Four in America*, and more. See http://writing.upenn.edu/library/Stein-Gertrude_Rose-is-a-rose.html. Date accessed: March 4, 2014.

2. The "Harvard Annex" for women opened in 1879 with twenty-seven students and became Radcliffe College in 1894 with an enrollment near 250. In 1886, the Board of Overseers officially considered admitting women into Harvard College where they could earn degrees but did not officially do so until 1894 when Radcliffe was founded. See Morison 360, 391–393.

3. For the definitive work on invention in modern rhetoric, see Sharon Crowley's *The Methodical Memory* and *Toward a Civil Discourse*, chapter 2.

4. Crowley calls "current-traditional rhetoric" an American school of rhetoric that is "a direct descendant of the work of the British new rhetoricians," including Hugh Blair, George Campbell, and Richard Whately (*Methodical* 56). Current-traditional rhetoric has the following characteristics: (1) emphasizes the product over the process of writing; (2) focuses on style and usage including spelling and punctuation; (3) classifies discourse into description, exposition, narration, and argument; (4) assesses clarity based on words, sentences, and paragraphs. Writing instruction based on this model of discourse favors research papers and essays.

5. Brereton dates the rise of modern composition in the United States to about 1875, when the focus was nearly entirely on rhetoric: "In 1875 there was no college reader, no college book of exercises, just Blair, Campbell, Whately, and their followers, authors of treatise like books explaining the subject of rhetoric" (314). The texts of these rhetoricians included little if any coverage of grammar or mechanics. However, with greater emphasis on grammatical correctness, increasing class size, and students with little experience in writing, overworked universities professors looked for "a new sort of textbook, one that would explain and exemplify the sorts of rules that teachers were increasingly asking their students to learn and practice" (Connors 67). See Connor's "Mechanical Correctness in Composition Instruction."

6. The earliest entrance exams at Harvard, between 1865 and 1866, were oral. By the end of the decade, students were still required to read aloud, but the content of the reading was specified as either Shakespeare or Milton. In the early 1870s, the formal written requirement was added. Students were expected to demonstrate "Correct spelling, punctuation, and expression, as well as legible handwriting." Several years later, correct paragraphing was added to the list of requirements, and, in the early 1880s, students were asked to correct "bad English." (qtd. in Kitzhaber 34–35). For a fuller discussion of English at Harvard, see Kitzhaber and Morison.

7. In "The Emergence of a Literate Rhetoric in Greece," Richard Lee Enos locates the function of the paragraph within the development of the alphabet and written rhetoric. He demonstrates how the paragraph "is not merely a formulaic convention but rather a conceptual notion in the inventive process of composition" (238). Stein's interest in the paragraph also moves beyond stylistic features and toward a heuristic for creating and organizing discourse.

8. Hill served as the Boylston Chair of Rhetoric from 1876 to 1904 and taught composition at Harvard for nearly three decades. Hill's text, *The Principles of Rhetoric and Their Application*, was used in English A from 1878 to 1914. Other common textbooks include what Kitzhaber calls "the big four," which were used most widely in composition courses at the end of the nineteenth century. These include Hill, John Franklin Genung's *The Practical Elements of Rhetoric, with Illustrative Examples* (1885), Barrett Wendell's *English Composition* (1891), and Fred Newton Scott's *Paragraph-Writing* (1893). See Kitzhaber 62, Brereton 313–327, and Wozniak 125–128.

9. Rhetoric, according to Hill's definition, "neither observes, nor discovers, nor classifies; but it shows how to convey from one mind to another the results of observation, discovery, or classification" (6). Crowley notes that Hill's definition of rhetoric "as an art of presentation" eliminated invention and "placed Hill firmly in the camp of those who subscribed to a modern model of knowledge generation." For a fuller discussion of invention in Hill's *Principles of Rhetoric*, see Crowley 85–86.

10. Stein received a "C" in English 22, her lowest grade in her first two years of college.

11. Rosalind Miller examines the connection between ideas originating in the Radcliffe themes and Stein's published works; see 103–105.

12. The fourth and final report to the Board of Overseers, in 1897, examined the writing of 1,300 essays of students; it contains the first comment on the writing of students at Radcliffe, what Brereton calls "a rare effort, however incomplete, to examine women's writing" (101). The work of students in advanced writing courses was compared with 70 themes written by the women at Radcliffe. The "mechanical execution—neatness, penmanship, punctuation and orthography" of the Radcliffe essays showed "a marked superiority in standard over the papers from the courses of the College proper" (Brereton 108).

13. JoAnn Campbell finds that although students asked "to express their ideas, to share important parts of their lives, to be heard," their writing instructors "ignored their ideas and commented on their writing performance or dismissed their thought and observations by labeling them 'feminine' and therefore nonacademic" (473).

14. Wozniak finds that Abbott's *How to Write Clearly* and Hill's *Principles of Rhetoric* were widely used in composition courses at Harvard after their publications, in 1875 and 1874 respectively. Other texts used throughout the decade of the 1870s include Whatley's *Elements of Rhetoric*, Trench's *On the Study of Words*, and Webster and Worcester's dictionaries. According to Wozniak, Abbott's text was no longer in use after 1880. However, Wozniak's research primarily considers Harvard's English A. Stein took English 22.

15. Blair argues that rhetoric teaches the management of arguments, not their discovery or creation. A rhetorician manages arguments through form and style. Invention is not part of the rhetorical process.

16. Stein examines the relation between human nature and the human mind, between identity and the self, between the public and private in *The Geographical History of America or The Relation of Human Nature to the Human Mind*, which, as its title suggests, considers the *relation* between these categories rather than how they are distinct.

17. Feminist literary critics began to take interest in Stein's writing in the 1980s. See Chessman, Marianne DeKoven's *A Different Language*, and Lisa Ruddick's *Reading Gertrude Stein*.

18. Stein took three classes with James, including an introductory course on philosophy in which James lectured largely from *The Principles of Psychology*. During Stein's years at Radcliffe, James published *The Will to Believe* (1897). Shortly after, he published *The Varieties of Religious Experience* (1901) and *Pragmatism* (1907). Stein took Santayana's year-long philosophy course in her first year.

19. Later in her life, Stein acknowledged the importance of William James's thinking to hers when she called him "the really lasting impression of her Radcliffe life" (*Autobiography* 96).

20. Royce taught his *The Spirit of Modern Philosophy* in which he explicates the

philosophies of Spinoza, Kant, and Hegel. Royce lectured on Kant's theory of transcendental unity of apperception, as taken from Kant's *Critique of Pure Reason*. See Kant 75.

21. In defining "What Pragmatism Means," James notes that new ideas might "stain" or change old ideas, but "New truth is always a go-between. . . . It marries old opinion to new fact so as ever to show a minimum of jolt, a maximum of continuity" (35).

22. For Quintilian, grammar was within the purview of the grammaticus, not the rhetor, a distinction that speaks to the current tension between "composition" and "rhetoric," between "composition" and "literature," and between "public speaking" and "communication studies." Susan Miller distinguishes between the two: "The *grammaticus* was to teach correct speech and proper grammar as well as the texts of the poets. But his work was not to overlap with the *rhetor*, who taught the invention and arrangement of compositions that effectively advised, praised, or decided legal business in the public realm" (49). A rhetor's work came after the grammaticus. A rhetor composed discourse and used language with the intent of reflecting and affecting a community along with the thinking and actions of its members. Stein's narrator—a grammarian and a teacher of grammar—refuses to separate the work of the grammaticus and the rhetor.

Chapter 3

1. In "The Form and Politics of Networks in Jean Toomer's *Cane,"* Wesley Beal recently identified the taxonomic challenges of *Cane's* compositional structure as "a network of forms" (658).

2. Early in the twentieth century, the Vienna Circle, responding to advances in science, worked to reconcile philosophy and science by dismissing metaphysics from the study of philosophy. Focusing on epistemological concerns, logical positivists claim that knowledge must be empirically verifiable. Forming the roots of the analytic philosophical tradition, logical positivism was imported to the English-speaking world largely with the publication of A. J. Ayer's *Language, Truth, and Logic* in 1936, the same year Stein published *The Geographical History of America.* The philosophy of Stein's friend, Alfred North Whitehead, followed a different trajectory, refusing to divorce metaphysics from philosophical inquiry. See *Process and Reality* (1929). Steven Meyer explored connections between Stein and Whitehead in *Irresistible Dictation*, 189–193.

3. In "Genres as Fields of Knowledge," Dimock introduces a special issue of PMLA devoted to genre.

4. Burke extends his discussion of form with his concept of symbolic action: "The main point is to note *what the poem's equational structure is.* This is a statement about its *form.* But to guide our observation of the form itself, we seek to discover

the *functions*, which the structure serves. This takes us into a discussion of purpose, strategy, and the symbolic act" (101). Two decades later, he further theorizes *Language as Symbolic Action* (1966). In *Kenneth Burke in Greenwich Village*, Jack Selzer locates Burke in the center of American modernism around the 1920s in Greenwich Village when he edited the modernist literary magazine, *The Dial*, and where he met many modernist writers, critics, and artists including Malcolm Cowley, Marianne Moore, Jean Toomer, Katherine Anne Porter, William Carlos Williams, Allen Tate, Hart Crane, Alfred Stieglitz, and many others. Selzer examines Burke's participation in and contributions to American modernism. More recently, Selzer extended his work on Burke into the 1930s in *Kenneth Burke in the 1930s*, which he coauthored with Ann George.

5. In *Seeing Gertrude Stein: Five Stories*, coauthors of and co-curators of an exhibit of the same name, Wanda Corn and Tirza True Latimer, "focuses on the 'visual' Stein buried in the archive, not the verbal or literary" by documenting Stein's developing understanding of the ways in which images construct identities.

6. Marshall McLuhan offered early analysis of cultural and cognitive shifts brought about by modern mass media's challenge to the linear, sequential presentation of information. See *Understanding Media*. Widely recognized for his pioneering studies of communication and technology, McLuhan's early intellectual work examined the history of the trivium, grammar, logic, and rhetoric, which was the focus of his dissertation completed at Cambridge University in 1942.

7. Here Quintilian is specifically referring to court cases. He goes on to describe various scenarios that might be faced in a courtroom and offers examples for addressing them. One's arrangement might not follow the standard form with an introduction, a statement of facts, a proof, a refutation, and a conclusion. If, for example, the case is complex, "the pleader will have to consider what requires refutation and where that refutation should be placed" (VII.1.–10). Quintilian maintains that "the order is subject to alteration" (VII.1.11–12).

8. In *The Discourse on Language*, Foucault notes that this "ancient elision" when the Sophist's "paradoxes were muzzled, more or less securely" (227) has occurred repeatedly throughout history and continually limits or excludes the possibility of discussing how and why this elision is itself embedded in social institutions and the orders of knowledge.

9. Although Blair devotes little attention to arrangement, his early lectures do address in detail "The Structure of Language" (Lectures VIII and IX) and the "Structure of Sentences" (Lectures XI, XII, XIII).

10. For example, Noah Webster's first dictionary, *The Compendius Dictionary of the English Language*, appeared in 1806. Research for the *Oxford English Dictionary* began in earnest in 1857. The *Encyclopedia Britannica*, published initially in 1768, increased to twenty volumes by 1809.

11. Hejinian also discusses the influence of William James's studies of perception

and consciousness on Stein; see 92–102. Steven Meyer offers a detailed description of James's scientific milieu and Stein's appropriation of and divergence from it on 22–32.

12. Scholars have long been interested in Stein in relation to Picasso and Cubism. Early work includes L. T. Fitz's "Gertrude Stein and Picasso: The Language of Surfaces," Edward Burns and Leon Katz's foreword to *Picasso: The Complete Writings*, Randa Dubnick's *The Structure of Obscurity*, and Marjorie Perloff's *The Poetics of Indeterminacy*, 6–85. For more recent explorations of Stein, Picasso, and Cubism, see Haselstein and Hilder.

13. Schmitz, "*tender buttons*, notwithstanding" in *Primary Stein*, edited by Janet Boyd and Sharon J. Kirsch.

14. Siraganian argues that Stein "simultaneously deemphasizes the beholder's role by suggesting that the spectator or reader is irrelevant to her meaning and emphasizes it in her aim to liberate the beholder's body through her poetry" (45). She reads Stein's paradoxical stance on the role of the reader as an explanation for "why critics often struggle to determine whether Stein is a cooperative conversationalist or an indifferent dictator" (45).

15. Random House intended the sales of *Everybody's Autobiography* to be a success on par with *The Autobiography*, but they ended production after the first print run of 3,000 copies.

16. In "Gertrude Stein's *Everybody's Autobiography* and the Art of Contradictions," Timothy Galow argues that Stein's second autobiography addresses the problem of identity by "creating an insistently illogical space of contradictions where Stein can both posit a self that exists only in the immediate present and cultivate a celebrity persona" (111).

17. This phrase occurs repeatedly throughout Stein's writing; it appears in *The Making of Americans*, "Matisse," "A Family of Perhaps Three," and "Orta or One Dancing," to name a few.

Chapter 4

1. In the context of Stein's lectures, Jennifer Ashton comments on Stein's efforts to be precise. See *From Modernism to Postmodernism* 53–56.

2. Marianne DeKoven argues that although Stein's importance is now clearly established, she "will never quite be canonical" (469). See "Introduction: Transformations of Gertrude Stein."

3. See Amy Lowell's 1915 preface to *Some Imagist Poets*.

4. In the field of rhetorical studies, a great deal of scholarly attention has recently been focused on style. In "The Stylistic (Re)Turn in Rhetoric and Composition," the introduction to *Style in Rhetoric and Composition*, Paul Butler argues, as

do many of the collections contributors, that style has recently emerged as "an area of significant interest" (1). Butler's *Out of Style* (2008) explores style's connection with invention. Jeanne Fahnestock's recent *Rhetorical Style* (2011) follows a long trajectory in the history of rhetorical style and offers a comprehensive guide to rhetorical stylistics including word choice, tropes, sentences, punctuation, and coherence. Barry Brummett's *A Rhetoric of Style* (2008) analyzes "style as a system of signification grounded largely in image, aesthetics, and extrarational modes of thinking" (xiii). Brummett explores the ways in which style "expresses social values, delimits categories, and organizes time and space" (xiii).

5. Although the author of *Rhetorica ad Herennium* remains anonymous, the work is often attributed to Cicero. Book IV offers an extended discussion of style. Quintilian also espoused a common view of style as a necessary element of rhetoric, claiming "without elocutio, our ideas are as useless as a sword kept concealed within its sheath" (*Institutio oratoria* 8, Prooemium 15. See also Cicero *De Oratore* 1.142).

6. For an early explication of the connections between poetics and the ordinary, see Marjorie Perloff's *Wittgenstein's Ladder*. See also Charles Bernstein's "The Art and Practice of the Ordinary," from *Attack of the Difficult Poems*.

7. See Ulla Dydo, *The Language That Rises* 417. Stein published *Lucy Church Amicably* and *How to Write* on Plain Edition in 1931. For a full list of Plain Edition publications, see Benstock's *Women of the Left Bank*, 391. In "Make It Plain," Gabrielle Dean examines the venture that produced the five books published in Stein and Toklas's Plain Edition.

8. In *Four in America*, General Grant becomes a religious leader who would become a saint; Wilbur Wright is a painter of art; Henry James transforms from novelist to military general; and George Washington transitions from president to a writer of novels. See Neil Schmitz's "Doing the Fathers: Gertrude Stein on U. S. Grant in *Four in America*."

9. Muckelbauer's persuasive and performative reworking of rhetorical invention to include an "affirmative style of engagement" draws on classical rhetorical texts by Aristotle, Plato, and the Sophists as well as key rhetorical concepts including kairos, topoi, and doxa.

10. Rhetoric as a field has a long-standing interest in repetition. Since antiquity it has been used to emphasize key points by using figures of speech or developing rhythms in the language for persuasive force. Jeanne Fahnestock discusses this strategic use of repetition in *Rhetorical Style*, 230–237.

11. Liesl Olson attributes Stein's attraction to habit and repetition to the influenced of William James. Olson also points out that repetition for Stein need not be philosophically rooted; rather, it can be pleasurable. Mr. and Mrs. Reynolds, for example, are "an example of not being consumed by the existential angst of repe-

tition; rather, they maintain a sense of control in repeating actions that give them pleasure" (*Modernism and the Ordinary* 108). See also Claudia Franken's discussion of habit and repetition in *Gertrude Stein*, 57–67.

12. In response to a question about his relationship with his "masters," which he defines as one of "fidelity and betrayal," Derrida comments on the inventive potential in repetition: "You cannot simply repeat the same thing, you have to invent, to do something else if only to respect the alterity of the other" (Payne 10).

13. Quoted in *The Cambridge History of Literary Criticism*, volume VII, 107. From a newspaper clipping dated November 2, 1934, in Yale Collection of American Literature.

14. In *The Language That Rises*, Dydo's reading of Stein's "An Elucidation" begins with the larger context of its writing in 1923, examines the manuscripts and publication history, and offers a lengthy section devoted to reading "the text itself." See 43–70.

15. Isocrates, Gorgias's most famous student, opened the first school of rhetoric in Athens around 393 BCE, several years prior to the opening of Plato's Academy.

16. Excellent orators, according to Isocrates, begin with natural ability, which they supplement with practical experience and formal training.

17. Quotations come from the new edition of *Stanzas in Meditation*, edited by Emily Setina and Susannah Hollister. This edition includes a textual history of the manuscript and two typescripts of the poem. Setina and Hollister meticulously trace changes Toklas made to the text when she discovered references to Stein's former lover.

18. Lyn Hejinian's "Rejection of Closure" in *The Language of Inquiry* identifies a kind of repetition that "challenges our inclination to isolate, identify, and limit the burden of meaning given to an event" (44). Stein's use of repetition continually offers the reader a range of options. Repetition multiplies and opens up possibilities rather than confines meaning to certain patterns, themes, or theses.

19. After deconstructing the metaphysics of presence in his monumental *Of Grammatology*, which was also a certain stylistic performance specifically at odds with standard modes of argumentation in the discipline of philosophy, Derrida addressed more directly the connection between what is said and how it is said as an ethical concern in his debate with Searle and in *The Gift of Death* (1995). In 2003, Derrida denied his work took an ethical turn. See *Voyous*, Paris: Galilee 2003: 64.

20. See Mackey.

Chapter 5

1. Stein's articulation of forgetting also critiques the failures of memory in masculine narratives. *Tender Buttons*, for example, recalls and records domestic objects

while *Lifting Belly* and *A Book Concluding with As a Wife Has a Cow* explore women's sexuality and lesbian identity. See DeKoven, Ruddick, and Chessman.

2. *Rhetorica ad Herennium* III.xvi–xxiv. See also Kennedy, *Classical Rhetoric*, 96–99. The second chapter of Yates's *The Art of Memory* offers detailed analysis of *Rhetorica ad Herennium*. Date accessed: March 4, 2014. www.archive.org/stream /adcherenniumdera00capluoft#page/n7/mode/2up.

3. Aristotle's *On Memory* (*De Memoria Et Reminiscentia*) treats memory as a mental faculty, not a category of rhetoric.

4. In "Plato's Pharmacy," Derrida famously deconstructs the privileging of speech over writing.

5. *Cicero De Oratore* II.Ixxxvi.351–54. See Jarratt on Cicero and Quintilian (33–34). The Latin root of *imagination* includes *imaginary* or to "picture oneself" from *imago* or image. Thus, even the act of forming mental images is an act of imagination even if those images are then placed in a "storehouse." Prior to storing them, images must be conjured or called to mind, which is an act of imagination. This seemingly simply mnemonic strategy has always been an act of the imagination.

6. Just as the author of the *Rhetorica ad Herennium* recognizes memory as "the custodian of all the parts of rhetoric," so too does Quintilian, who asserts, "Our whole discipline relies on memory" (11.2.1).

7. The Sophists, like Gorgias, based their rhetorical theory on kairos, acknowledging the contingency of situations, institutions, issues, and modes of argumentation. How one seizes a moment depends on how one analyzes the contingencies—the demands and opportunities—of a situation. For an overview of kairos and rhetoric, see Sipiora and Baumlin.

8. Historian of rhetoric, Wilbur Samuel Howell, credited for popularizing the moniker "New Rhetoric," defines it as a response to "the emergence of the new science . . . [when] rhetoric began to see itself as the rightful claimant to the methods of learned communication and as the still unrivaled master of the arts of popular discourse" (5–6).

9. Campbell's theory of the human mind—where it contains the separate faculties of the will, the imagination, the understanding, and the passions—arose from the eighteenth-century philosophy expressed in David Hume's *Treatise on Human Nature* and Thomas Reid's *An Inquiry into the Human Mind and on the Principles of Common Sense*.

10. Interestingly, Campbell says we need "faith in the clear representation of that faculty [memory]" or we cannot gain knowledge (80). Furthermore, in order to be successful, an orator requires more than understanding: "it is necessary that he engage in his service all these different powers of the mind, the imagination, the memory, and the passions" (94). These powers are *not*, Campbell stresses, "supplanters of reason . . . they are her handmaids" (94).

11. George Campbell alone "noticed that introspective invention fundamentally depends on the assumption that the mind's memory of an investigation is an accurate record of its manipulation of ideas" (23).

12. The trajectory of James's career, seen through changes in his academic titles, speaks to the disciplinary shifts occurring in higher education. Initially trained in medicine, James came to Harvard in 1873 as an instructor in physiology and later that year became an instructor of anatomy and physiology. Three years later, he became an assistant professor of psychology, and then in 1881 he became an assistant professor in philosophy. He earned an endowed chair in psychology in 1889 and returned to philosophy in 1897. After working on *The Principles of Psychology* for twelve years, James attached an exasperated letter to his 1000-page manuscript to his editor, Henry Holt, claiming "1st, that there is no such thing as a *science* of psychology, and 2nd, that W. J. is an incapable." See *The Letters of William James*, 393–394.

13. These studies were both published in the newly founded journal *Psychological Review* in 1896. "The Place of Repetition in Memory" confirmed "in general the accepted fact of the efficacy of continued repetition in impressing any kind of subject-matter on the memory" (27). See Smith.

14. Although the Johns Hopkins Medical School of Medicine admitted women on equal terms with men when it opened in 1893, they did so reluctantly, making the environment inhospitable to women. The members of the Women's Fund for Medical Education, including Bryn Mawr College president M. Carey Thomas, Mamie Gwinn, Bessie King, and railroad heiress Mary Elizabeth Garrett, were all daughters of Hopkins's trustees. Garrett offered $300,000 with several conditions. Not only did she insist that women "enjoy all the advantages on the same terms as men," including "all prizes, dignities, or honors" available to male students, she also required that her stipulation "shall be printed each year in whatever annual or semi-annual calendars may be issued announcing the courses of the Medical School" (183). For a complete account, see Sander.

15. By the end of the twentieth century, memory studies deconstructed even those modern paradigms of memory as a subjective phenomenon or an intersubjective social phenomena. The burgeoning field of memory studies explores memory as a culturally significant aspect of intellectual history. Groundbreaking studies looked back to ancient sources and helped to renew interest in the rhetorical canon of memory. Frances Yates's *The Art of Memory* provides comprehensive analysis of memory as a critical canon of rhetoric, which is central to the other canons. While Mary Carruthers's *The Book of Memory* (1990) explains the functions of memory in medieval society, she also attributes memory's demise to its being classified as a "technical" rather than a "philosophical" element of rhetoric by historians of rhetoric who "may have contributed to the impression that *memoria*, being merely

technical, was limited in its applicability to the conditions of oral debate" (Carruthers 13).

16. Here Franken echoes Allegra Stewart's claim that "memory (with its freight of the past) interferes with creation" (37). See Stewart.

17. The manuscript that was to become Stein's opus, *The Making of Americans*, was written between 1903 and 1911. Due to Ernest Hemingway's persistence, part of Stein's novel was published serially in monthly installments in the *Transatlantic Review*.

18. Richard Bridgman points out that Stein's story is drawn from Aristotle's *Nicomachean Ethics*, Book VII, chapter 6, lines 10–13. See Bridgman, *Gertrude Stein in Pieces*, 66–67. Neil Schmitz addresses Stein's reference to Aristotle in "Portrait, Patriarchy, Mythos: The Revenge of Gertrude Stein" 89. Clive Bush offers an extended reading on Stein's use of the opening folktale, its roots in Aristotle's *Nicomachean Ethics*, its echoes with Zukofsky's reference in *A*, and, finally, its "critique of American bourgeois society at the level of behavior and psychology" (364).; see 361–374.

19. The shortened title, *Pragmatism*, was used after its publication with *The Meaning of Truth*, a collection of three essays that respond to criticisms raised by James's treatment of truth in his lectures on pragmatism. James collected and published these essays in 1909. They have often subsequently been published together as *Pragmatism and Four Essays from The Meaning of Truth*.

20. In *Sister Brother*, Brenda Wineapple identifies "Two" as "among the most personal and variable of Gertrude Stein's early work" because of its "autobiographical urgency" and its heralding of "stylistic shifts" (348). Wineapple reads a longer section of the text in which this passage occurs as "a comic rendition of Sarah's ecstatic vision" (350). Sarah was Stein's sister-in-law.

21. Ruddick comments on Stein's interest in Christian themes and vocabulary in *Reading Gertrude Stein*, 233–236.

22. Brinnin comments on this passage and Stein's "emancipation" from Leo in *The Third Rose* 190–202. Neil Schmitz explores Leo's ever-present absence in *Tender Buttons* in "*tender buttons*, notwithstanding."

23. Dydo calls *Stanzas* "The Other Autobiography." See Ulla Dydo, "*Stanzas in Meditation*: The Other Autobiography."

24. Although Stein wrote *Stanzas* in 1932, it was not published in its entirety until 1956, after her death. Excerpts were published during her lifetime. For a detailed publication history, see Appendix A of *Stanzas in Meditation*, 259–260.

25. Dydo's chapter on *Stanzas in Meditation* in *Gertrude Stein: The Language That Rises* offers detailed and definitive analysis of Stein's composition process. See 487–525.

26. Stein's uses an antimetabole, a rhetorical figure of repeated words in reverse

grammatical order, which is sometimes incorrectly assumed to be synonymous with chiasmus. Antimetabole appeared in *Rhetorica ad Herennium*, Book IV. See Stein's "Listen to Me" 390.

Chapter 6

1. Loren Glass's *Authors Inc.* examines the ways in which "celebrity troubled many American authors' sense of their relation to their texts and audiences" (8). Richard Keller Simon's "Modernism and Mass Culture" provides an early, detailed overview of modernism and mass culture. Although Mark Morrisson's *The Public Face of Modernism* does not include Stein, Morrisson explores the "crisis of publicity" faced by modernist authors and artists who embraced mass marketing strategies. Karen Leick's recent *Gertrude Stein and the Making of an American Celebrity* considers the US response to Stein, arguing that modernist literature including Stein's became "mainstream public knowledge" through "the diverse and pervasive media that analyzed, reproduced or otherwise advertised modern literature" (3).

2. For an overview of Stein's theorization of and relationship to audience, see Peter Quartermain's *Disjunctive Poetics*, Harriet Chessman's *The Public Is Invited to Dance*, Lisa Ruddick's *Reading Gertrude Stein*, and the introduction to Joan Retallack's *Gertrude Stein*.

3. Vanderbilt made this comment to a reporter from the Chicago *Daily News*. He went on to say, "I don't take any stock in this silly nonsense about working for anybody but our own"—comments that would send any twentieth-century press agent into crisis communication mode. (Interview, Chicago *Daily News*, October 9, 1882).

4. See Roland Marchand's *Creating the Corporate Soul* for detailed account of how corporate entities were transformed through advertising and image making into "good neighbors."

5. For a detailed day-to-day chronology of Stein's lecture tour, see Appendix I by William Rice in Edward M. Burns and Ulla Dydo's *The Letters of Gertrude Stein and Thornton Wilder*, 333–353.

6. In *Kenneth Burke in the 1930s*, Ann George and Jack Selzer open with a fascinating account of "April 1935," where they place Burke within intellectual, political, and literary conversations of the 1930s, all of which provided the foundation for his writings in this decade.

7. See Kirk Curnutt's "Inside and Outside: Gertrude Stein on Identity, Celebrity, and Authenticity" and Joan Retallack's introduction to *Gertrude Stein*, 3–14, for specifics about the kinds of publicity used to promote Stein and her work.

8. Nearly one hundred years later, celebrities who are famous for being famous, like Paris Hilton and Kim Kardashian, manufacture and brand personalities worth

millions and can command hundreds of thousands of dollars simply for showing up at an event. See "Inside Kardashian Inc."

9. In an effort to shape her own legacy, Stein bequeathed her famous portrait by Picasso to the Metropolitan Museum of Art with instructions to display it within the museum's immense collection, not just with contemporary art. The images included in "Picturing Gertrude," the first in *Seeing Gertrude Stein*, provide a fascinating serial portrait and visual evolution of Stein's shifting public identity. See 8–59.

10. Olson's "'An invincible force meets an immovable object': Gertrude Stein come to Chicago" examines Stein's methods of self promotion to two audiences: mainstream reading public and the university crowd. In particular, she explores how Stein's visits to the University of Chicago "illuminate a tension between the avant-garde and the institutional, between Stein's radical experiments with language and the University of Chicago's curriculum of 'Great Books'" (332).

11. For discussion of Stein's anxiety about lecturing, see Mellow 292–296 and Dydo 78–82.

12. Romeike's clipping service began in 1881, the first of its kind to build a business on "the personal vanity of socialites, nouveaux riches, politicians, tycoons and stage folk," and writers like Stein and Hemingway, who made up the bulk of Romeike's business in the early twentieth century. By the early 1930s, the majority of the clipping bureau's revenue (75 percent) came from "Big Business," largely broadcasting, aviation, theater and cinema, automobiles, public utilities, and trade associations, further evidence of corporate America keeping track of and managing public opinion. See "Clipping Business," *Time*, Monday, May 30, 1932. For a fuller account of the newspaper coverage of Stein, see Tischler's "A Rose is a Pose."

13. Although Lenart-Cheng calls Stein's conscious manipulation of her image "debatable," I concur with Corn and Latimer that Stein was deeply engaged with the management of her public image even as early as her years at Harvard when Stein "manage[d] to push at the boundaries of studio conventions for women [portrait] sitters" (21).

14. Schoenbach examines Stein's sense of publicity and civilization within the social and institutional contexts of pragmatic modernism, including analysis of Stein's self promotion and "sophisticated marketing skills." See in particular 246–247.

15. This expanded sense of delivery has recently been explored by Lindal Buchanan in "Regendering Delivery," in which she analyzes the delivery by women speakers in "both a sexual and textual sense." More than just "the most material canon," Buchanan explores how delivery "becomes imbued with ideological concerns and ramifications" (53).

16. For an explanation of the historical and disciplinary disconnection between rhetorical studies and public relations, see my "PR Guns for Hire."

17. Wallis Simpson, 1896–1986, became the Duchess of Windsor in 1937 upon

her marriage to Edward VIII. She was named "Woman of the Year," by *Time* because "In a single year 1936 she became the most talked about, written-about, headlined and interest-compelling person in the world." See "Foreign News."

18. In "Gertrude Stein and the Radio," Sarah Wilson explores how "Stein wrestles with the idea of radio as a kind of public sphere—a forum in which self, other, and community can be constituted through talk" (260).

19. UbuWeb: Sound offers a number of audio clips of Stein reading her works: www.ubu.com/sound/stein.html. Date accessed: March 4, 2014. For further description of Stein's "unforgettable voice," see Corn 232.

20. Aristotle's *Rhetoric* 218 3.1.4; Cicero's *De Oratore* 179 III.223. Delivery has long been denigrated as a craft with its subordinate status rooted in Aristotle, who called it "vulgar" and acknowledged that "An Art concerned with [the delivery of oratory] has not yet been composed" (218). In *Rhetoric Beyond Words*, Carruthers identifies delivery as the "heart of rhetoric." Others have recently published important work "recovering" and "regendering" the canon of delivery. In "Composition and the Circulation of Writing," John Trimbur makes a compelling argument that the rhetorical canons of delivery and memory have been conceptually separated from the canons of invention, arrangement, and style. See also Porter and Buchanan. In *Electric Rhetoric*, Welch argues, "the disappearance of memory and delivery is not a benign removal" but "part of a larger movement in the United States to pablumize the humanities in general, and to vitiate writing in particular, . . . as if it were a mere skill, craft, or useful tool" (144–145).

21. In "The Gradual Making of The Making of Americans," Stein comments on her early interest in the types of characters that define individuals. In the Psychology Lab at Harvard, Stein conducted experiments to test "the average college student in a state of normal activity and in the state of fatigue" (137). While the intent of the study was to learn about their reactions, Stein was more interested "in the types of their characters that is what I even then thought of as the bottom nature of them" (137).

22. Stein often plays with the verb "to be" in all its grammatical and definitional complexity: to exist, to occur or take place, to have the state, quality, identity, or nature.

Chapter 7

1. Headlines surrounding the Stein exhibitions in New York make clear the allegations and vitriol leveled at Stein. For example, see Alexander Nazaryan's New York *Daily News* article "Gertrude Stein Exhibit at the Met Will Now Allude to Her Hitler-loving Past and Collaboration with Vichy Regime," Alan Dershowitz's charge that Stein was a "major collaborator," Barbara Will's repeated allegations, and

Emily Greenhouse's second *New Yorker* piece, "Why Won't the Met Tell the Whole Truth about Gertrude Stein?" A respondent to Greenhouse's article asked, "How about 'Two Jewish anti semitic Nazi's'—would that satisfy you—or do we need to add Lesbian and whether or not they bathed daily." See http://www.newyorker.com/online/blogs/culture/2012/06/why-wont-the-met-tell-the-whole-truth-about-gertrude-stein.html#ixzz2A98W0VnX. Date accessed: March 4, 2014.

2. Bernstein's dossier, with commentary by Edward Burns, Ulla Dydo, Marjorie Perloff, Joan Retallack, and Renate Stendahl, offers a nuanced look at Stein's often troubling wartime politics. See Bernstein's "Gertrude Stein's War Years."

3. *Yale Poetry Review* published this untitled manuscript in 1947 under the title "Reflection on the Atomic Bomb." See Stimpson and Chessman, *Gertrude Stein: Writings 1932–1946*, 823. For additional comments on Stein's relationship to war, see Brenda Wineapple's "The Politics of Politics; or, How the Atomic Bomb Didn't Interest Gertrude Stein and Emily Dickinson."

Works Cited

Abbott, Edwin A. *How to Write Clearly: Rules and Exercises on English Composition*. Boston: Roberts Brothers, 1876.

Adams, Charles Frances, Edwin Lawrence Godkin, and Josiah Quincy. "Report of the Committee on Composition and Rhetoric." *The Origins of Composition Studies in the American College, 1875–1925: A Documentary History*. Ed. John C. Brereton. Pittsburgh: U of Pittsburgh P, 1995. 73–100.

Anderson, Sherwood. "The Work of Gertrude Stein." Introduction. *Geography and Plays. By Gertrude Stein*. Madison: U of Wisconsin P, 1993.

Aristotle. *Nicomachean Ethics*. Trans. Joe Sachs. Newport, MA: Focus Publishing, R. Pullins Company, 2002.

———. *On Memory*. Ed. Richard Sorabji. 2nd edition. Chicago: U of Chicago P, 2006.

———. *On Rhetoric: A Theory of Civic Discourse*. Trans. George A. Kennedy. Oxford: Oxford UP, 1991.

Arnold, Matthew. "The Function of Criticism at the Present Time." 1864. *Lectures and Essays in Criticism. The Complete Prose Works of Matthew Arnold*. Ed. R. H. Super, Vol. 3. Ann Arbor: U of Michigan P, 1962. 258–90.

Ashton, Jennifer. *From Modernism to Postmodernism: American Poetry and Theory in the Twentieth Century*. Cambridge: Cambridge UP, 2005.

———. "Gertrude Stein for Anyone." *ELH* 62.1 (spring 1997): 289–331.

Axelrod, Steven Gould. "*Mrs. Reynolds*: Stein's Anti-Nazi Novel." *Primary Stein: Returning to the Writing of Gertrude Stein*. Eds. Janet Boyd and Sharon J. Kirsch. Lanham: Lexington Books, 2014 259–76.

Barnard, G. William. *Living Consciousness: The Metaphysical Vision of Henri Bergson*. Albany: SUNY Press, 2011.

Beal, Wesley. "The Form and Politics of Networks in Jean Toomer's *Cane*." *American Literary History* 24.4 (Sept. 2012): 658–79.

Benstock, Shari. *Women of the Left Bank: Paris, 1900–1940*. Austin: U of Texas P, 1986.

Bergson. Henri. *Matter and Memory: Essay on the Relation between the Body and the Spirit*. 1896. Translated by N. M. Paul and W. S. Palmer. New York: Zone Books, 1990.

Berlin, James. "Revisionary Histories of Rhetoric: Politics, Power, and Plurality." *Writing Histories of Rhetoric*. Ed. Victor J. Vitanza. Carbondale: Southern Illinois UP, 1994. 112–27.

———. *Rhetoric and Reality: Writing Instruction in American Colleges, 1900–1985*. Carbondale: Southern Illinois UP, 1987.

———. "Richard Whately and Current-Traditional Rhetoric." *College English* 42 (1980): 10–17.

Bernays, Edward. *Propaganda*. 1928. Brooklyn, NY: Ig Publishing, 2005.

Bernstein, Charles. "Gertrude Stein's War Years: Setting the Record Straight, A Dossier." *Jacket2* May 9, 2012. Date accessed: Dec 11, 2012. https://jacket2.org/feature/gertrude-steins-war-years-setting-record-straight.

———. "Inventing Wordness: Gertrude Stein's Philosophical Investigations." *Gertrude Stein Advanced: An Anthology of Criticism*. Ed. Richard Kostelanetz. Jefferson, NC: McFarland and Co., 1990.

———. *A Poetics*. Cambridge: Harvard UP, 1992.

———. *Recalculating*. Chicago: U of Chicago P, 2013.

Bialostosky, Don. "Rhetoric in Literary Criticism and Theory." *The Sage Handbook of Rhetorical Studies*. Eds. Andrea A. Lundsford, Kirt H. Wilson, and Rosa A. Eberly. Thousand Oaks, CA: Sage Publishing, Inc., 2009. 215–26.

Bizzell, Patricia, and Bruce Herzberg. *The Rhetorical Tradition: Readings from Classical Times to the Present*. 2nd ed. Boston: Bedford/St. Martin's, 2001.

Blair, Hugh. *Lectures on Rhetoric and Belles Lettres*. 1783. Ed. Harold F. Harding. Carbondale: Southern Illinois UP, 1965.

Booth, Wayne. *The Rhetoric of Rhetoric: The Quest for Effective Communication*. Oxford: Blackwell Publishing, 2004.

———. *The Vocation of a Teacher: Rhetorical Occasions, 1967–1988*. Chicago: U of Chicago P, 1988.

Brazier, Michelle. "The Making of Gertrude Stein: Reading, Writing, and Radcliffe." Diss. Rutgers U, 2010.

Brereton, John C. *The Origins of Composition Studies in the American College, 1875–1925: A Documentary History*. Pittsburgh: U of Pittsburgh P, 1995.

Bridgman, Richard. *Gertrude Stein in Pieces*. New York: Oxford UP, 1979.

Briggs, Le Baron Russell. "The Harvard Admission Examination in English." *The*

Origins of Composition Studies in the American College, 1875–1925: A Documentary History. Ed. John C. Brereton. Pittsburgh: U of Pittsburgh P, 1995. 57–73.

Brinnin, Malcolm. *The Third Rose: Gertrude Stein and Her World*. Boston: Little Brown, 1959.

Bromfield, Louis. "Gertrude Stein, Experimenter with Words." *New York Herald Tribune*. Sept. 3, 1933.

Brooke, Collin Gifford. "Making Room, Writing Hypertext." *JAC* 19.2 (1999): 253–68.

Brown, Stuart C., Theresa Enos, David Reamer, and Jason Thompson. "Portrait of the Profession: The 2007 Survey of Doctoral Programs in Rhetoric and Composition." *Rhetoric Review* 27.4 (2008): 331–40.

Brown, Stuart C., Rebecca Jackson, and Theresa Enos. "The Arrival of Rhetoric in the Twenty First Century: The 1999 Survey of Doctoral Programs in Rhetoric." *Rhetoric Review* 18.2 (2000): 233–42.

Brummett, Barry. *A Rhetoric of Style*. Carbondale: Southern Illinois UP, 2008.

Buchanan, Lindal. "Regendering Delivery: The Fifth Canon and the Maternal Rhetoric." *Rhetoric Society Quarterly* 32.4 (2002): 51–73.

Burke, Kenneth. *The Philosophy of Literary Form*. 1941. Berkeley: U of California P, 1973.

———. *Language as Symbolic Action: Essays on Life, Literature, and Method*. Berkeley: U of California P, 1966.

Burns, Edward, ed. *The Letters of Gertrude Stein and Carl Van Vecthen Vol. 1: 1913–1935*. New York: Columbia UP, 1986.

Burns, Edward, and Ulla Dydo, eds. *The Letters of Gertrude Stein and Thornton Wilder*. New Haven: Yale UP, 1996.

Burns, Edward, and Leon Katz. "Foreword: 'The Walk in the Light.'" *Picasso: The Complete Writings*. Boston: Beacon P, 1970.

———. "Gertrude Stein: A Complex Itinerary, 1940–1944." *Jacket2* May 9, 2012. Date accessed: Dec 11, 2012. https://jacket2.org/article/gertrude-stein-complex-itinerary-1940%E2%80%931944.

Bush, Clive. *Halfway to Revolution: Investigation and Crisis in the Work of Henry Adams, William James and Gertrude Stein*. New Haven: Yale UP, 1991.

Butcher, Fanny. "Gertrude Stein Is Pleased With Success in U. S.," *Chicago Tribune*. Dec. 2, 1933: 13. Date accessed: Mar. 3, 2013. http://pqasb.pqarchiver.com/chicagotribune/doc/181501879.html?FMT=ABS&FMTS=ABS:AI&type=historic&date=Dec+2%2C+1933&author=F+B%3B+Stein%2C+Gertrude&pub=Chicago+Daily+Tribune+(1923–1963)&edition=&startpage=&desc=Gertrude+Stein+Is+Pleased+with+Success+in+U.+S.

Butler, Paul. *Out of Style: Reanimating Stylistic Study in Composition and Rhetoric*. Logan: Utah State UP, 2008.

———. "The Stylistic (Re)Turn in Rhetoric and Composition." *Style and Rhetoric in Composition: A Critical Sourcebook.* Boston: Bedford/St. Martin's, 2009.

Campbell, George. *The Philosophy of Rhetoric.* Ed. Lloyd Bitzer. Carbondale: Southern Illinois UP, 1963.

Campbell, JoAnn. "Controlling Voices: The Legacy of English A at Radcliffe College 1883–1917." *College Composition and Communication* 43.4 (1992): 472–85.

Campbell, Karlyn Kohrs. "Biesecker Cannot Speak for Her Either." *Philosophy and Rhetoric* 26 (1993): 153–59.

———. *Man Cannot Speak for Her.* 2 vols. New York: Praeger, 1989.

Carlo, Roseanne, and Theresa Jarnagin Enos. "Back-Tracking and Forward-Gazing: Marking the Dimensions of Graduate Core Curricula in Rhetoric and Composition." *Rhetoric Review* 30.2 (2011): 208–27.

Carruthers, Mary. *The Book of Memory: A Study in Memory in Medieval Culture.* Cambridge: Cambridge UP, 1990.

———. *Rhetoric Beyond Words: Delight and Persuasion in the Arts of the Middle Ages.* Cambridge: Cambridge UP, 2010.

Cerf, Bernard. *At Random: The Reminiscences of Bennett Cerf.* New York: Random House, 1977.

Chessman, Harriet. *The Public Is Invited to Dance: Representation, the Body, and Dialogue in Gertrude Stein.* Stanford: Stanford UP, 1989.

Cicero. *De Oratore.* Trans. E. W. Sutton and H. Rackham. 2 vols. 1977. Cambridge, MA: Harvard UP, 1988.

Clark, Timothy J. *Farewell to an Idea: Episodes from a History of Modernism.* Yale UP, 1997.

"Clipping Business." *Time Magazine.* May 30, 1932.

Connors, Robert J. "Mechanical Correctness as a Focus in Composition Instruction." *College Composition and Communication* 36.1 (1985): 61–72.

Cope, Karin. *Passionate Collaborations: Learning to Live with Gertrude Stein.* Victoria, BC: U of Victoria P, 2005.

Copeland, Carolyn Faunce. *Language and Time and Gertrude Stein.* Iowa City: U of Iowa P, 1975.

Corbett, Edward P. J. *Classical Rhetoric for the Modern Student.* 2nd ed. New York: Oxford UP, 1972.

Corn, Wanda, and Tirza Latimer. *Seeing Gertrude Stein: Five Stories.* Berkeley: U of California P, 2011.

Cowley, Malcolm. "Gertrude Stein, Writer or Word Scientist?" *The New York Herald-Tribune Weekly Book Review* Nov 24, 1946: 1. In *The Critical Response to Gertrude Stein.* Ed. Kirk Curnutt. Westport, CT: Greenwood Publishing, 2000. 147–50.

Cox, J. R. "Memory, Critical Theory, and the Argument from History." *Argument and Advocacy* 27 (1990): 1–13.

Creel, George. *Rebel at Large: Recollections of Fifty Crowded Years.* New York: G.P. Putnam's Sons, 1947.

Cronkite, Walter. "Daily Texan Talks Great Depression with Author." *Daily Texan* Mar. 22, 1935.

Crowley, Sharon. *The Methodical Memory: Invention in Current-Traditional Rhetoric.* Carbondale: Southern Illinois UP, 1990.

———. "A Plea for the Revival of Sophistry." *Rhetoric Review* 7.2 (1989): 318–34.

———. *Toward a Civil Discourse: Rhetoric and Fundamentalism.* Pittsburgh: U of Pittsburgh P, 2006.

Crowley, Sharon, and Debra Hawhee. *Ancient Rhetorics for Contemporary Students.* 3rd ed. New York: Longman Pearson, 2003.

Curnutt, Kirk, ed. *The Critical Response to Gertrude Stein.* Westport, CT: Greenwood Publishing, 2000.

———. "Inside and Outside: Gertrude Stein on Identity, Celebrity, and Authenticity." *Journal of Modern Literature* 23.2 (1999): 291–308.

Dean, Gabrielle. "Make It Plain: Stein and Toklas Publish the Plain Edition." *Primary Stein: Returning to the Writing of Gertrude Stein.* Eds. Janet Boyd and Sharon J. Kirsch. Lanham: Lexington Books, 2014 13–35.

DeKoven, Marianne. *A Different Language: Gertrude Stein's Experimental Writing.* Madison: U of Wisconsin P, 1983.

———. "Introduction: Transformations of Gertrude Stein." *Modern Fiction Studies* 42.3 (1996): 469–83.

———. "Modernism and Gender." *The Cambridge Companion to Modernism.* 2nd ed. Ed. Michael Levenson. Cambridge: Cambridge UP, 2011. 212–31.

Derrida, Jacques. *The Gift of Death.* Chicago: U of Chicago P, 1991.

———. "The Law of Genre." Trans. Avital Ronell. *Critical Inquiry* 7.1 (autumn 1980): 55–81.

———. *Of Grammatology.* Baltimore: Johns Hopkins UP, 1976.

———. "Plato's Pharmacy." *Dissemination.* Trans. Barbara Johnson. Chicago: Chicago UP, 1981. 61–117.

———. "Structure, Sign and Play in the Discourse of the Human Sciences." *Writing and Difference.* Trans. Alan Bass. London: Routledge, 1994. 278–94.

Dershowitz, Alan. "Suppressing Ugly Truth for Beautiful Art. *Huffington Post* May 1, 2012. Date accessed: Nov 23, 2012. http://www.huffingtonpost.com/alan-dershowitz/met-gertrude-stein-collaborator_b_1467174.html.

Dimock, Wai Chee. "Introduction: Genres as Fields of Knowledge." *PMLA* 122.5 (Oct. 2007): 1377–88.

Doane, Janice. *Silence and Narrative: The Early Novels of Gertrude Stein.* Westport, CT: Greenwood Press, 1986.

Donawerth, Jane. *Conversational Rhetoric: The Rise and Fall of a Woman's Tradition, 1600–1900.* Carbondale, IL: Southern Illinois UP, 2012.

———. *Rhetorical Theory by Women before 1900: An Anthology*. Lanham, MD: Rowman & Littlefield Publishers, Inc., 2002.

Dubnick, Randa. *The Structure of Obscurity: Gertrude Stein, Language, and Cubism.* Urbana: U of Illinois P, 1984.

Dydo, Ulla. *Gertrude Stein: The Language That Rises 1923–1934.* Evanston, IL: Northwestern UP, 2003.

———. "*Stanzas in Meditation*: The Other Autobiography." *Chicago Review* 35.2 (1985): 4–20.

———. *A Stein Reader*. Evanston, IL: Northwestern UP, 1993.

Ebert, Roger. Review *Midnight in Paris.* Rogerebert.com. May 25, 2011. Date accessed: Jun 5, 2011. http://www.rogerebert.com/reviews/midnight-in-paris-2011.

Enos, Richard Lee. "The Emergence of Literate Greek Rhetoric in Greece." *Rhetoric Society Quarterly* 36.3 (2006): 223–41.

———. "I Remember Edward P. J. Corbett." *JAC: Journal of Rhetoric, Culture, and Politics* 18.3 (Fall 1998): 395–96.

Ewen, Stuart. *PR! A Social History of Spin.* New York: Basic Books, 1996.

Fahnestock, Jeanne. "Arrangement." *Encyclopedia of Rhetoric and Composition: Communication from Ancient Times to the Information Age.* Ed. Theresa Enos. New York: Garland, 1996.

———. *Rhetorical Style: The Uses of Language in Persuasion.* Oxford: Oxford UP, 2011.

Fifer, Elizabeth. "Is Flesh Advisable? The Interior Theater of Gertrude Stein." *Signs.* 4 (1979): 472–83.

Fish, Stanley. "Rhetoric." *Doing What Comes Naturally: Change, Rhetoric, and the Practice of Theory in Literary and Legal Studies.* Durham: Duke UP, 1989.

Fitz, L. T. "Gertrude Stein and Picasso: The Language of Surfaces." *American Literature* 45.2 (May 1973): 228–37.

"Foreign News: Woman of the Year." *Time* Jan 4, 1937.

Foucault, Michel. *The Archeology of Knowledge* and *The Discourse on Language.* Trans. A.M. Sheriden Smith. New York: Pantheon Books, 1972.

———."The Order of Discourse." 1970. Rpt. in *Untying the Text: A Post-Structuralist Reader.* Ed. Robert Young. Boston: Routledge & Kegan Paul, 1981. 48–78.

Fox, Margalit. "Wayne C. Booth, Critic that Analyzed Rhetoric, Dies at 84." *New York Times* Oct. 11, 2005.

Franken, Claudia. *Gertrude Stein: Writer and Thinker.* Piscataway, NJ: Transaction, 2000.

Friedman, Susan Stanford. "Definitional Excursions: The Meanings of Modern/Modernity/Modernism." *Modernism/modernity* 8.3 (2001): 493–513.

Galow, Timothy. "Gertrude Stein's *Everybody's Autobiography* and the Art of Contradictions." *Journal of Modern Literature* 32.1 (2008): 111–28.

Gaonkar, Dilip. "Close Readings of the Third Kind: Reply to My Critics." *Rhetorical Hermeneutics; Invention and Interpretation in the Age of Science*. Eds. Alan Gross and William Keith. Albany: SUNY P, 1997. 330–56.

Gass, William. *The World within the Word.* New York: Basic Books, 2000.

Genung, John Franklin. *The Practical Elements of Rhetoric, with Illustrative Examples.* Boston: Ginn, 1885.

———. "The Study of Rhetoric in the College Course." (1887). *The Origins of Composition Studies in the American College, 1875–1925: A Documentary History*. Ed. John C. Brereton. Pittsburgh: U of Pittsburgh P, 1995.

George, Ann, and Jack Selzer. *Kenneth Burke in the 1930s*. Columbia: U of South Carolina P, 2007.

"Gertrude Stein: A Radio Interview in 1934." *Paris Review* 116 (fall 1990): 88–89.

Glass, Loren. *Authors Inc.: Literary Celebrity in the Modern United States, 1880–1980*. New York: New York UP, 2004.

Goodspeed-Chadwick, Julie. *Modernist Women Writers and War: Trauma and the Female Body in Djuna Barnes, H.D., and Gertrude Stein*. Louisiana State UP, 2011.

Graff, Gerald G. *Professing Literature: An Institutional History*. Twentieth Anniversary Edition ed. Chicago: U of Chicago P, 2007.

Greenhouse, Emily. "Why Won't the Met Tell the Whole Truth about Gertrude Stein?" *New Yorker*, June 8, 2012. Date accessed: Nov. 23, 2012. http://www.newyorker.com/online/blogs/culture/2012/06/why-wont-the-met-tell-the-whole-truth-about-gertrude-stein.html.

Guerlac, Suzanne. *Thinking in Time: An Introduction to Henri Bergson*. Ithaca, NY: Cornell UP, 2006.

Guthrie, W. K. C. *History of Greek Philosophy*. 6 vols. Cambridge: Cambridge UP, 1969.

Gutting, Gary. "Bridging the Analytic-Continental Divide." *New York Times* Feb. 19, 2012. Date accessed: May 3, 2012. http://opinionator.blogs.nytimes.com/2012/02/19/bridging-the-analytic-continental-divide/?_r=0.

Haas, Robert Bartlett. *A Primer for the Gradual Understanding of Gertrude Stein*. Los Angeles: Black Sparrow P, 1974.

Haselstein, Ulla. "Gertrude Stein's Portraits of Matisse and Picasso." *New Literary History* 34.4 (2003): 723–43.

Hawhee, Debora. "Kairotic Encounters." *Perspectives on Rhetorical Invention*. Eds. Janet M. Atwill and Janice M. Lauer. Knoxville: U of Tennessee P, 2002. 16–35.

Hejinian, Lyn. *The Language of Inquiry*. Berkeley: U of California P, 2000.

———. "Two Stein Talks." *The Language of Inquiry*. Berkeley: U of California P, 2000. 83–130.

Hemingway, Ernest. *A Moveable Feast*. New York: Scribner's, 1964.

Hilder, Jamie. "'After all one must know more than one sees and one does not see a cube in its entirety': Gertrude Stein and Picasso and Cubism." *Critical Survey*. 17.3 (2005): 66–84.

Hill, Adams Sherman. *Principles of Rhetoric*. 1878. New York: American Books Co., 1895.

Hoffman, Michael J. "Gertrude Stein and William James." *Personalist* 47 (1966): 226–33.

Horner, Winifred. *Nineteenth-Century Scottish Rhetoric: The American Connection*. Carbondale: Southern Illinois UP, 1992.

Howe, Susan. *My Emily Dickinson*. Berkeley: U of California P, 1985.

Howell, Wilbur Samuel. *Eighteenth-Century British Logic and Rhetoric*. Princeton: Princeton UP, 1971.

Hudson, Hoyt H. "Rhetoric and Poetry." *Quarterly Journal of Speech Education* 10.2 (1924): 143–54.

Hume, David. *A Treatise on Human Nature*. Eds. David Fate Norton and Mary J. Norton. Oxford: Oxford UP, 2000.

"Inside Kardashian Inc.: How the Kardashians Made $65 Million Last Year." Feb 16, 2011. Date accessed: Aug. 21, 2012. http://www.hollywoodreporter.com/news/how-kardashians-made-65-million-100349.

"Interview with William H. Vanderbilt." *Chicago Daily News* Oct 9, 1882.

Isocrates. *Isocrates in Three Volumes*. Trans. George Norlin and Larue van Hook. Vol. 2. Cambridge: Loeb-Harvard UP, 1929.

James, William, ed. *The Letters of William James*. Boston: Little Brown, 1926.

———. *Pragmatism and the Meaning of Truth*. Cambridge, MA: Harvard UP, 1978.

———. *The Principles of Psychology*. Cambridge, MA: Harvard UP, 1983.

———. *Talks to Teachers on Psychology and to Students on Some of Life's Ideals*. 1899. New York: Henry Holt and Company, 1901.

———. *The Varieties of Religious Experience*. Ed. Martin E. Marty. New York: Penguin Books, 1982.

———. *The Will to Believe and Other Essays in Popular Philosophy*. Cambridge, MA: Harvard UP, 1979.

Jarratt, Susan. *Rereading the Sophists: Classical Rhetoric Refigured*. Carbondale: Southern Illinois UP, 1998.

Johnson, Nan. *Nineteenth-Century Rhetoric in North America*. Carbondale: Southern Illinois UP, 1991.

Kant, Immanuel. *Critique of Pure Reason*. 1781. Trans. Norman Kemp Smith. New York: St. Martin's P, 1965.

Karl, Alissa. *Modernism and the Marketplace: Literary Culture and Consumer Capitalism in Rhys, Woolf, Stein, and Nella Larsen*. New York: Routledge, 2008.

Keith, William. "On the Origins of Speech as a Discipline: James A. Winans and Public Speaking as Practical Democracy." *Rhetoric Society Quarterly* 38.3 (2008): 239–58.

Kellner, Bruce, ed. *A Gertrude Stein Companion: Content with the Example*. New York: Greenwood P, 1988.

Kennedy, George A. *Classical Rhetoric and its Christian and Secular Tradition from Ancient to Modern Times*. 2nd ed. Chapel Hill: U of North Carolina P, 1999.

Kirsch, Sharon J. "PR Guns for Hire: The Specter of Edward Bernays in Gadhafi's Libya," *Present Tense: A Journal of Rhetoric in Society*. 2.1 (fall 2011): n.p. Date accessed: Sep 14, 2011. http://www.presenttensejournal.org/volume-2/pr-guns-for-hire-the-specter-of-edward-bernays-in-gadhafi%E2%80%99s-libya.

———. "'Suppose a Grammar Uses Invention': Gertrude Stein's Theory of Rhetorical Grammar." *Rhetoric Society Quarterly* 38.3 (July 2008): 283–310.

Kitzhaber, Albert R. *Rhetoric in American Colleges, 1850–1900*. Dallas: Southern Methodist UP, 1990.

Kostelanetz, R., ed. *Gertrude Stein Advanced: An Anthology of Criticism*. Jefferson, NC: McFarland and Co., 1990.

Leick, Karen. *Gertrude Stein and the Making of an American Celebrity*. New York: Routledge, 2009.

Lenart-Cheng, Helga. "Autobiography as Advertisement: Why do Gertrude Stein's Sentences Get Under our Skin?" *New Literary History* 34.1 (winter 2003): 117–31.

Lippmann, Walter. "Blazing Publicity: Why we Know so Much about 'Peaches' Browning, Valentino, Lindbergh and Queen Marie." Eds. Cleveland Armory and Frederic Bradlee. New York: Viking P, 1927; 1960. 121–22.

———. *The Phantom Public: A Sequel to Public Opinion*. New York: MacMillan, 1927.

———. *Public Opinion*. 1922. New York: Free Press Paperbacks, 1997.

Litz, A. Walton, Louis Menand, and Rainey Lawrence, eds. *The Cambridge History of Literary Criticism, Vol. 7: Modernism and the New Criticism*. VII Vol. Cambridge: Cambridge UP, 2000.

Liu, Yameng. "Invention and Inventiveness: A Postmodern Redaction." *Perspectives on Rhetorical Invention*. Eds. Janet M. Atwill and Janice M. Lauer. Knoxville: U of Tennessee P, 2002. 53–95.

Locke, John. *An Essay Concerning Human Understanding*. Ed. Peter H. Nidditch. Oxford: Oxford UP, 1975.

Lowell, Amy. Preface. *Some Imagist Poets*. Boston: Houghton Mifflin Co. Riverside P, 1915. v–viii.

Loy, Mina. "Communications: Gertrude Stein." *The Critical Response to Gertrude Stein*. Ed. Kirk Curnutt. Westport, CT: Greenwood Publishing, 2000. 178–82.

Lundell, William. "Gertrude Stein: A Radio Interview." *Paris Review* 32 (fall 1990): 85–97.

Lyne, John, and Carolyn R. Miller. "Introduction: Rhetoric, Disciplinarity, and Fields of Knowledge." *The Sage Handbook of Rhetorical Studies*. Eds. Andrea A. Lundsford, Kirt H. Wilson, and Rosa A. Eberly. Thousand Oaks, CA: Sage Publications, Inc., 2009. 167–74.

Mackey, Louis H. "An Exchange on Deconstruction Reply by John R. Searle." *New York Review of Books* Feb. 2, 1984. Date accessed: May 3, 2012. http://www.nybooks.com/articles/archives/1984/feb/02/an-exchange-on-deconstruction/?pagination=false.

Maillioux, Steven. *Disciplinary Identities: Rhetorical Paths of English, Speech, and Composition*. Modern Language Association of America, 2006.

———, ed. *Rhetoric, Sophistry, Pragmatism*. Cambridge: Cambridge UP, 1995.

Marchand, Roland. *Creating the Corporate Soul: The Rise of Public Relations and Corporate Imagery in American Big Business*. Berkeley: U of California P, 1998.

McComiskey, Bruce. *Gorgias and the New Sophistic Rhetoric*. Carbondale: Southern Illinois UP, 2002.

McKeon, Richard. "Pluralism of Interpretation and Pluralism of Objects, Actions, and Statements Interpreted." *Critical Inquiry* 12.3 (1986): 576–96.

McLuhan, Marshall. *Understanding Media: The Extensions of Man*. 1964. Cambridge, MA: MIT Press, 1997.

Mellow, James. *Charmed Circle: Gertrude Stein and Company*. New York: Praeger, 1974.

Meyer, Steven. *Irresistible Dictation: Gertrude Stein and the Correlations of Writing and Science*. Stanford: Stanford UP, 2001.

Miller, J. Hillis. "Moving Critical Inquiry On." *Critical Inquiry* 30.2 (2004): 414–20.

Miller, Rosalind S. *Gertrude Stein: Form and Intelligibility*. New York: Exposition P, 1949.

Miller, Susan. "Classical Practice and Contemporary Basis." *The Rhetorical Tradition and Modern Writing*. Ed. James Murphy. New York: Modern Language Association, 1982. 46–57.

———. *Textual Carnivals: The Politics of Composition*. Carbondale: Southern Illinois UP, 1991.

Mitchell, W. J. T., ed. *Critical Inquiry*, http://www.journals.uchicago.edu/page/ci/brief.html. Date accessed: May 1, 2012.

Morison, Samuel Eliot, ed. *Three Centuries of Harvard College, 1636–1936*. Cambridge, MA: Harvard UP, 1936.

Morrisson, Mark. *The Public Face of Modernism: Little Magazines, Audiences, and Reception, 1905–1920*. Madison: U of Wisconsin P, 2000.

Muckelbauer, John. *The Future of Invention: Rhetoric, Postmodernism, and the Problem of Change*. Albany: SUNY P, 2008.

Murphy, James. "The Codification of Roman Rhetoric: With a Synopsis of the *Rhetorica ad Herennium*." 3rd ed. *A Synoptic History of Classical Rhetoric*. Eds. James Murphy and Richard Katula. Mahwah, NJ: Lawrence Earlbaum, 2003. 127–49.

Nazaryan, Alexander. "Gertrude Stein Exhibit at the Met Will Now Allude to Her Hitler-loving Past and Collaboration with Vichy Regime." *New York Daily News*. May 2, 2012. Date accessed: Nov 12, 2012. http://www.nydailynews.com/blogs/pageviews/2012/05/gertrude-stein-exhibit-at-the-met-will-now-allude-to-her-hitler-loving-past-and—0.

"Not an Admirer of G. Stein." *Chicago Daily Tribune* Nov. 3, 1934.

Ohmann, Richard M. *English in America: A Radical View of the Profession*. New York: Oxford UP, 1996.

Olson, Liesl. "'An Invincible Force Meets an Immovable Object': Gertrude Stein Comes to Chicago." *Modernism/modernity* 17.2 (2010): 331–61.

———. "Gertrude Stein, William James, and Habit in the Shadow of War." *Twentieth Century Literature* 49.3 (Fall 2003): 328–59.

———. *Modernism and the Ordinary*. Oxford: Oxford UP, 2009.

Osborne, Peter. "Philosophy After Theory: Transdisciplinarity and the New." *Theory After Theory*. Eds. Jane Elliot and Derek Attridge. New York: Routledge, 2011.

O'Sullivan, Brian. "'Raid[s] on the Inarticulate': Modernist Scene[s] of Rhetoric." Diss. Temple U, 2002.

Payne, Michael, and John Schad, eds. *Life.After.Theory*. London: Continuum, 2003.

Perloff, Marjorie. *The Poetics of Indeterminacy*. Princeton: Princeton UP, 1981.

———. *Wittgenstein's Ladder: Poetic Language and the Strangeness of the Ordinary*. Chicago: U of Chicago P, 1996.

Plato. *Phaedrus*. Trans. H. N. Fowler. 1914. Loeb Classical Library. London: G.P. Putnam's Sons, 1960.

Porter, James. "Recovering Delivery for Digital Rhetoric." *Computers and Composition* 26.4 (2009): 207–24.

Posman, Sarah. "Modernist Energia: Henri Bergson and the Romanic Idea of Language." *Understanding Bergson, Understanding Modernism*. Eds. S.E. Gontarski, Paul Ardoin, and Laci Mattison. New York: Bloomsbury Academic, 2013. 213–27.

Poulakos, John. *Sophistical Rhetoric in Classical Greece*. Columbia: U of South Carolina P, 1995.

———. "Toward a Sophistic Definition of Rhetoric." *Philosophy and Rhetoric* 16 (1983): 35–48.

Preston, John Hyde. "A Conversation." *The Atlantic Monthly* 156.1 (August 1935): 187–94.

Quartermain, Peter. *Disjunctive Poetics: From Gertrude Stein and Louis Zukofsky to Susan Howe*. Cambridge: Cambridge UP, 1992.

Quintilian. *Institutio Oratoria*. 4 vols. Trans. H. E. Butler. Cambridge: Harvard UP, 1920.

Rainey, Lawrence. *Institutions of Modernism: Literary Elites and Public Culture*. New Haven: Yale UP, 1998.

Reid, Thomas. *An Inquiry into the Human Mind and on the Principles of Common Sense*. Ed. Derek R. Brooks. Edinburgh: Edinburgh UP, 2000.

Retallack, Joan, ed. *Gertrude Stein: Selections*. Berkeley: U of California P, 2008.

———. "Introduction: Essay as Wager." *The Poethical Wager*. Berkeley: U of California P, 2003. 1–20.

Rhetorica ad Herennium. Trans. Henry Caplan. Loeb Classical Library. Cambridge, MA: Harvard UP, 1952.

Rice, William. "Gertrude Stein's American Lecture Tour." *The Letters of Gertrude Stein and Thornton Wilder*. Eds. Edward Burns and Ulla Dydo. New Haven: Yale UP, 1996. 333–53.

Ritchie, Joy, and Kate Ronald, eds. *Available Means: An Anthology of Women's Rhetoric(s)*. Pittsburgh: U of Pittsburgh P, 2001.

Rogers, W. G. *When this You See Remember Me: Gertrude Stein in Person*. New York: Rinehart, 1948.

Ronald, Kate, and Joy Ritchie, eds. *Teaching Rhetorica: Theory, Pedagogy, Practice*. Portsmouth, NH: Boyton/Cook, 2006.

Royce, Josiah. *The Spirit of Modern Philosophy: An Essay in the Form of Lectures*. Boston: Houghton Mifflin Company, 1892.

Ruddick, Lisa. *Reading Gertrude Stein: Body, Text, Gnosis*. Ithaca: Cornell UP, 1990.

———. "Stein and Cultural Criticism in the Nineties." *Modern Fiction Studies* 42.3 (1996): 647–59.

Sander, Kathleen Walters. *Mary Elizabeth Garrett: Society and Philanthropy in the Gilded Age*. Baltimore: Johns Hopkins UP, 2008.

Santayana, George. "Literary Form." *Essays in Literary Criticism*. Ed. Irving Singer. New York: Charles Scribner's Sons, 1956. 336–60.

Schiappa, Ed. *The Beginnings of Rhetorical Theory in Classical Greece*. New Haven, CT: Yale UP, 1999.

Schmitz, Neil. "Doing the Fathers: Gertrude Stein on U. S. Grant in Four in America." *American Literature* 65.4 (Dec. 1993): 751–60.

———. "Gertrude Stein as Post-Modernist: The Rhetoric of *Tender Buttons*." *Journal of Modern Literature* 3.5 (July 1974): 1203–18.

———. "Portrait, Patriarchy, Mythos: The Revenge of Gertrude Stein." *Salmangundi* 40 (winter 1978): 69–91.

———. "*tender buttons*, notwithstanding." *Primary Stein: Returning to the Writing of Gertrude Stein*. Eds. Janet Boyd and Sharon J. Kirsch. Lanham: Lexington Books, 2014.

Schoenbach, Lisi. "'Peaceful and Exciting': Habit, Shock and Gertrude Stein's Pragmatic Modernism." *Modernism/modernity* 11.2 (2004): 239–59.

———. *Pragmatic Modernism*. Oxford: Oxford UP, 2012.

Scott, Fred Newton. *Paragraph-Writing: A Rhetoric of Colleges*. Ann Arbor, MI: Register Publishing, 1891.

Selzer, Jack. *Kenneth Burke in Greenwich Village: Conversing with the Moderns, 1915–1931*. Madison: U of Wisconsin P, 1996.

Shaw, Patrick. "The (Re)Birth of the Author: A Rhetoric of Gertrude Stein." Diss. U of Missouri, 1992.

Sidney, Philip. *An Apology for Poetry*. 3rd ed. Ed. R. W. Maslen. Oxford: Manchester UP, 2002.

Silliman, Ron. *The New Sentence*. New York: Roof, 1987.

Simon, Richard Keller. "Modernism and Mass Culture." *American Literary History* 13.2 (2001): 342–53.

Sipiora, Phillip, and James S. Baumlin, eds. *Rhetoric and Kairos: Essays in History, Theory, and Praxis*. Albany: SUNY P, 2002.

Siraganian, Lisa. *Modernism's Other Work: The Art Object's Political Life*. Oxford: Oxford UP, 2012.

Small, Jocelyn P. *Wax Tablets of the Mind: Cognitive Studies of Memory and Literacy in Classical Antiquity*. London: Routledge, 1999.

Smith, W. G. "The Place of Repetition in Memory." *Psychological Review*, 3.1 (Jan. 1896): 21–31.

Spahr, Juliana. *Everybody's Autonomy: Connective Reading and Collective Identity*. Tuscaloosa: U of Alabama P, 2001.

Stein, Gertrude. *The Autobiography of Alice B. Toklas*. 1933. New York: Vintage, 1963.

———. *A Book Concluding with As a Wife Has a Cow a Love Story*. 1926. Boston: Something Else Press, 1973.

———. "Composition as Explanation." *Gertrude Stein: Selections*. Ed. Joan Retallack. Berkeley: U of California P, 2008. 215–25.

———. "An Elucidation." *Gertrude Stein: Selections*. Ed. Joan Retallack. Berkeley: U of California P, 2008. 174–89.

———. *Everybody's Autobiography*. 3rd ed. Cambridge: Exact Change, 1993.

———. *Four in America*. New Haven, CT: Yale UP, 1947.

———. *The Geographical History of America or The Relation of Human Nature to the Human Mind*. 1936. Baltimore: Johns Hopkins UP, 1995.

———. *Geography and Plays*. 1922. Madison: U of Wisconsin P, 1993.

———. "The Gradual Making of the Making of Americans." *Lectures in America*. 1935. London: Virago, 1988. 135–61.

———. "History or Messages from History." *Gertrude Stein: Selections*. Ed. Joan Retallack. Berkeley: U of California P, 2008. 254–73.

———. *How to Write*. Ed. Patricia Meyerowitz. 1931. New York: Dover Publications, 1975.

———. *How Writing is Written*. Ed. Robert Bartlett Haas. Los Angeles: Black Sparrow P, 1974.

———. "If I Told Him, A Completed Portrait of Picasso." *Gertrude Stein: Selections*. Ed. Joan Retallack. Berkeley: U of California P, 2008. 190–93.

———. *Lectures in America*. 1935. London: Virago, 1988.

———. "Listen to Me." *Last Operas and Plays*. 1949. Ed. Carl Van Vechten. New York: Vintage-Random House, 1979.

———. *Lucy Church Amicably*. Paris: Plain Edition, 1931.

———. *The Making of Americans: Being a History of a Family's Progress*. 1925. Normal, IL: Dalkey Archive P, 2006.

———. "A Message from Gertrude Stein." 1946. In *Selected Writings of Gertrude Stein*. Ed. Carl Van Vechten. New York: Vintage Books, 1990, vii.

———. "*The Mother of Us All*. 1949." *Gertrude Stein: Writings, 1932–1946*. New York: Library of America, 1998. 779–819.

———. *Narration: Four Lectures by Gertrude Stein*. 1935. Chicago: U of Chicago P, 2010.

———. "And Now." *How Writing is Written*. Los Angeles: Black Sparrow P, 1974.

———. *Paris France*. New York: Liveright, 1970.

———. "Poetry and Grammar." *Lectures in America*. 1935. London: Virago, 1988. 209–46.

———. "Portraits and Repetition." *Lectures in America*. 1935. London: Virago, 1988. 165–208.

———. "Reread Another." *A Stein Reader*. Ed. Ulla Dydo. Evanston, IL: Northwestern UP, 1993. 347–55.

———. *Stanzas in Meditation: The Corrected Edition*. Eds. Susannah Hollister and Emily Setina. New Haven, CT: Yale UP, 2012.

———. *A Stein Reader*. Ed. Ulla Dydo. Evanston, IL: Northwestern UP, 1993.

———. *Tender Buttons*. 1914. Los Angeles: Sun & Moon P, 1990.

———. *Three Lives*. 1909. New York: Vintage, 1936.

———. "A Transatlantic Interview." 1946. *A Primer for the Gradual Understanding of Gertrude Stein*. Ed. Robert Haas. Los Angeles: Black Sparrow P, 1974. 11–35.

———. *Two: Gertrude Stein and Her Brother and Other Early Portraits, 1908–1912*. Ed. Carl Van Vechten. New Haven: Yale UP 1951.

———. "We Came. A History." *Gertrude Stein: Selections*. Ed. Joan Retallack. Berkeley: U of California P, 2008. 274–80.

———. "What Are Masterpieces and Why Are There So Few of Them." *Gertrude Stein: Selections*. Ed. Joan Retallack. Berkeley: U of California, 2008. 308–18.

Stevens, Anne H., and Jay Williams. "The Footnote, in Theory." *Critical Inquiry* 32.2 (2006): 208–25.

Stewart, Allegra. *Gertrude Stein and the Present*. Cambridge, MA: Harvard UP, 1967.

Sutherland, Donald. "Gertrude Stein and the Twentieth Century." *A Primer for a Gradual Understanding of Gertrude Stein*. Ed. Robert Bartlett Haas. Los Angeles: Black Sparrow P, 1974. 139–56.

———. "An Interview with Gertrude Stein." *Gertrude Stein: A Biography of Her Work*. New Haven, CT: Yale UP, 1951. 173–203.

Tischler, Alyson. "A Rose is a Pose: Steinian Modernism and Mass Culture." *Journal of Modern Literature* 26.3/4 (spring 2003): 12–27.

Trimbur, John. "Composition and the Circulation of Writing." *College Composition and Communication* 52.2 (2000): 188–219.

Turner, Catherine. *Marketing Modernism Between the Two World Wars*. Amherst: U of Massachusetts P, 2003.

"Understand Einstein? Just Try Stein-Stein." *Chicago Herald*. Nov 8, 1934. Yale, MSS 76, box 145, folder 3355.

Vitanza, Victor. "Some Rudiments of Histories of Rhetoric and Rhetorics of History." *Rethinking the Rhetorical Tradition: Multidisciplinary Essays on the Rhetorical Tradition*. Boulder: Westview Press, 1992. 193–240.

Wagner-Martin, Linda. *Favored Strangers: Gertrude Stein and Her Family*. New Brunswick: Rutgers UP, 1995.

"Wayne Booth, Professor Emeritus of English, 1921–2005." *University of Chicago News Office* Oct. 11, 2005.

Welch, Kathleen. *Electric Rhetoric: Classical Rhetoric, Oralism, and a New Literacy*. Cambridge, MA: MIT P, 1999.

Wendell, Barrett. *English Composition*. New York: Charles Scribner's Sons, 1891.

Whately, Richard. *The Elements of Rhetoric*. Ed. Douglas Ehninger. Carbondale: Southern Illinois UP, 1963.

White, Ray Lewis, ed. *Sherwood Anderson/Gertrude Stein: Correspondence and Personal Essays*. Chapel Hill: U of North Carolina P, 1972.

Whittier-Ferguson, John. "Stein in Time: History, Manuscript, and Memory." *Modernism/modernity* 6.1 (1999): 115–51.

Wichlen, Herbert A. "The Literary Criticism of Oratory." *Studies in Rhetoric and Public Speaking in Honor of James Albert Winans*. Ed. A. M. Drummond. New York: Century Co., 1925. 181–215.

Wilson, Edmund. "27 Rue De Fleurus." *New Republic* October 11, 1933: 246–47.

Wilson, Robert A. *Gertrude Stein: A Bibliography.* New York: Phoenix Bookshop, 1974.

Wilson, Sarah. "Gertrude Stein and the Radio." *Modernism/modernity* 11.2 (2004): 261–78.

Winter, Jay. *Remembering the War: The Great War between Memory and History in the Twentieth Century.* New Haven, CT: Yale UP, 2006.

Winterowd, W. Ross. "Dispositio: The Concept of Form in Discourse." *College Composition and Communication* 22 (1971): 39–45.

———. *Rhetoric. A Synthesis.* New York: Holt, Rinehart & Winston, 1968.

Wollaeger, Mark. *Modernism, Media and Propaganda: British Narrative from 1900–1945.* Princeton, NJ: Princeton UP, 2006.

Wozniak, John Michael. *English Composition in Eastern Colleges, 1850–1940.* Washington, DC: UP of America, 1978.

Yates, Frances. *The Art of Memory.* Chicago: U of Chicago P, 1966.

Index

Abbott, Edwin A., *How to Write Clearly*, 22, 28–29, 35, 59, 60, 63, 129n14
Adams, John Quincy, 16
advocacy, 65–66
Allen, Woody, 115
Alsop, Joseph, 110
analytic philosophy, 130n2; versus continental philosophy, 71–72
Anderson, Sherwood, 30, 103; *Winesburg, Ohio*, 41
antimetabole, 137n26
apperception, theory of, 34, 36, 37
Aristotle, 13, 20, 78, 110; classification of poetry in *Poetics*, 42; definition of rhetoric, 2, 118; definition of style emphasizing clarity, 63; four-part arrangement, 46; *On Memory*, 79–80, 135n3; *Nicomachean Ethics*, 137n18; *Rhetoric*, 45, 63, 79, 123n4, 140n20
arrangement, rhetorical canon of, 1, 4, 41–42, 45–49; ancient, 45–47; as effective order of arguments in speech or writing, 45; modern approach as textual auxiliary to reason, 47–49. *See also* Stein, Gertrude: rhetorical canon of arrangement
Ashton, Jennifer, 51
Austin, J. L., 8
Axelrod, Steven Gould, "*Mrs. Reynolds*," 116
Barthes, Roland, 7
Bates, Kathy, 115
Beaton, Cecil, 44
Bergson, Henri: *Matter and Memory*, 82; Stein's connection with, 81–82
Berlin, James, 17, 40, 47, 125n15
Bernays, Edward, 104
Bernstein, Charles, 5, 8, 52; definition of poetics, 120; *Gertrude Stein's War Years*, 116
Bieseceker, Barbara, debate with Karlyn Kohrs Campbell, 9
Blair, Hugh: *Lectures on Rhetoric and Belles Lettres*, 14–15, 19, 25, 31, 47–48, 64, 126n24, 129n15, 131n9; as "new rhetorician," 80, 127n4
Bloom, Harold, 8
Booth, Wayne: founding member of *Critical Inquiry*, 12; identification of "major rescuers" of rhetoric, 8, 14; and problem of defining rhetoric, 1; as rhetorician, 125n17
Bradley, William, 105
branding of images, 100. *See also* Stein, Gertrude: rhetorical canon of delivery
Braque, Georges, 41
Brereton, John C., 28, 129n11
Bridgman, Richard, 82, 92, 137n18
Brinnin, Malcolm, 82, 102, 137n22
Bromfield, Louis, 104

Brooke, Collin Gifford, 45
Buchanan, Lindal, "Regendering Delivery," 139n15
Burcher, Fanny, 103
Burke, Kenneth, 12, 130n4, 138n6
Bush, Clive, 137n18
Butler, Judith, 12

Cambridge History of Literary Criticism, The, 10
Campbell, George, 3, 127n4; *The Philosophy of Rhetoric*, 17, 25, 49, 80; theory of the human mind, 135n9, 135n10, 136n11
Campbell, JoAnn, 129n13
Campbell, Karlyn Kohrs: debate with Barbara Biesececker, 9; *Man Cannot Speak for Her*, 9
Carruthers, Mary: *The Book of Memory*, 136n15; *Rhetoric Beyond Words*, 140n20
Cerf, Bennett, 104, 105
Channing, Edward, 16
Chaplin, Charlie, 97
Child, Francis, 16
Cicero: canon of arrangement, 46; canon of delivery, 110; canons of rhetoric, 4; definition of rhetoric, 2; *De Oratore*, 78, 135n5, 140n20; on "embellishment of discourse," 63
classification, of literary texts, 42
Committee on Public Information (CPI), 100, 101
communication departments, shift of oratory to, 15, 23
composition: course developed at end of nineteenth century, 24, 127n30; five-part essay, 46; rise of within departments of English, 15; separation from literature, 17. *See also* Stein, Gertrude: education; compositional practices
Connors, Robert J., 22, 28
continental theory, 71–72, 74, 125n15
continuous present, 2, 75, 76, 80, 83, 119, 120
Copeland, Carolyn Faunce, *Language & Time & Gertrude Stein*, 5
Corbett, Edward P. J., *Classical Rhetoric for the Modern Student*, 77, 80–81
Corn, Wanda, 44, 98, 124n8, 130n5
Creel, George, 100, 101, 102
Criterion, 101
Critical Inquiry, 11–14; lack of attention to rhetoric, 11, 12, 14, 16, 17; lack of women theorists cited in, 12, 126n19; and literary theory, 12, 13
Cronkite, Walter, 106
Crowley, Malcolm, 62
Crowley, Sharon, 11, 32, 47, 73, 80, 123n2; *The Methodical Memory*, 31, 127n4
Cubism, 51, 54
Curnutt, Kirk, 107–8
current-traditional rhetoric, 23, 26, 27, 31, 127n4, 127n28

Davidson, Jo, 44
deconstruction, 11, 13
DeKoven, Marianne, 8, 66, 132n1
Deleuze, Gilles, 125n15
delivery, rhetorical canon of, 1, 4, 45; Cicero and, 110; delivery by women speakers, 139n15; "recovery" of, 140n20. *See also* Stein, Gertrude: rhetorical canon of delivery
De Man, Paul, 11
Derrida, Jacques, 8, 11, 36, 42, 67, 125n15; "Afterword," 71–72; debate with John Searle, 71–72, 134n19; *The Gift of Death*, 134n19; *Of Grammatology*, 134n19; on inventive potential of repetition, 134n12; "Plato's Pharmacy," 123n3, 135n4
Descartes, René, 37, 69, 80
Dewey, John, 8
Dial, The, 130n4
dialectical negation, 66
Dickinson, Emily, 8
Dimock, Wai Chee, 42
disjuncture, 47
Doane, Janice, 66
Dodge, Mabel, 82
Donawerth, Jane, 9, 124n12, 125n13
Duchamp, Marcel, *Nude Descending a Staircase*, 51
Dydo, Ulla, 9, 40, 68, 82, 85, 93–94, 95, 134n14, 137n23

Ebert, Roger, 115
Eliot, Charles, 24–25
Eliot, T. S., 7, 61; *Ash Wednesday*, 101; "The Love Song of J. Alfred Prufrock," 85; *The Waste Land*, 41, 62

English departments, 15, 126n20
Enos, Richard Leo, "The Emergence of Literate Rhetoric in Greece," 47, 77, 128n7
entity writing, 32, 42, 92–93, 94
Ewen Stuart, 102

faculty psychology, 48, 80
Fahnestock, Jeanne, 45, 133n10
feminism: feminist historians of rhetoric, 9; feminist literary criticism, 129n17; poststructuralist feminism, 10, 125n15
figurative language, 15, 61, 63, 127
Fish, Stanley, 11
"Footnote, in Theory, The" (Stevens and Williams), 12–13
Foucault, Michel, 47, 125n15, 130n8
Franken, Claudia, 83, 137n16
Frankfurt School, 125n15
Friedman, Susan Stanford, "Definitional Excursions," 7

Galow, Timothy, 132n16
Gaonkar, Dilip, 111
Garrett, Mary Elizabeth, 136n14
genre, 42, 43, 47, 52, 57, 61, 99
Genung, John Franklin: *The Practical Elements of Rhetoric*, 25, 128n8; "The Study of Rhetoric in the College Course," 127n28
George, Ann, 138n6
Glass, Loren, *Authors Inc.*, 138n1
Gorgias, 134n15, 135n7; *Encomium of Helen*, 3; theory of invention, 36–37
Graff, Gerald, 71–72
Great Depression and increasing hostility toward big business, 101
Gutting, Gary, "Bridging the Analytic-Continental Divide," 72, 74
Gwinn, Mamie, 136n14

Harvardization of English, 22, 23–25
Harvard University: Committee on Composition and Rhetoric reports on writing instruction, 24, 35, 129n12; entrance exams, 24, 35, 128n6; initiation of "current-traditional" first-year composition model, 23; and split between literature and composition, 16; use of Hill's rhetoric handbook in late nineteenth and early twentieth century, 128n8, 129n14
Hawhee, Debra, 36–37, 39
H.D., 61
Hejinian, Lyn: "Rejection of Closure" in *The Language of Inquiry*, 134n18; "Two Stein Talks," 8, 50, 130n11
Hemingway, Ernest, 137n17; *A Moveable Feast*, 115–16
Hill, Adams Sherman, *The Principles of Rhetoric and Their Application*, 25, 32–33, 128n8, 128n9, 129n14
Holt, Henry, 136n12
Horner, Winifred, *Nineteenth-Century Scottish Rhetoric*, 14, 126n25
Howe, Susan, 8
Howell, Wilbur Samuel, 135n8
human mind: assumptions about in eighteenth-century discourse theory, 31, 80; Campbell's theory of, 135nn9–10, 136n11; and memory, 94–95; and modern approach to arrangement, 48–49; relation to human nature, 79, 92–94, 129n16; and Scottish Common Sense Realism, 15; Stein's investigation of in *How to Write*, 23, 31
human nature: and identity writing, 92; relation to the human mind, 79, 92–94, 129n16
Hume, David, 34, 37, 135n9
hypertext, 45

identity writing, 42, 92
Imagist, 61
insistence vs. repetition, 67–68
invention, rhetorical canon of, 1, 4, 18, 30, 35; discovery and creation models of, 36, 37; "invention-in-the-middle," 37; subsumed by arrangement in eighteenth century, 47, 64. *See also* Stein, Gertrude: rhetorical canon of invention
Isocrates, 134nn15–16; "Against the Sophists," 68–69

James, William, 6, 8, 30, 63, 81; "the art of remembering," 87; pragmatic notion of grammar, 33; *Pragmatism*, 85, 137n19; *The Principles of Psychology*, 136n12; sense

of truth, 92, 137n19; *Talks to Teachers*, 34, 36; theory of apperception, 34, 36; "What Pragmatism Means," 130n21
Jarratt, Susan, 11
Johns Hopkins Medical School of Medicine, 136n14
Joyce, James, 7; *Dubliners*, 85; *Finnegan's Wake*, 101; *Ulysses*, 85

kairos: sense of time identified in Ancient Greece, 80, 133n9; Sophists' rhetorical theory based on kairos, 3, 68, 135n7; Stein's kairotic arrangement, 58; Stein's kairotic articulation of forgetting, 76; Stein's kairotic art of rhetoric, 2, 3, 4; Stein's kairotic rhetorical invention, 2, 18, 38–39, 118; Stein's kairotic sense of memory, 19, 77, 93, 96 (*See also* continuous present); Stein's kairotic sense of time, 65, 76; Stein's kairotic style, 74; Stein's public speaking as kairotic opportunity for invention, 99, 111, 113–14
Kant, Immanuel, transcendental theory of apperception, 34, 37
Karl, Alissa, 107
Kellner, Bruce, 92–93, 93
Kennedy, George, 118
Kenner, Hugh, 8
King, Bessie, 136n14
Kitzhaber, Albert R., 25, 128n8

Language poetry, 8
Latimer, Tirza True, 44, 124n8, 130n5
Lawrence, D. H., 7
Leick, Karen, *Gertrude Stein and the Making of an American Celebrity*, 138n1
Lenart-Cheng, Helga, 106, 139n13
linguistics, departments of, and scientific study of language, 15
Lipchitz, Jacques, 44, 103
Lippmann, Walter: "Blazing Publicity," 102; *The Phantom Public*, 102
literary analysis/criticism, 16–17, 44; distancing from teaching of composition, 17
literature, historical grounding in rhetoric, 13
Liu, Yameng, 35
Locke, John, 1–2, 15, 48–49, 72; *Essay Concerning Human Understanding*, 63
logic, shift to departments of mathematics or philosophy at end of nineteenth century, 15, 23
logical argumentation, order of, 41
logical positivism, 130n2
Loy, Mina, 82
Lyotard, Jean-Francois, 125n15

Mailloux, Steven, 11; *Disciplinary Identities*, 126n23
Man Ray, 44, 103
mass culture, and modernism, 124n10, 138n1
mass media and diminishing invention potential of spoken language, 109. *See also* public relations, mass mediated; Stein, Gertrude: rhetorical canon of delivery
McComiskey, Bruce, 11
McKeon, Richard, 13
McLuhan, Marshall, 130n6
Mellow, James, 110
memory, rhetorical canon of, 1, 4, 45; early twentieth-century view of, 81; memory-as-storage-container, 79, 84, 135n5; nineteenth-century view of as rote data retrieval, 80–81; as rhetoric's forgotten canon, 77; role for Greek and Roman rhetoricians, 77–80; shifted to disciplines of psychology and philosophy by end of nineteenth century, 77, 81; view of as memorization, 77. *See also* Stein, Gertrude: rhetorical canon of memory
memory studies, 77, 136n15
Meyer, Steven, 130n11
Midnight in Paris (film), 115
Miller, J. Hillis, 13
Miller, Rosalind, 28, 129n11
Miller, Susan, 17, 130n22
modernism, 42, 63, 73; Burke and, 130n4; and clarity, 60–61; definitional challenge of, 7; and formal innovation, 44, 49, 50; inception of, 85; and mass culture, 124n10, 138n1; pragmatic, 139n14; Stein in canon of, 1, 5, 7–8, 9, 11, 41, 50, 51, 57, 60, 73, 84–85, 97–98, 106, 107
Moody, William Vaugh, 27

Morrison, Mark, *The Public Face of Modernism*, 138n1
Muckelbauer, John, *The Future of Invention*, 62, 65–66, 68, 73, 74, 133n9
Munsterberg, Hugo: "The Place of Repetition in Memory," 81; and Stein at Radcliffe, 63
Murphy, James, 45

Nation, The, 101
negative dialectics, 73
Neo-Aristotelian literary critics, 13
New Criticism, 44
New Masses, 101
New Republic, The, 101
New Rhetoric, 80, 127n4, 135n8
Nietzsche, Friedrich, 11

Olson, Liesl, 124n10, 133n11, 139n10
oratory, 135n10; reduction of rhetoric to, 16, 23; shift of rhetoric away from and toward composition, 24; shift to departments of speech communication, 15; for Stein, 98–99, 110, 113
ornamentation, 4, 15, 63

Pagany, 101
paragraph, function of, 47, 128n7
Phelan, James, 125n17
philology, shift to departments of linguistics at end of nineteenth century, 23
philosophical inquiry, 92–93
philosophy, and rhetoric, 12–13
Picasso, Pablo, 41, 44, 83; *Gertrude Stein*, 51, 103; *Les Demoiselles d'Avignon*, 51
Plain Edition, 62–63, 133n7
Plato: criticism of Sophism, 2, 18, 20, 46, 75; definition of rhetoric, 2; *Euthydemus*, 75; *Gorgias*, 13; *Phaedrus*, 14, 45–46, 78; view of essential work of memory, 78
poetics, 5, 8, 17, 120
poetics of invention, 9, 10, 15, 18, 73, 116, 117
Poetry, 101
postmodernism, styles of engagement, 65–66
poststructuralist feminism, 10, 125n15
Poulakos, John, 3, 76
Pound, Ezra, 7, 60; *The Cantos*, 41
prescriptive grammar, 22
Psychological Review, 136n13
public relations, mass mediated, 100–104; during World War I, 100, 101; emotional appeals in managing of public opinion, 102; and mediation of discourse in America, 102; and role of individual "personality," 101. *See also* Stein, Gertrude: rhetorical canon of delivery
public speaking: as kairotic opportunity for invention, 99, 111, 113–14; shift to departments of speech communication at turn of twentieth century, 15

Quartermain, Peter, *Disjunctive Poetics*, 65, 138n2
Quintilian, 130n7, 130n22, 135n6; architectural metaphor for storing and retrieving memory, 78–79, 93; and canon of arrangement, 46; definition of rhetoric, 2; *Institutio Oratoria*, 46; view of style, 133n5

Radcliffe College, 127n2; evaluation of women's writing at, 129n12; Stein at, 5, 18, 22, 23, 26–27, 34, 63, 77
radio, Stein and, 105–6, 140n18
Rainey, Lawrence, *Institutions of Modernism*, 124n10
Reid, Thomas, 135n9
repetition, Stein's use of, 5, 21; as aid to clarity, 68; as aid to composition, 90–91; as central feature of style, 66–67; and opening up of possibilities, 134n18; and recreation of ideas in language, 32, 61; vs. insistence, 67–68
Retallack, Joan: *Gertrude Stein*, 8; *The Poethical Wager*, 80, 119
rhetoric: and "belles lettres," 14, 30–31; classical canons of, 1; and cultural and linguistic norms, 2; definitional challenges of, 1–2; feminist historians of, 9; focus on perspicuity, 61; and inventional theory of nineteenth century, 31; kairotic art of, 2; modern affiliation with composition, 14, 16, 22, 24; "new rhetoricians," 80, 127n4, 135n8; and philosophy, 12–13; and poetics, 116, 1115; reduction to oratory

and shift to speech communication departments, 16, 23; separation from literature at turn of twentieth century, 22, 23–24; shift from theoretical to practical, 25; Sophist, 3
Rhetorica ad Herennium, 4, 45, 47, 62, 78, 133n5, 135n6
rhetorical canons, 1; arranged by Roman rhetoricians, 45; as invented structure, 3; renewed popularity in late nineteenth and early twentieth century, 4. *See also* arrangement; delivery; invention; memory; style
rhetorical historiography, essentialist vs. constructionist debate, 123n2
rhetorical studies: across disciplines, 125n15; attention to style, 132n4; fragmented in twentieth century, 15, 16, 23–24, 126n23; interest in repetition, 133n10; and literary studies, 13, 14, 18; place of women in, 9, 125n13; uncoupling of speaking from writing, 16, 23
rhetorical theory, 11; modern, and elimination of invention from rhetorical process, 47; modern, subsumed under composition, 15; nineteenth-century affiliation with belles lettres, 15; poetics of, 73; of women, 9
Rhetoric Review, 127n29
Rhetoric Society Quarterly, 9
Richard, I. A., 8; *Practical Criticism*, 16
Ritchie, Joy, 124n16, 125n13
Rogers, William G., 105
Romeike clipping bureau, 105, 139n12
Ronald. Kate, 124n16, 125n13
Roosevelt, Eleanor, 97
"a rose is a rose is a rose," 21, 42, 50, 66, 103, 107, 127n1
Royce, Josiah, 34, 129n20
Ruddick, Lisa, 5, 6, 137n21

Santayana, George, 30, 32, 63
Schiappa, Ed, 11
Schmitz, Neil, 6–7, 52, 98, 137n18, 137n22
Schoenbach, Lisi, 139n14
Scott, Fred Newton: *Paragraph-Writing*, 128n8
Scottish Common Sense Realism, 15, 48, 80
Scottish Enlightenment, 14, 49
Searle, John, 71–72
Seeing Gertrude Stein (Corn and Latimer), 103, 124n8, 130n5, 139n9, 139n13
"Seeing Gertrude Stein" (exhibit), 115
Selzer, Jack, 130n4, 138n6
Sidney, Sir Philip, 3
Silliman, Ron, *The New Sentence*, 8
Simon, Richard Keller, "Modernism and Mass Culture," 138n1
Siraganian, 132n14
Sitwell, Edith, 104
Small, Jocelyn Penny, 78
Socrates, 14, 78, 96
Sophists, 69, 76, 120; banishment of, 47, 131n8; emphasis on self improvement and gaining facility with language, 69, 99; Isocrates, 68–69, 134n15, 134n16; as itinerant intellectuals, 20; late twentieth-century revival, 11, 123n3; Plato's criticism of, 2, 18, 20, 46, 75; rhetorical theory based on kairos, 2, 3, 135n7
Spahr, Juliana, *Everybody's Autonomy*, 8
Stein, Gertrude
—*How to Write*, 2, 16, 18, 21, 22, 33, 34, 41, 59, 61, 97, 121; arrangements as agreed upon actions or processes, 43; epistemic rhetoric, 40; exploration of possibilities of language through rhetorical classical canons, 9; "A Grammarian," 37–40, 56; investigation of workings of human mind, 23, 31; on rhetorical invention and grammar, 4, 35–36, 119; satiric commentary on Edwin Abbott's handbook of writing, 29; on the sentence, 54–55, 56; "Sentences and Paragraphs," 29, 32, 56; theory of rhetorical grammar, 27–28; traditional arrangement of, 28, 46; on use and function of vocabulary in relation to grammar, 6, 21
—canon of modernism, 1, 5, 7–8, 9, 11, 41, 50, 51, 57, 60, 73, 84–85, 97–98, 106, 107; as a contemporary Sophist, 3–4, 18, 20, 68–69, 70, 76, 99, 120; and *Gertrude Stein* (Picasso), 51, 103, 139n9; interest in Christian themes, 88, 137n21; legacy in

academic and popular circles, 20; ongoing celebrity, 115–16; and philosophical inquiry, 92–93; self-positioning among men of letters and innovators, 64; wartime allegations directed at, 140n1; war writing, 116–17, 141n3
—compositional practices: antimetabole, 137n26; arrangement of sentences, 52–55, 56; connections of geography and literature, 51; embracing of difficulty, 119–20; experiments with verb "to be," 140n22; identity writing and entity writing, 42; nineteenth-century obsession with clarity, 60; reflection of nineteenth-century composition theory and practice, 5–7, 22, 30; relation between act of writing and invention, 4, 37; rhetorical approaches to composition, 8–9; simplicity of diction, 62; variety of literary and artistic forms, 61; view of self and writing as historical, 6
—education: experiments on memory in Harvard Psychological Laboratory, 81, 140n21; feedback on Stein's compositions showing current-traditional approach, 26, 27; formal education in composition at Radcliffe College, 5, 18, 22, 23, 26–27, 63, 77; grade in English 22 at Radcliffe, 128n10; influence of William James upon, 6, 63, 124n6, 129nn18–19, 131n11, 133n11; medical education at Johns Hopkins School of Medicine, 81; and Munsterberg, 63; and Santayana, 129n18; writing assignments exploring issues central to later writing, 26, 129n11; writing assignments housed at Stein archive, Beinecke Library, Yale University, 26
—rhetoric, grammar, and language: arrangement (*See* Stein, Gertrude: and rhetorical canon of arrangement); definition of grammarian, 37–40; delivery (*See* Stein, Gertrude: and rhetorical canon of delivery); epistemic rhetoric, 40; and generative grammar, 30, 35–37; on importance of grammar to English language, 35; interest in cultural function of language, 40, 98; interrelation of grammar, language, and thought as philosophical effort, 32; invention (*See* Stein, Gertrude: rhetorical canon of invention); language as intellectual recreation, 18, 40; linguistic innovation, 42, 50; memory (*See* Stein, Gertrude: rhetorical canon of memory); overlooked in field of rhetorical studies, 8–9; reinvention of classical canons of rhetoric, 1, 2, 9, 10–11, 18, 119; and relationship between language and history, 36, 40; rhetorical theory, 2, 5, 9–10, 11, 15, 16, 18, 22, 119; rhetoric of supposition, 116, 118–19, 120; style (*See* Stein, Gertrude: rhetorical canon of style); theory of rhetorical grammar, 22, 27–28, 29–30, 32, 36–37; work within dominant rhetorical discourse of late nineteenth century, 9
—rhetorical canon of arrangement: arrangement as agreements, 43, 58; arrangement as site of invention, 19, 42–45, 50–58; arrangement in *Tender Buttons,* 51–54; on arrangement's change between nineteenth and twentieth century, 57; arrangements of narrative and historical knowledge, 57; distinction between "writing" and its forms, 61
—rhetorical canon of delivery: adept handling of hecklers, 104; *Autobiography* as rhetorical act of public relations, 106; and celebrity culture, 100, 107–8; delivery as textual and inventional process, 107; experiments with aesthetics of delivery, 99, 110; exploration of how the relation between audience and speaker affects writing and speaking, 111; image of self as active listener and teacher, 112; initial reluctance as public speaker, 104; invitation to audience to participate, 112; logo and tagline, 106–7; mass media ridicule of Stein with parodies of her style, 103; paradoxical stance on spectator or reader, 132n14; public speaking as kairotic opportunity for invention, 111, 113–14; radio interviews as means to influence relations with public, 105–6, 140n18; response to au-

dience questions after lectures, 111; retheorizing of delivery in age of mass media and publicity, 99; rhetorical performance of delivery, 19–20, 99–100, 109–14; self-positioning as itinerant intellectual, 99; self-promotion to mainstream public and academics, 139n10; self-referential delivery, 112; staying "with the language," 113; use of public relations strategies to brand herself, 98, 99, 102, 103–9, 139nn13–14; view of mass media as diminishing the invention potential of spoken language, 109; view of publicity as communicative substitute for novel, 108–9

—rhetorical canon of invention: connection of grammar to invention, 16, 21, 22, 23, 28, 35, 39, 76; invention and rhetorical identity, 30–35; invention as catalyst for other rhetorical canons, 4, 18; invention as discovery and creation, 35, 39; kairotic rhetorical invention, 38–39, 118; linking of invention and rhetorical style, 61–62

—rhetorical canon of memory: "continuous present," 2, 75, 76, 80, 83, 119, 120; distinction between habit and movement, 82; geographic mnemonic of place, 93–95; and the human mind and human nature, 92–94, 129n16; memory and history in *The Making of Americans*, 84–87; memory as articulation of forgetting, 75, 76, 84, 86–87, 88–89, 96, 134n1; memory in "Portraits and Repetition," 87–91; memory in *Stanza in Meditation*, 95–96; memory in *The Geographical History of America*, 91–96; memory lessons, 75–76, 82–84, 85–86; memory without certainty, 87–91; and repetition, remembering, and confusion as aids to composition, 90–91; warning against view of memory as mimesis, 77, 83

—rhetorical canon of style: approach to style through rhetoric, 19; commitment to and questioning of assumptions about clarity, 72–73; conception of style, 62, 64–65; distinction between repetition and insistence, 67–68; ethic of style, 71–74; linking of rhetorical style and invention, 61–62; and repetition, 5, 21, 32, 61, 66–68, 90–91, 134n18; simplicity of diction, 62; style as core of rhetorical theory, 73–74

—works: *The Autobiography of Alice B. Toklas*, 7, 75–76, 82, 95, 97–98, 101, 103, 106, 116; *Brewie and Willie*, 116; "Composition as Explanation," 2, 46, 55, 104; "An Elucidation," 68–71; *Everybody's Autobiography*, 6, 30, 31, 33, 34, 54, 55, 107, 132n15; *Four in America*, 64, 133n8; *The Geographical History of America or The Relation of Human Nature to the Human Mind*, 2, 27, 30, 31, 33, 42, 78, 82, 91–96, 129n16; *Geography and Plays*, 2, 82; "The Gradual Making of the Making of Americans," 109, 112, 140n21; "History of Messages from History," 56–57; *How to Write* (*See* Stein, Gertrude, *How to Write*); *How Writing is Written*, 30, 59–60, 75, 76; "Identity a Poem," 42; "If I Told Him, A Completed Portrait of Picasso, 60; "Jenny, Helen, Hannah, Paul, and Peter," 88–89; *Lectures in America*, 4, 7, 40, 59, 97–114; *The Making of Americans*, 2, 5, 26–27, 41, 42, 50, 51, 80, 82, 83, 97, 111, 119, 137n17; "Melanctha," 5; *The Mother of Us All*, 27; *Mrs. Reynolds*, 116; *Narration*, 2, 31, 62, 63, 64, 77, 115; *Operas and Plays*, 84; "Pictures," 54, 97; "Plays," 112, 113; "Poetry and Grammar," 40, 71, 115; "Portraits and Repetition," 2, 60, 64, 65, 67, 69, 73, 76, 83, 88–91, 97, 112; "Reflections on the Atomic Bomb," 117–18, 141n3; "Reread Another," 84; "Sacred Emily," 127; *Stanzas in Meditation*, 2, 6, 16, 41, 44, 80, 82, 95–96, 134n17, 137nn23–24; *Tender Buttons*, 3, 6–7, 41, 42, 51, 60, 61, 63, 97, 134n1; *Three Lives*, 5, 27, 97, 105; "A Transatlantic Interview," 97; *Two*, 6, 75, 76, 87, 137n20; *Wars I Have Seen*, 7, 63, 116–17; "We Came. A History," 36, 43–44; "What Are Masterpieces and Why Are There So Few of Them," 84, 113

Stein, Leo, 87, 88, 137n22

"Steins Collect, The" (exhibit), 115

Stevens, Anne H., 12, 126n18, 126n19

Stevens, Wallace, 61
Stewart, Allegra, 137n16
style, rhetorical canon of, 1, 4; ancient, 62–63, 133n5; focus of rhetorical studies on, 132n4; modern, 63–74. *See also* Stein, Gertrude: rhetorical canon of style
Sutherland, Donald, "Gertrude Stein and the Twentieth Century," 5, 50, 57

theory, rise of in late twentieth century, 12
Thomas, M. Carey, 136n14
Tischler, Alyson, 103
Toklas, Alice B., 44, 62, 87, 88, 104, 107, 110, 134n17
Toomer, Jean, *Cane*, 41, 130n1
Transatlantic Review, 137n17
Trench, Richard C., *On the Study of Words*, 129n13
Trimbur, John, "Composition and the Circulation of Writing," 140n20
Turner, Catherine, 106

Vallotton, Félix, 103
Vanderbilt, William H., 100, 138n3
Van Vechten, Carl, 104
Vienna Circle, 130n2
Vitanza, Victor, 16

Wagner-Martin, Linda, 32, 82
Welch, Kathleen, *Electric Rhetoric*, 140n20
Wendell, Barrett, *English Composition*, 128n8
Whately, Richard, *Elements of Rhetoric*, 129n14; as "new rhetorician," 80, 127n4
Whitehead, Alfred North, 130n2
Whittier-Ferguson, John, 82–83
Willard, George, 41
Williams, Jay, 12, 126n18, 126n19
Williams, William Carlos, 61
Wilson, Edmund, 98
Wilson, Sarah, "Gertrude Stein and the Radio," 140n18
Wilson, Woodrow, 100
Wineapple, Brenda, 137n20
Winterowd, W. Ross, 45
Wollaeger, Mark, *Modernism, Media, and Propaganda*, 102
Women's Fund for Medical Education, 136n14
Woolf, Virginia, 85; *The Waves*, 100–101
Wozniak, John Michael, 129n14

Yale Poetry Review, 117
Yates, Frances, *The Art of Memory*, 136n15
Yeats, W. B., 7